Life behind
Barbed Wire

D1602749

Life behind Barbed Wire

THE WORLD WAR II
INTERNMENT MEMOIRS
OF A HAWAI'I ISSEI

YASUTARO (KEIHO) SOGA

TRANSLATED BY
KIHEI HIRAI

WITH AN INTRODUCTION BY
TETSUDEN KASHIMA

UNIVERSITY OF HAWAI'I PRESS
HONOLULU

Library of Congress Cataloging-in-Publication Data
Soga, Keiho, 1873–1957.
    [Tessaku seikatsu. English]
    Life behind barbed wire : the World War II internment memoirs of
a Hawai'i Issei / Yasutaro (Keiho) Soga ; translated by Kihei Hirai ;
with an introduction by Tetsuden Kashima.
        p. cm.
    Includes index.
    ISBN 978-0-8248-2033-6 (pbk. : alk. paper)
    1. Soga, Keiho, 1873-1957. 2. Japanese Americans—Evacuation and
relocation, 1942–1945. 3. World War, 1939-1945—Personal narratives,
American. 4. World War, 1939–1945—Japanese Americans. 5. Japanese
Americans—Ethnic identity. 6. Japanese Americans—Hawaii—Biography.
I. Title.
    D769.8.A6S66 2007
    940.53'18978956092—dc22
                                                    2007031672

Designed by Liz Demeter

Printed by Versa Press, Inc.

CONTENTS

FOREWORD

DENNIS M. OGAWA

"Please don't get cold" were Sei Soga's last words to her husband as he was being arrested and taken away. At the time, Soga found himself unable to respond; a half-year would pass before he was allowed to see or speak to her. In a poem he expresses his feelings for his wife:

After a long half-year
I take my wife's hand into mine
And for at least half a day
I do not wash away her touch

Soga was one of 1,466 Hawai'i Japanese who were imprisoned during World War II. He was arrested on the day of the Pearl Harbor attack, incarcerated at Sand Island, O'ahu, and placed in camps on the Mainland.

This book, *Life behind Barbed Wire,* is a daily record of Soga's internment experiences. In his preface, he writes: "In what follows I have tried to record my observations and experiences as truthfully, fairly, and simply as possible." Regarding his description of internee life, Soga more often wrote about what he saw than what he felt. However, one can gain some insight into his personality in portions of the text and by reading between the lines.

Soga loved nature and was fond of walking in the evening. He found great solace in the wildflowers and gardens raised by internees. One Christmas Eve, eight inches of snow fell at Santa Fe Camp: "As the sun gradually rose the snow began to glisten. The beauty of the scene was beyond my words. I took a solitary walk in the snow. I was able to enjoy the beauty of nature even while I was interned."

Soga's personality comes through in his poems, which he wrote all through his internment. Early on he writes of an encounter with a young MP who ordered internees at bayonet point, as if they were "dogs": "I was so upset by his treatment that I felt as if my blood would run backward in my veins":

> Like a dog
> I am commanded
> At bayonet point.
> My heart is inflamed
> With burning anguish.

Yasutaro Soga was born in Tokyo on March 18, 1873, the first son of Kisaburo and Kura Soga. He studied English and later British law at Tokyo Law School. In his junior year, he decided to study medical chemistry, but his poor eyesight forced him to give it up. On February 18, 1896, Soga emigrated to Hawai'i aboard the *China Go,* intending to stay just long enough to work and pursue an education in America. On March 5, 1896, he began his first job as manager of a store in Wai'anae owned by Chuzaburo Shiozawa. He wore the same clothes as his customers, who were mostly plantation workers, and earned a similar wage, $12.50 a month. He worked daily from 6:00 A.M. to 10:00 P.M. On Sundays, when the store was closed, he helped Japanese laborers write letters and learn English. He later worked at Shiozawa's Waipahu store, then at a store on Moloka'i, eventually becoming its bookkeeper and manager.

Upon his return to O'ahu in October 1899, Soga was persuaded by Shojiro Takahashi, editor of the *Hawaii Shimpo,* to use his language skills and become a newspaper reporter. During the Russo-Japanese War of 1904–1905, the *Hawaii Shimpo* and the *Pacific Commercial Advertiser* worked together to publish war news in Japanese in the English-language paper for the hundreds of Japanese domestic servants working in Caucasian homes. Every day Soga worked until after midnight in the *Advertiser's* downtown office, translating telegrams then taking his translations to the *Hawaii Shimpo* to be printed. After proofreading his copy, he returned home on his bicycle.

In May 1905, Soga became managing editor of the Japanese newspaper *Yamato Shimbun.* In 1906, he reorganized the paper as a joint-stock enterprise, completely changed its editorial policy, and renamed it *Nippu Jiji.* At the time, the six-page semiweekly paper had a circulation of three hundred and fifty. The *Nippu Jiji* took an active role in the 1909 strike led by Japanese sugar plantation laborers who were being paid $18 a month while others received $22.50 for the same work. Although the industry-wide strike involved all of O'ahu's major plantations and was supported by laborers on the other islands, it ended without a settlement.

A dedicated journalist, Soga was also a gifted tanka poet. He helped found Choon Shisha (The Sound of the Sea Tanka Club), the first of its kind in Hawai'i. Writing under the pen name Keiho, he produced an anthology entitled *Keiho Kashu,* which included more than eight hundred poems. When he was not writing, Soga was fond of reciting *yōkyoku* (*noh* chants) and playing *go* (Japanese chess).

Most of Soga's published work, however, is autobiographical. *Sen-Man-Shi No Hatsutabi—Nira no Nioi* (My First Trip to Korea–Manchuria–China: The Smell of Chives) and *Nichi-Man O Nozoku* (My Visit to Japan and China) both appeared before the war. After the publication of *Life behind Barbed Wire,* Soga went on to write *Gojunenkan No Hawaii Kaiko* (Fifty Years of Hawai'i Memories) and *Hawaii Sono Oriori* (Life in Hawai'i).

Yasutaro Soga married Sei Tanizawa in 1911. They had a child, Shigeo, who took over the *Nippu Jiji* while his father was interned and changed the paper's name to the *Hawaii Times.* Shigeo and his wife, Miya, had four children: Helen Yasuko, Walter Ichiro, Jean Ruriko, and Roy Kazuo.

On December 7, 1941, at the age of sixty-eight, Soga was arrested and interned for the duration of the war, first on O'ahu at Sand Island, then on the Mainland at Lordsburg and Santa Fe camps. He was sustained during those four long years by acknowledging his destiny: "The fish on a cutting board cannot escape no matter how much it struggles. We all tried to accept what was happening to us calmly." Soga returned to Hawai'i on November 13, 1945. During the postwar period he continued to write editorials and columns for the *Hawaii Times* and helped to reactivate Choon Shisha. In 1952 he and his wife, both longtime members of Makiki Christian Church, became naturalized citizens. Yasutaro Soga died on March 7, 1957, at the age of eighty-three.

Of Soga's many achievements, this book is perhaps one of the most significant. Writing about his own experience and his observations of what happened to the victims imprisoned in Hawai'i and interned on the Mainland constitute an invaluable firsthand, detailed account of a tragic episode in the history of our nation when American justice failed and people were imprisoned solely because of their race.

Tessaku Seikatsu (Life behind Barbed Wire) was translated by Kihei Hirai. Mr. Hirai was born in Tokyo, Japan, graduated from Tokyo University of Education and, after serving as a chief economist and executive for Mitsui

Bank, retired in Honolulu where his last position was executive vice president, City Bank. Currently, Mr. Hirai volunteers as a bilingual translator at the Japanese Cultural Center of Hawai'i. The intellectual debt owed to Mr. Hirai for his scholarly translating work and dedication to helping the greater community understand Hawai'i's Japanese American history is beyond measure.

The introduction to this book was written by Dr. Tetsuden Kashima, professor of ethnic studies at the University of Washington and author of *Judgement Without Trial: Japanese American Imprisonment during World War II*. His overview of the WRA (War Relocation Authority) camps and U.S. Army and Justice Department camps such as Lordsburg (an Army-run camp) and Santa Fe (Justice Department) helps the reader appreciate fully the significance of Soga's book. For Dr. Kashima, "The Issei and Nisei story is incomplete without an understanding of both the War Relocation Authority incarceration and the U.S. Army and Justice Department's Internment camp experience where Mr. Soga was taken. This book will be read by those who heretofore thought that the WRA camps exemplified the entire experience."

Of the 120,000 Japanese Americans who were interned, up to now the focus has been on the two-thirds who were American citizens—that is, the Nisei or second generation. But how about the other one-third—the Issei, first-generation Japanese who were ineligible for citizenship? Their experiences in the camps have been ignored, their voices rendered silent. Soga's book, written from an Issei point of view, provides us with a more complete history of the incarceration.

Tessaku Seikatsu (Life behind Barbed Wire), as translated by Kihei Hirai with additional text by Dr. Tetsuden Kashima, is a notable book. For the first time, a text is now available in English that can help us understand what happened to the Hawai'i internees: what their feelings and reactions were to the confinement they experienced; what they would never forget.

* * *

In the text, parentheses are used to include what Mr. Soga wrote; brackets enclose interpolations the translator added for clarification.

ACKNOWLEDGMENTS

Although my name appears as the translator for this book, acknowledgment and deep gratitude are owed to the following persons and institutions:

The family of the late Yasutaro Soga, with special thanks to his granddaughter, Helen Soga Sato, for working with us throughout the publication process.

The Japanese Cultural Center of Hawai'i (JCCH) and its Resource Center, for assistance and support. The following individual Resource Center volunteers: Yaeko Habein for checking the accuracy of the translation against the original text; Florence Sugimoto for proofing the grammar and writing; and Shigeyuki Yoshitake for verifying the accuracy of names and historical facts.

Dr. Dennis M. Ogawa, professor in and chair of the American Studies Department, University of Hawai'i, for playing a major role in supporting the publishing of this book.

I especially want to thank Jane Kurahara, who not only gave freely of her time and talents to help with checking the grammar but assisted Dr. Dennis M. Ogawa and the JCCH Resource Center volunteers with regard to the editorial and publishing needs of the University of Hawai'i Press and its conscientious and patient editors, Masako Ikeda, Ann Ludeman, and Barbara Folsom.

Last, I cannot forget my longtime friend Mr. Tatsumi Hayashi, who invited me to join the Japanese Cultural Center of Hawai'i's Resource Center as a volunteer translator. Working with Tatsumi and all the great volunteers at the JCCH has been a most rewarding experience.

Funding for this book was provided in part through the University of Hawai'i Press' Extraordinary Lives series.

Beyond the forbidding fence
Of double barbed wire,
The mountain, aglow in purple,
Sends us its greetings

YASUTARO (KEIHO) SOGA*

INTRODUCTION

TETSUDEN KASHIMA

During the Second World War two dramatically different scenarios confronted persons of Japanese ancestry in the United States and the territories of Alaska and Hawai'i. Many knowledgeable Americans now understand that in the continental United States and Alaska, their resident persons of Japanese ancestry, identified as the Nikkei, became involuntary victims of a tragic and gross violation of civil liberties and personal freedom. They suffered a mass expulsion from their homes and confinement in ten incarceration centers for periods ranging from months to, for many, three years. It was military necessity, President Franklin Delano Roosevelt declared on February 19, 1942, when he signed Executive Order (EO) 9066 authorizing this action. Forty years later, in 1982, a government commission charged with investigating the actions following upon this order concluded that the stated rationale had not been justified. The root historical causes, it elaborated, had been "race prejudice, war hysteria, and a failure of political leadership." [1] It was at this point that President Ronald Reagan signed the Civil Liberties Act of 1988, which proferred a presidential apology and required a $20,000 monetary redress payment to the surviving persons affected by that 1942 presidential order.

In the Territory of Hawai'i, the picture was dramatically different. There was no mass incarceration in the Islands, although the secretary of the navy, Frank Knox, argued for one, and President Roosevelt, in effect, ordered it. What did take place, in all three places—Hawai'i, Alaska, and the continental United States—was a priori systematic arrest and confinement, referred to here as "the internment," of initially preselected nationals of Germany, Italy, and Japan, starting on December 7, 1941. Relatively few people are aware of this internment episode, and Yasutaro Soga's *Life Behind Barbed Wire* focuses on this important, intriguing, and engrossing chapter of World War II. At that time, he was sixty-eight years old and had lived in Hawai'i for forty-five years since his initial emigration from Japan. As an immigrant Japanese national, he was an Issei, or first-generation Nikkei, and on that December seventh, he was also managing editor of the *Nippu Jiji*, a Hawai'i Japanese vernacular newspaper. For these reasons, and not because he had committed any criminal or other untoward acts against the United States, the Hawai'i military authorities immediately arrested him. How was this possible?

This introduction attempts to deal with this question and situates Soga's internment account within the *Nikkei* World War II experience that includes both the mass incarceration epic and the separate and distinctive set of actions that resulted in the internment of foreign nationals designated as "alien enemies." These two events are related like complementary tiles of a panoramic mosaic depicting the United States imprisonment picture during World War II. Soga's work is important because it brings to light a personal and heretofore little understood internment experience that took place during the dark days of World War II. Moreover, Soga's own story reveals the important interplay between the internment and incarceration as it affected Nikkei from both Hawai'i and the continental United States, the latter hereafter also referred to as the Mainland. This introduction, will then, start with Yasutaro Soga's internment experience, touch on the larger incarceration epic, and briefly examine an Issei writer's style.

The Internment Experience

Although Soga's actual narrative begins on December 7, 1941, preparations for his arrest started years earlier. What follows in this section provides the background to the Issei transferral from Hawai'i to the Mainland. In the 1920s, various United States military and government officials became concerned about Hawai'i's position as a vulnerable and strategic outpost in the midst of the Pacific Ocean. The U.S. Navy, even at this early period, was also interested in Japan's military and political activities. Then, starting in the 1930s both the navy and the army indicated a growing concern about the activities of the Issei. For example, President Roosevelt in August 1936 wrote to his chief of naval operations: "One obvious thought occurred to me—that every Japanese citizen or non-citizen on the Island of O'ahu who meets these Japanese ships [arriving in Hawai'i] or has any connections with their officers or men should be *secretly* but definitely identified and his or her name placed on a *special list* of those who would be the first to be placed in a concentration camp in the event of trouble." [2]

Such sentiments resulted in the intelligence agencies in the territories of Alaska and Hawai'i and the Mainland constructing lists of suspect organizations and the names of potentially "dangerous" individuals—in the latter case, mostly nationals and men, but including some women and American citizens as well.

"A-B-C" AND THE CUSTODIAL DETENTION LIST

The main agencies responsible for the creation and evaluation of this information were the military's intelligence units, especially the Office of Naval Intelligence (ONI) and agencies within the Justice Department such as the Federal Bureau of Investigation (FBI) and the Special Defense Unit. They eventually compiled a "Custodial Detention" list of organizations and individuals they deemed to be actual or potential "threats to the internal security of the United States."[3]

The listed organizations and names were differentiated by an "A-B-C" hierarchical designation based on their degree of perceived perfidiousness. The navy's ONI A-listed organizations and its members, for example, were viewed as constituting an actual threat to the United States. They were comprised of twelve Japanese organizations, such as the Kokoryukai (or Black Dragon Society); in the case of the Germans, it was the German American Bund; and the Federation of Italian War Veterans in the U.S.A., Inc., for the Italians.[4] The B-listed organizations were considered "potential threats to the national security" and included certain religious organizations, such as the Japanese Konko Church headquartered in San Francisco. The C-listed organizations were seen as having only some ties to the foreign nationals' homelands, and their officials and members were thought to engage in activities possibly inimical to the best interests of the United States. These included selected vernacular-language newspapers along with their officers, judō clubs, and names of Japanese-language schoolteachers. Hawai'i's A, B, and C list also included voluntary consular agents, business leaders, and priests.

In most instances, it was a case of "guilt by organizational association." Simply being a member or an officer of these organizations, or subscribing to a particular magazine, could be sufficient reason to have one's name classified and placed on the list. For the resident Issei, there was never any specific act or action deemed to be criminal in nature or construed to be an act of espionage or sabotage. Rather, merely attending a banquet sponsored by a listed Japanese organization, donating to a charitable organization, participating in a sports activity such as judō, or innocently attending a meeting could result in one's name being included on such a list. Obviously, however, paid staff members of a foreign government's embassy or legation constituted a separate category altogether.

What can be said about the inherent quality of these lists? Nineteen months after the start of the war, in July 1943, the Justice Department conducted an internal review of the A-B-C classification system and its validity when applied to American citizens. It concluded that the rating system was without merit and that the manner of assigning the A-B-C classification was based on "wholly inadequate evidence gathered and analyzed by persons suffering from serious misconceptions as to what evidence should be sought. . . . [It was based on] the use of patently unreliable hearsay, and other varieties of dubious information."[5] However, this review was not extended to foreign national cases, perhaps because of the differences in their legal status. The initial collection of derogatory information and those who evaluated it did not differentiate between citizens and nationals in assigning a particular classification. There is little reason to doubt that the same conclusion about the rating system as applied to citizens would also apply to the procedures used to classify alien nationals. For the Japanese, the method used to assess Issei organizations, and especially the actions of particular individuals, was usually implemented by American officials who had little or no knowledge about this ethnic group, its organizations, or its activities.

The purpose of the list was to pre-identify individuals who would be arrested and interned in the event of a war, and by the late 1930s the spotlight was turned on nationals from Germany, Italy, and Japan. The authority for the subsequent arrests resided in the Alien Enemies Act (1918 and 1798) that read, in part: "upon the declaration of war . . . [when] the President makes a public proclamation of the event . . . natives, citizens, denizens or subjects of the hostile nation . . . [can be] apprehended, restrained, secured, and removed as alien enemies."[6]

The Justice and War Departments were the two agencies assigned the main responsibility to plan for and, if necessary, implement the Alien Enemies Act. From April through July 1941, they met to spell out the conditions for the activation of such a program. To be brief, the Justice Department agreed to make recommendations and carry out the arrest of designated foreign alien enemies from countries with which the United States was at war and, once the Alien Enemies Act was invoked, to create and institute "hearing" boards to recommend a final status for those nationals. At the hearings, three recommendations were available: release, parole, or permanent internment. If the last recommendation was made, Justice would turn responsibility of the individual over to the army for safekeeping for an indeterminate time period. Their status became, in essence, that of civilian prisoners of war, and their treatment was subject to the articles of the Geneva Convention. The War Department, for its part, agreed to hold these "alien enemies" in camps and centers in the United States. It also accepted primary responsibility for the United States territories and, after their hearings, if the recommendation was for permanent interment, for transporting them to the contiguous United States for placement in a U.S. Army-run internment camp. Yasutaro Soga and others from Hawai'i were subject to this prewar agreement.

On December 7, 1941, even as Japanese planes were dropping bombs on Pearl Harbor, the military and FBI ordered their agents to arrest all persons on the Custodial Detention list regardless of the A, B, or C classification. By December 9, in Hawai'i those arrested included 345 Issei, 22 Nisei, 74 German nationals, 19 German Americans, 11 Italian nationals, and 2 Italian Americans; by the end of the war, for the Issei, the numbers had risen to 875, with a few Nisei out of a total Japanese ancestry population of 157,905. In contrast, of 126,948 Nikkei on the Mainland, 6,978 Issei were so interned.[7] The total number of "alien enemies" interned or placed under the jurisdiction of the Justice Department during the war by the United States government came to 39,899, of which 17,477 were Nikkei, mostly Issei; 11,507 mainly German nationals; and 2,730 mainly Italian nationals. Although everyone in this total came under the responsibility of the Justice Department during World War II, and the majority placed in US Army or Justice Department camps, not all of them were so interned. Within the Nikkei group, not a single Issei or Nisei was found guilty of committing any acts of espionage or sabotage, or of hindering the war efforts of the United States.

THE HEARINGS

Once arrested, the Hawai'i Issei, now referred to as "detainees," were eventually brought to and held at the Sand Island military detention camp, across the bay from Honolulu. The army determined their ultimate status through a hearing, which, although unlike a civil legal procedure, was considered to be an "administrative proceeding" and a "privilege," rather than a right accorded to those arrested. In it, they were questioned about their past activities and allowed to offer their personal testimonies. In the continental United States, the detainees could not be represented by counsel, whereas in Hawai'i they were granted this privilege. Also in Hawai'i, the detainees were given two hearings: the first with a civilian board and the second with a military panel. On the Mainland there was only a civilian board; the hearing "judges" were mainly local leaders—for example, a Mainland board consisted of a college professor, the editor of a local newspaper, and a local lawyer. Their instructions specified that the recommendation could be based only upon the presented information, usually drawn from the FBI files that had led to the detainee's inclusion on the Custodial Detention list in the first place. The detainees could not confront their accusers and, in essence, had to "prove their innocence" rather than entering with a presumption of innocence. The hearing board's recommendation of release, parole, or internment then determined the next step in the detainee's fate.

HAWAI'I AND MAINLAND JUSTICE AND WAR DEPARTMENT CAMPS

If the hearing board members recommended a permanent internment status for a Hawai'i detainee—a recommendation not told to the internee—he or she was then taken eventually to a War Department camp on the Mainland and held for an unspecified duration of time. Mr. Soga was thus interned for four years, and during his captivity he and the other internees were shifted between various camps. He probably knew that two agencies, the military and the Justice Department were most involved in his internment, but he could not have known the extent to which these two and other government and civilian-run agencies cooperated and competed to control the government's internee population.

Recall that the Justice Department, in their prewar talks, had agreed that with an internment recommendation that responsibility for the internee would transfer to the U.S. Army. From December 1941 to 1943, this was the usual pathway; however, in 1943, with the arrival of a growing number of German and Italian prisoners-of-war brought for internment from the European theater, the War Department asked Justice to take back the civilian internees. The Justice Department agreed to do so, which explains why Soga's journey started at his Hawai'i camp at Sand Island under the U.S. Army's Hawai'i Command, his initial Mainland stay was at Angel Island under the Justice Department until his transfer to the army's Lordsburg, New Mexico, camp, and in 1943 he was transferred back to the Justice Department camps at Santa Fe, New Mexico. Here he remained until the end of the war, when he was released on October 30, 1945, and took a train to Seattle, Washington, to board his Hawai'i-bound ship. Yasutaro Soga could not have known the reason for his many transfers, because even the interning authorities were often unaware of the many changes to which they had to adapt in an ever-changing wartime situation.

Soga mentions the names of numerous camps that held the detainees and internees during World War II.[8] The character of these camps and centers differed according to their controlling agencies, the type of internees they held, and the duration of time they stayed in operation. Some were under the Justice Department's Immigration and Naturalization Service (INS) Stations, or other Army-run temporary detainee holding places, while others were considered permanent camps. Two had very unique functions, such as the Seagoville, Texas, INS internment camp created to hold women internees and their children, and the INS "family reunification" center that Yasutaro Soga called a "cohabitation" camp at Crystal City, Texas. There were numerous camps holding Nikkei internees under army authority, although many of them also held at the same time Issei, Italian, and/or German internees. The two largest centers designated to hold mainly Japanese internees were the army's Lordsburg internment camp and Justice's Santa Fe internment center, both located in New Mexico.

What might be confusing to some readers is Soga's mention of certain incarceration camps run by the War Relocation Authority (WRA). Although more will be said about these centers in the next section, a few words about their relationship with the Justice and War Departments' internee camps is relevant here. First, the government, perhaps in response to the internees' and families' pleas, decided in late 1942 to initiate a family reunification program. From November 1942 until 1945, the largest group from Hawai'i sent to the Mainland was composed of the internees' wives and children. Although the wives were usually Issei, their names were not on a Custodial Detention list, nor had they been accorded a hearing. Moreover, the children were Nisei, and therefore outside the interning authority of the Alien Enemies Act. So, those from Hawai'i were initially held at a WRA incarceration center awaiting the resolution of various details—for example, completion of the Crystal City camp, waiting for the transfer of their husband or father into the Crystal City camp, and the processing of the dependent's agreement to accept voluntarily the same internee status as that of their husband or father. The WRA camps mentioned in passing by Soga that held the majority of those from Hawai'i were Minidoka (Idaho), Topaz (Utah), Tule Lake (California), and Heart Mountain (Wyoming). Second, after the Issei internees requested a second hearing and it resulted in a change of status from internee to "parolee" or "release" from the internment camp, their usual destination was a WRA incarceration camp. Here they again found themselves behind barbed-wire fences.

In the internment centers, the internees continually tried to obtain their freedom. As Soga points out, however, there were few options open to them. If the second hearing did not result in a change of status, they could request repatriation to Japan. Some died for medical reasons, and others took more drastic measures—a few attempted or committed suicide, and three were shot and killed by the guards.

ISSEI IN THE WAR AND JUSTICE DEPARTMENT CAMPS

The Issei internees were not simply docile and submissive throughout their internment. Although Soga was not himself present, he points out that an Issei internee collective mass protest arose in June 1942 at the army's Lordsburg, New Mexico, internment camp. At this camp, the Issei protested work orders that they considered were in contravention of the articles of the Geneva Convention. What Soga does not mention is that their protest eventually led to the transfer of this particular camp commander out of the Lordsburg center. However, during this time of turmoil, two internees, H. Isomura and T. Kobata (mistakenly identified as T. Obata in the text), were shot and killed for allegedly trying to escape, and subsequent research reports that the court-martial board acquitted on both counts the soldier who had committed the homicides.[9] In other camps, internees were beaten or kept in solitary confinement because they refused to obey orders mandated by their jailers. Confinement life was difficult, and the ever-present barbed-wire fence reminded all internees of their prisoner status. As Soga writes, "While we were detained, our minds grew dissolute. The joyless and dreary life continued day after day."[10] The Japanese internees spent their days waiting, hoping perhaps to be released, repatriated to Japan, or for a cessation of hostility between the United States and Japan. This is Yasutaro Soga's story—a participant-observer's voice for this intrepid Issei group.

The Incarceration Experience

Conceptually separate from but intertwined with the actions in the internment camps for the Nikkei were the mass incarceration centers run by the U.S. Army's Wartime Civil Control Administration (WCCA) and the civilian War Relocation Authority (WRA). Briefly, after December 7, 1941, there were no immediate plans to remove en masse those Issei not already interned or their citizen children. On the West Coast there existed from the early 1900s a history of anti-Japanese sentiment and an extensive array of discriminatory legal and political policies and actions. This ethnic group had been effectively contained and constrained, physically and socially, from large-scale acceptance by members of the larger society. By 1942, they were a segregated ethnic group of whom most of the Mainland population had little knowledge, nor with whom they sought acquaintance. After the attack on Pearl Harbor, the flames of racial animosity were fanned by leading West Coast politicians, military officials, and the general public, and the public silence of President Roosevelt on the subject of the Nikkei group became stronger and drifted over the entire West Coast Nikkei population.[11] Although the historic anti-Japanese forces clamored for the government to solve their "Japanese problem," President Roosevelt, the US Navy's ONI, and the Justice Department's FBI had contrary intelligence reports attesting to the basic loyalty of this ethnic population. Nevertheless, for political reasons, Roosevelt signed an order resulting in the mass incarceration of almost all Nikkei from designated areas of Washington, Oregon, California, and Arizona. The authority for this action was Executive Order 9066 (EO 9066), signed on February 19, 1942, authorizing the secretary of war "or any military commander he so designated to prescribe military areas . . . from which any or all persons may be excluded, and with respect to which, the right of any person to enter, remain in, or leave shall be subject to whatever restriction [he] may impose in his discretion."[12] Although the United States was also at war with Germany and Italy, the initiation and implementation of EO 9066 targeted the Nikkei—American citizens and the remaining Issei who were not interned under the Alien Enemies Act. Because the incarceration story under EO 9066 on the Mainland is well known, my focus will now shift to the effects of EO 9066 on Hawai'i.

Before the start of World War II the Nikkei in Hawai'i were not excluded from the taint of racial hostility and suspicion as exemplified earlier by the 1939 statement of President Roosevelt. On December 18, Roosevelt accepted his cabinet's recommendation that all Japanese aliens in Hawai'i be removed and placed on an island other than O'ahu. The reply of Lieutenant General Delos C. Emmons, commander of Hawai'i's martial law government, to this order stressed the military and logistical difficulties of carrying out this maneuver, and so the War Department gave him permission to send only "those Issei he deemed dangerous to the mainland."[13] In compliance, Emmons sent to the Mainland on January 21, 1942, 156 Issei, 16 Nisei, and a few others such as 10 German nationals and 14 German Americans.[14] When they arrived on the West Coast, the Justice Department refused to accept the Nisei and German Americans, citing the inadvisability of a Mainland detention because their arrests had been conducted under martial law. Consequently they were returned to Hawai'i. Later, after the signing of EO 9066, President Roosevelt agreed with Frank Knox's recommendation to have all persons of Japanese ancestry in Hawai'i removed and incarcerated on another Hawai'i island, stating that "I do not worry about the constitutional question—first because of my recent order (EO 9066) and second because Hawaii is under martial law." [15] The Joint Chiefs of Staff on March 18 issued an order to General Emmons that "Japanese residents (either U.S. citizens or nationals) as are considered . . . to constitute a source of danger be transported to the U.S. mainland and placed under guard in concentration camps." [16] Because of the earlier objection of the Justice Department to interning American citizens, the War Department then ordered a selective removal of up to 15,000 Nikkei to the Mainland into "resettlement" areas, but that these areas are not to be called "internment camps." Besides the 875 Issei internees, 1,217 Hawai'i Nikkei came to the Mainland and were placed in the WRA incarceration camps, producing a total of 2,092 Hawai'i Nikkei so removed. In addition, about 300 Nikkei remained in Hawai'i and were interned at the army's Honouliuli Gulch, O'ahu, internment camp after the Sand Island detention center was closed. The total Hawai'i Nikkei detained in either the Hawai'i or Mainland imprisonment facilities came to about 2,392.

What accounts for the differential treatment of the Hawai'i Nikkei when compared to the mass incarceration of those on the Mainland? The reasons are complex and an extended discussion is beyond the scope of this introduction. Certainly, in Hawai'i interethnic tensions did exist between the various ethnic groups, but arguably the degree of racial hostility and legal, political, and economic exclusion was considerably less than that faced by Nikkei on the Mainland. However, Hawai'i's social history also includes many instances of positive social interrelationships among the island Nikkei and others of the island population. It was at this level of interpersonal relationships, especially between the Nisei generation and members of other racial and ethnic groups in Hawai'i, that made for a better basis of interethnic understanding and trust. Specifically, Hawai'i had a group of influential individuals who were knowledgeable about the Nikkei and were careful to treat persons as individuals rather than subjecting them to collective suspicion and fearful attitudes on the basis of their ethnicity. Members of this group had since the late 1930s created a Council for Interracial Unity that quietly but effectively worked to counter efforts toward mass internment and incarceration in Hawai'i. The members of this committee came from many sectors of the Hawai'i population, including, for example, Charles Hemenway, a University of Hawai'i regent; Hung Wai Ching, YMCA executive; Shigeo Yoshida, a Hilo-born writer and teacher; and John A. Burns, Honolulu police detective. Later, key individuals in Hawai'i included Robert Shivers, FBI agent, and General Emmons. Within three days of Emmons' assuming the command of the Hawai'i's martial law government on December 18, he created a Morale Committee headed by Ching, Yoshida, and Charles Loomis. This committee became instrumental in capturing and expressing the patriotism and loyalty of the Hawai'i Nikkei such that by January 16, 1942, General Emmons decided against the president and War Department wish to intern the Issei and their citizen children.[17]

Another important factor that mitigated the decision for a large-scale internment and incarceration of the Hawai'i Nikkei was its significant presence in the population and labor force. *Nikkei* constituted 37.3 percent of the World War II island population, while on the Mainland it was always less than 1 percent. General Emmons used this potential loss-of-labor issue as an important reason to forego immediate compliance with the order for the wholesale incarceration of the Hawai'i Nikkei. There were undoubtedly other factors, although perhaps of lesser consequence, such as the imposition of martial law allowing for a tighter control of the Nikkei population and the early and impressive showing of the Nisei in creating and participating in a voluntary labor group that was noticed by authorities in both Hawai'i and Washington, D.C. And finally, the differing personalities and perceptions of the military commanders on the West Coast and Hawai'i, especially as they assessed the Nikkei populace, undoubtedly played an important role in the differential treatment of this group within their command area.

An Issei Narrative

Inside the entryway of the Japanese Cultural Center of Hawai'i in Honolulu are twelve square granite pillars standing side by side. Above the stones is the adage "Values create a people and help them survive and thrive," and on each column are etched the following in Japanese characters: *KōKō* (filial piety), *On* (debt of gratitude), *Gaman* (quiet endurance), *Ganbari* (perseverance), *Shikata Ga Nai* (acceptance with resignation), *Kansha* (gratitude), *Chūgi* (loyalty), *Sekinin* (responsibility), *Haji/Hokori* (shame/pride), *Meiyo* (honor), *Giri* (sense of duty), and *Gisei* (sacrifice). Each of these Japanese concepts represents core values brought by the Japanese immigrants to their new Hawai'i home, and these concepts resonate throughout Yasutaro Soga's narrative. Although Soga does not explicitly refer to these values, an understanding of them helps one to enter into the Issei life-world and illuminates how he understood and made sense of his social world. For example, throughout the narrative, there is a noticeable positive stress on the importance of quiet endurance, displeasure when individuals unduly place their personal welfare before the good of the group, an emphasis on maintaining one's personal honor, and the necessity of persevering and accepting life's conditions while cherishing moments of hope and beauty even in the most difficult of conditions and times.

The reader may also observe that, in contrast to remembrances written in a European literary tradition, there appears to be an absence of heightened drama. Soga's narrative tone appears to be more monotonic, so that in many sections the mundane aspects of life take and hold center stage. There seems to be an inordinate stress on the daily vicissitudes of life—the weather, flowers, food, and even the pettiness of other internees. The names of people also appear at times to crowd the text. However, rather than seeing these as stylistic liabilities, the reader might recall that this is not a diary but personal recollections initially penned for the 1946 Japanese newspaper-reading audience. Soga's audience is attuned to this Japanese writing style, and it allows us in the present day to appreciate both the Issei perspective and his framing of his personal and eyewitness experiences as an internee in the World War II army and Justice Department camps. What is quite exceptional is his detailed account of almost all the major events encountered by the Hawai'i Issei internee—Hawai'i's Sand Island, Angel Island, California, Lordsburg, and Santa Fe in New Mexico. This is a rare and valuable addition to understanding the complete World War II story.

Again, perhaps because of the journalistic origin of this narrative, Soga appears reluctant to let the reader into his emotional state during his four years of internment. Two examples in the narrative, however, offer tantalizing glimpses of the inner world of the Issei male. When the first Hawai'i Issei group was told that they would be shipped to the Mainland, he observes that "Many of the men grew desperate and felt that no one cared if they lived or died. One man, who had been so brazen and such a troublemaker before the war, broke down in tears. On the night of the 19th, at the [Hawai'i] Immigration Office, some men sang, some cried, and some fell deep into thought." Then, when it was Soga's time to leave Hawai'i, he tells us: "The day before I left [August 7, 1942], I asked Dr. Mori to give my wife the ninety poems I had composed while in the camp. I felt like the aimless wanderer in the old Japanese tales. I carried a suitcase in each hand and asked a young man to carry the big barracks bag for me. When we passed in front of the women's barracks, they called out, 'Good luck!' I heard Mrs. Mori say, 'Mr. Soga, be strong.' A tear fell in spite of myself. We boarded ship at four that afternoon."

However, Yasutaro Soga was not timid in his depiction and antagonistic portrayal of a few Issei figures in the internment camps. Considering that his initial audience would be a Japanese readership, he was quite willing to castigate others when they showed less than proper deference or concern about what he considered to be shameful behavior *(Haji),* or when they failed to do their expected duty *(Giri)* with honor *(Meiyo).* This provides us with an entrance into the mind of an educated Japanese Issei, and thus is valuable in its own right. That "Values create a people and help them survive and thrive" is a fitting maxim to keep in mind when striving to understand Soga's public face while in an internment camp.

Soga's mention of the ninety poems that he sent to his wife the day before he left Hawai'i gives reason to believe that it was not out of personal reluctance that he limited the expression of his intimate thoughts. He was an accomplished and published poet, and through some poems of Keiho Soga, his pen name, the reader may better understand his innermost sentiments about the internment experience. His separation from his wife, for example, is expressed through the image of someone who is as close as his memory though remaining far-distant:[18]

As I doze at dawn,	akatsuki no
My wife comes to me	utsuro kokoro ni
Our hands lightly touch,	te to te o furete
The dream is no more.	yume samenikeri

At the Santa Fe, New Mexico, camp, Soga saw the effect of the internment and time on the internee's inner spirit:

Many a friend	toraware no
Who is incarcerated	tomo no oku wa
Ages visibly.	me ni shiruku
Summer is passing by.	oini keru kamo
	natsu nakaba sugu

And for others, their deaths are memorialized:

The barren wasteland	suna kuruu
Raged by sandstorm,	areno ni toha ni
I weep for my friend	nemuritaru
Who sleeps there alone,	tomo no sabishisa
Eternally.	omoi namidasu

and,

When the war is over   warera mina
And after we are gone   sarinishi ato no
Who will visit   kono mushiro
This lonely grave in the wild   tare ka touran
Where my friend lies buried?   ikusa hate naba

The Issei internees felt keenly their change of status from able-bodied, fully functioning family providers, husbands, and fathers to a vulnerable state imposed through no fault of their own but based only on an accident of ethnicity and generation. The internment camp authorities continued to reinforce this position, and the internees tried continually to find meaning and hope in their daily existence. And so, their daily concerns, petty as they might appear to those outside the system, became the reality of their lives. Soga's Issei narrative reflects this perspective; yet forever present in the background and brought strategically at times to the foreground by Soga are instances of huge and momentous events such as death, physical assaults, internee resistance, and a seemingly interminable separation of time and distance from their wives and families.

Conclusion

Today, in America's post-September 11, 2001 days, we have become hyper-vigilant about the possible harmful actions of people about whom we know very little. This was the situation of the Nikkei in Hawai'i and on the Mainland during World War II, and especially in the case of the Issei, who were all assumed to have unfathomable loyalties toward an enemy nation. This sweeping generalization was not imposed wholesale on the Italian and German nationals in the United States. However, regardless of the perceptions of those in Washington, D.C., about the Nikkei, there were significantly fewer Issei interned in Hawai'i compared with their mainland compatriots. The incarceration saga likewise offers an even more starkly different picture. Whereas in Alaska and the continental United States almost all the remaining Nikkei group were expelled from their homes and put into "relocation" camps, only a comparative handful were so treated in Hawai'i. And even among these few individuals, most were voluntary internees hoping to reunite with their husbands and or fathers. It is important to understand at least one important lesson stemming from the differential treatment of this group—that alternatives to mass internment or incarceration do exist and that such actions should not be predicated simply on the basis of ethnicity or race. It is conceivable that a call for similar actions might arise toward a group if another fanatical-based attack occurs in or to the United States. When fear and prejudice are directed at a vulnerable group—a group that few can claim friendships with or knowledge about—then the result may again mirror the catastrophic actions taken on the U.S. West Coast against their Nikkei population. Hawaiʻi demonstrated that knowing people before a shattering event occurs can affect the process generated to deal with difficult situations. Castigating an entire group on the basis of religious affiliation, national origin, ethnicity, race, or other social categories rather than on individual behavior could again result in draconian measures taken in the name of "national security" and "military necessity."

To this point, George Santayana offers an appropriate remark: "Progress, far from consisting in change, depends on retentiveness . . . when experience is not retained, as among savages, infancy is perpetual. Those who cannot remember the past are condemned to repeat it. . . . This is the condition of children and barbarians, in whom instinct has learned nothing from experience." [19] The lessons that can be learned from Hawaiʻi and its treatment of their Nikkei population offers an acceptable alternative to the World War II internment and incarceration instituted in the Territory of Alaska and on the mainland United States. That fewer Issei and Nisei had to endure the difficult journey of internment and incarceration, however, does not alleviate the pain and suffering felt by Yasutaro Soga:

There is nothing	ikusa hodo
More sorrowful than war.	kanashiki wa nashi
Here alone,	sekaijyu no
All of life's sadness	kanashiki koto no
Is brought together.	koko ni atsumaru

Seattle, Washington
October 13, 2006

Notes

*Yasutaro (Keiho) Soga, in Jiro Nakano and Kay Nakano, eds., *Poets Behind Barbed Wire: Tanka Poems by Keiho Soga, Taisanboku Mori, Sojin Takei, and Muin Ozaki* (Honolulu: Bamboo Ridge Press, 1983), 58. Poems quoted with permission of the publisher.

1. Commission on Wartime Relocation and Internment of Civilians, *Personal Justice Denied* (Seattle: University of Washington Press, 1982), 18.

2. Gary Okihiro, *Cane Fires: the Anti-Japanese Movement in Hawaii, 1865–1945* (Philadelphia: Temple University Press, 1991), 173.

3. Tetsuden Kashima, *Judgment without Trial: Japanese American Imprisonment during World War II* (Seattle: University of Washington Press, 2003).

4. Ibid., 32, 38, 231.

5. Memorandum, July 13, 1943, Justice Department, file number 44-3-31, Record Group 85, National Archives, quoted in Kashima, *Judgment without Trial,* 33.

6. Kashima, *Judgment without Trial,* 23–27.

7. Ibid., 124–125.

8. Jeffrey F. Burton, Mary M. Farrell, Florence B. Lord, and Richard W. Lord, *Confinement and Ethnicity: An Overview of World War II Japanese American Relocation Sites* (Seattle: University of Washington Press, 2002).

9. Kashima, *Judgment without Trial,* 186–191.

10. Soga, in Nakano and Nakano, *Poets Behind Barbed Wire,* 36.

11. Greg Robinson, *By Order of the President: FDR and the Internment of Japanese Americans* (Cambridge, MA: Harvard University Press, 2001).

12. Commission on Wartime Relocation and Internment of Civilians, *Personal Justice Denied.*

13. Kashima, *Judgment without Trial,* 77.

14. Ibid., 78.

15. Quoted in ibid., 80.

16. Quoted in ibid.

17. Tom Coffman, "The First Battle: A Fight for Justice and Equality in Hawaii," documentary, Honolulu, Hawai'i, 2006. See also Kashima, *Judgment without Trial,* 77.

18. The following poems by Yasutaro (Keiho) Soga are published in Nakano and Nakano, *Poets Behind Barbed Wire.* A Japanese *tanka* poem "consists of 31 syllables (5-7-5-7-7)" and "speaks of nature and human emotions and allows the reader to perceive the unsaid and the intimated unsaid" (p. viii).

19. George Santayana, *Life of Reason,* vol. 1, chap. 12, p. 248; 1905.

Life behind
Barbed Wire

Tessaku Seikatsu

YASUTARO (KEIHO) SOGA

I dedicate this book to
those who died in the camps.

PREFACE

AFTER FOUR years, I returned to this green island in the Pacific Ocean from the snowy mountains of Santa Fe. The differences between this world near sea level and where I had been, 7,500 feet above the sea and surrounded by the Rocky Mountains, were never so apparent to me than upon my return. Honolulu seems to have changed much, but I truly believe that it is still a beautiful place—as it has always been. Coming home to a warm, loving family after living day in and day out with only men in a barracks was a dream come true. Only those who shared our fate can truly understand this feeling.

Time flies. Our group of 450 came back by way of Seattle on November 13, only a little more than a month and a half ago. With the return of 900 Issei and Nisei and their families on December 10, all who had been sent to the Mainland from Hawaii were finally home except for those who had chosen to go on to Japan. For the first time in a long while we could rest easy. When I reflect on my life as an internee during those four years, many images cross my mind like those on a revolving shadow lantern. Of course life was not easy, but the camps proved to be an invaluable training ground for the human spirit. The fallout from war hysteria threw us—innocent victims—together in a place of exile where we shared a common experience. I had presumed that a war between Japan and the United States would never come to pass, no matter how tense the situation became, but it was just wishful thinking. Of course I was prepared to accept my fate should the unthinkable happen.

The fish on a cutting board cannot escape no matter how much it struggles. We all tried to accept what was happening to us calmly. Moreover, we used this "forced vacation" to read and meditate, activities we had been neglecting. Thanks to this attitude, I kept quite busy and was not *21* troubled much. Many people try to be sympathetic and say, "You must have been bored." But I never found internee life tedious. Fortunately my health was always good except for the occasional light cold or minor stomach trouble. I was never hospitalized and could easily have kept up this record of good health. In the camp I was too busy to fall ill.

After we were forced to move to the Mainland, all of us—Japanese from every conceivable background, from Alaska down to South America—were obliged to live in groups, fenced in by barbed wire: In the camps, we represented the Japanese community of the Americas in miniature. In what follows I have tried to record my observations and experiences of that time and place as truthfully, fairly, and simply as possible. I sometimes felt, however, that I was writing too much—particularly in the beginning, where I describe the frightening time we spent detained on Sand Island. For this I sincerely beg the reader's forgiveness.

Yasutaro (Keiho) Soga
Honolulu, Hawaii
January 9, 1946

THE BOMBING
OF PEARL HARBOR

"Like a thunderbolt out of the blue" literally describes the news of Japan's attack on Pearl Harbor. Near the end of 1941, the situation between Japan and the United States had become serious, but most of the people in Hawaii believed something would be done at the last moment and war would be avoided. This was the thinking not only of Japanese here, but also of high-ranking military officials. At around nine o'clock in the morning on December 7 (December 8 in Japan), I was sitting on my porch, relaxing in a *yukata* (cotton kimono) and reading a magazine as was my habit on Sundays. The telephone rang. It was a coworker calling to say that Japanese planes were attacking Pearl Harbor and that war had broken out. "That's ridiculous. It must be a training exercise," I replied, refusing to discuss it further.

Sensing that something unusual was up, however, I ran upstairs to the second-floor veranda and looked toward Pearl Harbor, several miles away.[1] Antiaircraft guns were roaring; every burst of fire blackened the sky with smoke, which temporarily froze, then formed big, dark clouds. At first I thought these were smoke screens. Huge columns of water were erupting everywhere, just like the ones I had seen during a torpedo exercise on the Sumida River when I was a child. The ghastly black smoke grew thicker and began covering the sky over the harbor. I could hear the thunder of cannon fire. This was quite a bit different from the usual military maneuvers. Soon a big fire was raging near the McCully Tract. More black smoke rose and red flames shot up, but no fire engines rushed to the scene as expected. I

---

1. Soga lived in a residential area east of downtown Honolulu known as Kaimuki. It is located approximately twelve miles from Pearl Harbor.

felt this was very strange. About an hour later the news confirmed that the Japanese naval force had launched a surprise attack on Pearl Harbor at 7:55 that morning. The fire in McCully had been caused by a shell from an American antiaircraft gun. All the fire engines in the city were called to the naval port, so nothing was done about the blaze in town. Several dozen children and adults, most of them Japanese, were killed or injured by shell fragments at the Hawaii Chuo Gakuin (a Japanese language school) in Nuuanu and other places. Many Hawaii Japanese suffered that day.[2]

I ran down the stairs immediately and switched on the radio. Both KGU and KGMB stations were already broadcasting news about the attack. It must be the real thing, I thought to myself, but I was still not convinced. When I heard "The enemy airplanes bore the mark of the Rising Sun," my heart began to pound. At the same time, I thought that perhaps they had been German planes in disguise or that the Japanese naval artisans had attacked rashly.

I listened to the radio, straining my ears. Orders from the military were read in succession by the announcer. One was for doctors in the city to report at once to various hospitals. Dr. Miyamoto and other Nisei physicians were among those called.[3] The orders continued. Civilians were not allowed to use telephones or cars. Although some Japanese had been taken into custody, there was no need for panic because not all Japanese were under arrest. Listeners were advised to boil drinking water because Japanese paratroopers might have poisoned the reservoirs. Finally, it was announced that Governor Poindexter had proclaimed martial law and that it was effective immediately.[4]

By this time, one of the biggest news stories of the century—the outbreak of war between the United States and Japan—had been broadcast not only in Hawaii, but all over the world. At about 10:00, as I was reading the first extra edition of the *Honolulu Star-Bulletin* (brought to me by Mr. A of Yokohama Specie Bank), I had a premonition that something was going to happen to me. I usually wore a *kimono* on Sundays, but I changed to a suit

2. According to documents in the Hawai'i War Records Depository at the University of Hawai'i, approximately seventy-two civilians were killed as a result of the Pearl Harbor attack, all by American antiaircraft fire. Thirty-two had Japanese surnames.

3. Dr. Miyamoto was Kazuo Miyamoto (1900–1988), who is subsequently mentioned a number of times in Soga's account. Miyamoto wrote a fictionalized version of his internment experience in the novel *Hawaii: End of the Rainbow* (Tokyo: Charles E. Tuttle, 1964).

4. Joseph Poindexter was appointed by President Franklin D. Roosevelt as territorial governor of Hawai'i in 1934 and served in that position until August of 1942, when he was succeeded by Ingram Stainback.

and put on a pair of shoes so that I would be ready to go out at any time. My family regarded me with suspicion, but I acted as though nothing was out of the ordinary and read a book with feigned calm. Later that day the Red Cross' surgical supplies department chief called my wife and asked her to increase her volunteer bandaging from once to several times a week. He also asked her to report for work the next day and to speak nothing but English in the workroom. He gave her some other advice as well.

From December 7, 1941, the Hawaiian Islands were under strict blackout orders from 6:00 P.M. to 7:00 A.M. Mr. A and his family lived near Fort Ruger. Because they felt unsafe with so many soldiers close by, I offered them our second floor and took in the couple and their two children. Usually I had dinner with my family, but that night I ate alone, explaining that I wanted to finish my meal before it got dark. While the evening dusk was gathering, a car with blue lights suddenly stopped in front of our yard. My son, Shigeo, went to the entrance hall to meet the visitors, three military policemen. They were six feet tall and young and wore MP armbands. They said they were taking me to the Immigration Office. I immediately answered, "All right," and went to the bedroom to get a vest. The three MPs barged in and followed me. My wife helped me put on the vest and a coat. I picked up three handkerchiefs, placed on top of the bureau earlier, and put them in my pocket. I also hid a tiny book containing the *noh* song "Yoroboshi" (Blind Priest) in another pocket. Helen, Walter, and the other children had not gone to bed yet; while both families stood dumbfounded, I was escorted out of the house. My wife came with me as far as the entrance hall and whispered, "Please be careful not to catch a cold." I tried to say something but could not utter a word and silently went to the car. Two of the MPs sat in the front, and one sat beside me in the back with a pistol in his hand.

There were no cars or pedestrians on the street: My neighborhood resembled a ghost town. The car quickly turned from 11th Avenue to Kilauea Avenue and sped toward town. One of the MPs asked if I knew where "William Ido" lived. From his pronunciation of the name, I thought it was Portuguese, so I replied, "No." They eventually found the house. The man who ended up seated behind me looked like Mr. Toka Ida, but I could not tell in the darkness. After him, they arrested Mr. Ryoichi Tanaka and Mr. Soichi Obata of my newspaper and squeezed them into the back seat. We were ordered not to speak to each other, so we kept silent. The MPs also drove to the former residence of Mr. Takashi Wada, who had since moved to the Waikiki area. They could not locate him. Finally, the car headed toward Ala Moana Boulevard and the Immigration Office.

Without light from street lamps or houses, I could not tell where we were headed. At every street corner, armed guards challenged us, brandishing their bayonets. One of the MPs was constantly getting out of the car to explain where they were going: "We are taking prisoners to the Immigration Office." In the distance we could hear the roar of cannon fire coming from Pearl Harbor. The only lights we saw were the blue lights of military cars. The MPs who were accompanying us snapped, "Japs are attacking Pearl Harbor again." Within the space of a day, we had been forced from our Pacific Ocean paradise and now found ourselves in hell.

At the Immigration Office

It was now just past eight o'clock in the evening on December 7. From the Immigration Office's rear entrance, we were taken to an underground room. Many MPs and other soldiers were there. Each of us was searched and everything, including money and identification papers, was confiscated. I saw a pile of knives on the floor, which led me to believe that many people had already passed through here. The only things I was allowed to keep with me were my wristwatch, fountain pen, and handkerchiefs.

Next we were sent to an upper floor. With an MP holding me by the arm, I went up a dark, narrow staircase. He opened the door to a room and practically threw me in. I was surprised by the rank and sultry air. I could not see how many people were in the room, but I quickly discovered there was almost no place for me to stand. The following morning I discovered there were 164 of us, all Japanese, packed like sushi into a space for about half as many. No wonder the room was so stifling. There were several rows of three-story beds, and the remaining floor space was filled with more beds—three or four people to each. A washroom and toilets were next door, but they were always crowded and soon became dirty and foul-smelling beyond description.

Soon after I entered the room, I think it was Mr. Kyoichi Hamamura who guided me to the uppermost bunk of an already occupied bed near a window. I could hear whispering. In time I heard Dr. Iga Mori inquire, "Mr. Soga?" and the thin voice of the owner of the Komeya Hotel call out, "I am here, too." I felt especially sorry for these sickly elders who were sharing my fate. It was very hot and someone opened the windows, but later that night it turned cold. Before I could get a decent bit of sleep, it was dawn. Everyone else must have passed the night in the same way.

When we could finally see each other, we realized that most of us were old acquaintances. One of the first to be brought here was the Reverend Kuchiba of the Honpa Hongwanji Hawaii Betsuin Mission. He had arrived at around three o'clock that afternoon. Dr. Tokue Takahashi, Mr. Manzuchi Hashimoto, Mr. Tetsuo Toyama, and others were later brought in handcuffed. Dr. Takahashi's residence was located on Alewa Heights, which looks down on Pearl Harbor. As soon as he heard of the attack, he went to his veranda to watch the drama unfold in detail through a telescope, taking note of what he saw. Just then the military police arrived and arrested him. Dr. Takahashi was the elder brother of Mr. Ibo Takahashi, a vice admiral in the Japanese navy. The owner of a speedboat, he had spent many Sundays cruising near his home. The authorities had probably kept a keen eye on him.

Two ministers, Buntetsu Miyamoto and Ryuten Kashiwa of Waialua, were brought in handcuffed, as was Mr. Takegoro Kusao, my newspaper's bureau chief.[5] The drive from Waialua to Honolulu usually takes about an hour and a half, but on the day of the attack it took about five hours. The car the three men were riding in passed the devastated Pearl Harbor naval port. At the sound of cannon fire, their guards would stop the car and dive under it. They arrived at the Immigration Office later that night, badly shaken.

The stories of those arrested were all different. It seems that much depended on the discretion of the military police, policemen, or FBI agents who made the arrest. Generally speaking, in cases where the officer in charge was either a Chinese or a Korean, treatment seemed unnecessarily harsh. The Immigration Office was located near Pearl Harbor, so it was reasonable to expect the staff there to be entirely unsympathetic to enemy aliens. The manner of the military police toward us was such that anything could have happened. I was prepared for the worst.

At mealtimes, we lined up single file and were led to a backyard under the strict surveillance of military police. Anyone who stepped out of line came face to face with the point of a bayonet. At the entrance to the yard, each of us got a mess kit and food. Then we sat down on the ground and ate. Although there was a covered rest area nearby, we were forbidden to use it. Even if the ground was wet or it had begun to rain, we were forced to eat sitting on the ground. After ten or twenty minutes, we were taken back to the room. We were not allowed an occasional breath of fresh air or exercise at all. Of course we had to wash our own utensils. After we

---

5. The Reverend Ryuten Kashiwa was the resident minister of the Waialua Hongwanji [Buddhist] temple on Oʻahu. Upon the cessation of the war, he returned to his former post in Waialua. Subsequently, he was asked to serve as acting bishop of the Hawaii Mission [Honpa Hongwanji].

returned to our room, a few of us were called in turn and ordered to clean our area and the toilets.

On the very first morning, a cocky young MP, apparently fresh from the Mainland, ordered us around like dogs with his bayonet. Once, with the blood surging in my veins, I was on the verge of throwing a dish at him, but at the last moment I regained my composure. Mr. Matsui, the general manager of Pacific Bank, was in front of me and also pale with anger. Later I found out that he and I had shared the same violent impulse. It was good that we endured the MPs' insults. If we had given in to our anger, we would have been run through—gored like potatoes—and would have died needlessly. Given my circumstances, I could not complain about the unpalatable food or the dirty tableware. However, some things were extremely unpleasant. Hawaiian, Portuguese, and sometimes Chinese and Nisei convicts did menial work at the Immigration Office and had their meals in the yard before us. We were forced to clean our tableware in the dirty water left from their washing. Thus even convicts belittled us.

On the morning of the third day, December 9, about half of us were loaded into covered trucks in groups of twelve. I was among those taken. We were driven to Pier 5 and directed aboard a big scow. Machine guns and bayonets surrounded us. I thought we were being sent to Lanai or Molokai, but shortly thereafter we tied up at Sand Island. In the old days, Sand Island had been called Sennin Koya (shack for a thousand people) because quarantined immigrants were housed there. Later it became the U.S. Quarantine Station and was put under military control.

2

SAND ISLAND
DETENTION CAMP

SAND ISLAND LIES just a short distance away from Honolulu. From the pier, we walked for about thirty minutes before we were lined up in front of the barracks. The 35th U.S. Army Regiment Commander, who was responsible for the security of the area, addressed us: "The United States and Japan are at war. I am aware of the outstanding characteristics of the Japanese, but you are now detainees. In due time each of you will get a hearing. Some of you may be released while others may be detained during the war. You are not criminals but prisoners of war. Thus we will treat you equally in accordance with military rules." His demeanor was pleasant enough, but I felt uneasy when I heard the phrase "prisoners of war." [1]

In one of the barracks we were ordered to take off our clothes and were thoroughly searched; they even checked the soles of our shoes. My wristwatch and the small book in my pocket were confiscated. We barely escaped with our fountain pens, pencils, and handkerchiefs. As for our living quarters, there was only one dining room and one building for showers and toilets in a fifteen-acre wilderness. Both were concrete; nearby there were a few small tents. We immediately began pitching more tents under the supervision of soldiers. After a quick meal, we continued working feverishly at this unaccustomed task. Night came, but lights were not allowed. It also began to rain. We had to assemble one tent for every eight people, about twenty tents in all, and set up army cots in each tent. It was not easy work. Soaked with rain and sweat, I think we completed the work at around nine o'clock that night. Just before we finished, a second group

---

1. The captain was identified by Patsy Sumie Saiki as John J. Coughlin of the 111th Military Police Company. This unit could have been attached to the 35th Regiment, as written here. See Saiki's *Ganbare! An Example of Japanese Spirit* (Honolulu: Kisaku, Inc., 1982), p. 30.

arrived from the Immigration Office. Among them was the frail, elderly owner of the Komeya Hotel, who had fainted on the dark camp road and had to be carried in by the others. That night, like sewer rats, we slept just as we were.

On the morning of the tenth, camp life began in earnest. We were granted conditional autonomy. About 160 men were divided into four companies of 40 each, with a commander. Each company was further divided into four squads of 10 men, including a squad leader. Finally, a battalion commander was elected as our liaison with the military authorities. No one was eager to take on the task, but Mr. George Genji Otani volunteered. The commanders were Mr. Sasaki, the principal of Makiki Japanese Language School; Mr. Kimura, the branch manager of Nippon Yusen Kaisha; and Mr. Harry Shiramizu and Mr. Kensaku Tsunoda, English reporters for the *Nippu Jiji*. Mr. Kawasaki of Dai-jingu was chosen as secretary.

Every morning and evening we lined up for roll call and companies received assignments for kitchen, toilet, and general cleaning jobs in turn. Mr. Otani, our battalion commander, was given the nickname "Admiral" by the military personnel, possibly because he had once been a sailor. We elected our own officers, but given our conditional autonomy, they first had to be approved by the authorities. We were forced to find replacements for those who were rejected. A few days after our arrival, the regimental commander in charge was suddenly reassigned and Captain E succeeded him.[2]

"The Okano Incident"

Captain E, the newly appointed commander, was formerly a chief inspector at the Honolulu Customs Office, where he was known as a faultfinder. The outgoing camp commander, a career military officer, told us that his successor was one of the toughest men in Honolulu. Captain E's attitude toward us was indeed very stern. We could accept someone who administered rules strictly but fairly. Captain E, however, intentionally made mountains out of molehills and deliberately presented a defiant attitude to irritate us. After he assumed command, a series of unpleasant incidents occurred one after another in the camp. His fat and arrogant figure, walking around the camp and jangling a bunch of keys, still lingers in my memory.

The first of these was "The Okano Incident." From the beginning, we

---

2. According to Saiki, "Captain E" was Carl F. Eifler. See *Ganbare!* p. 32.

were not allowed to keep anything that might be used as a weapon: knives, scissors, shaving blades, even nails. Some of the men, however, picked up the strips of metal used to bind crates to make tongue cleaners and knives, which they secretly sharpened on stones. On the evening of December 14, several men were taken outside to work beyond the barbed-wire fence. Upon their return, one of them, a young preacher named Ryoshin Okano, was found with a handmade knife. Instantly several guards sounded alarms, surrounded him, and stripped him completely naked while brandishing their pistols at him.

It was already nightfall, but Captain E called all of us out of our tents and into the yard, where he lined us up and had us strip to nothing, leaving us at attention while guards searched our clothing. They confiscated practically everything, including fountain pens and pencils. Even in Hawaii it gets cold at night in the middle of December. It was especially cold that winter, the year the war began. We were kept standing for a long time; a dry wind blew and we all shivered with cold. When we finally returned to our tents, we found all of our belongings scattered about. A handmade knife had also been found in the coat of Mr. Serizawa, a school principal from Kalihi. Although he claimed the knife was not his, he was ordered to perform hard labor for three days.

Around that time, we were assigned various chores in turn. We were also ordered to weed, pick up trash, and swat flies: There was never a free moment. Guards constantly walked between the tents. Unless you were sick, you were not allowed to remain in your tent. We were forced to exercise twice a day. If more than three of us gathered to talk, we were yelled at and ordered to disperse. (When the Reverend Kuchiba; Mr. Matsuda, the branch manager of Yokohama Specie Bank; and another man were seen talking together, they were obliged to carry picks and shovels to an area outside the barbed-wire fence and dig for unexploded ordnance.) We were not allowed paper or pencils or newspapers. At night there was no light. Even if we wanted to smoke, matches were forbidden at night. After dinner, from eight o'clock on, we could not leave our tents except to go to the toilet. If you were on your way to the toilet at night and a guard suddenly ordered "Stop!" you had to answer "Prisoner!" immediately. If you kept silent, you could be shot dead.

Our Status Is Corrected

The newly appointed army commander in Hawaii, Lieutenant General Delos C. Emmons, came to Sand Island for an inspection as soon as he arrived here. I think it was around December 20. He was a small but capable-looking man. On the twenty-second, his assistant announced: "You are neither criminals nor prisoners of war but merely detainees. Thus you are not governed by military rules. However, we would appreciate it if you would show respect when our flag is lowered at sunset." Up to that point, we had been regarded as prisoners of war. We had all thought the designation a strange one, and I think Commander Emmons noted it upon his arrival. On the other islands, we would have been considered detainees from the start. It seems that only the military authorities in Honolulu had thought otherwise. Once our status was changed, the tight grip on us loosened.

There were eight cots to a tent, and only a minimum of personal articles was allowed. Suitcases, trunks, and other items that we had brought with us were kept in a separate storage area. It was very humid in the tents because there was no flooring: Cots were placed directly on the ground, and the two blankets allocated to each of us were often damp by morning. When it rained at night, water sometimes flowed into the tents. Those who suffered from hemorrhoids or arthritis were especially affected by the damp. We lived in tents for six months before barracks were built.

Although Honolulu was within plain view, we were at first denied any contact with our families and the outside world. Our present conditions were never communicated to others beyond the barbed-wire fence. This tiny island, separated from Oahu by a narrow stretch of water, was a world unto itself. On both sides there was much speculation. In the camp rumors persisted that so-and-so had been shot dead or run through with a bayonet. Living under these circumstances was enough to drive anyone crazy.

Most of the men had arrived with only the clothes they were wearing at the time of their arrest. It was December and sandstorms raged constantly, which seemed appropriate in a place called "Sand Island." Behind the barbed wire we shivered with cold. At the time, we did not know what was going to happen to us and did not want to die unseemly deaths, so we slept in our clothes. Because we did not have any spare clothing, we washed our underwear and outer garments alternately. Dr. Takahashi tied up the torn sleeve of his overshirt with string. Mr. Taichi Sato was without a coat and was wearing only a pair of slippers when he was arrested. He did not have a handkerchief, so I gave him one of mine. He kept the handkerchief even after it had become tattered, saying it was a good memento. There are many such stories of people helping one another in small ways. All of a sudden we went from being "haves" to "have-nots." We endured many harsh and bitter experiences on Sand Island, but when we reflect on them now, we find much cause for laughter too. Many comical situations resulted from our having to adjust to a world without women.

Cigarette Hell

Although liquor was forbidden in the camp, the military is always compassionate toward cigarette smokers, so a small amount of Bull Durham tobacco and cigarettes were distributed. Most of us, however, were not allowed to have matches; only commanders could keep a few at a time. So while drinkers resigned themselves to living without liquor, smokers developed a stronger craving for cigarettes here in the camp, where there was no other pleasure. Due to the permanent shortage of cigarettes, seven or eight people would take turns smoking one cigarette. When that proved inadequate, they collected discarded cigarette butts, broke them up, then rerolled and smoked them, just like the Portuguese boys who scavenged for butts on the street. When cigarette paper was not available, they used toilet paper. Matches were split in two and later used as toothpicks. These people had lived respectable lives outside; here they were beyond all sense of shame. While in the camp, I clearly saw what it was like to be trapped in "cigarette hell." I had been a smoker in the old days, but more than ten years had passed since I stopped. I did want a puff once in a while and, given my dreary situation, I was tempted to smoke again. "Bad" friends also tempted me. Nevertheless, I stubbornly abstained from smoking throughout my four-year internment. I consider it to my advantage that I did and regard my obstinacy as a source of pride.

Somewhat apart from our camp lived seventy to eighty German and Italian detainees. We were prohibited from visiting each other, and conversation between the groups was discouraged. The mess hall chief was German, and his assistant and the other KP workers were Japanese. The food served was completely Western. For Japanese, there was too much fat and too few vegetables and fruits. I was accustomed to having fruit at every meal and liked vegetables, so the meals here pained me the most. Some spiteful guards forced us to eat what was left on our plates and watched us as we ate. They carefully monitored the amount of food we threw in the garbage can. If we threw out too much, they objected. There were instances when some ill-natured guards made whoever had thrown out leftovers eat them there, right in front of them. Every morning the authorities checked the toilets and other places that had been cleaned, even the beds. They were very strict; we were not allowed to use the toilets or showers until inspection was over.

In the beginning receiving mail from home was difficult. Letters had to be written in English. Of course both outgoing and incoming mail was inspected and confiscated at will. When the mail arrived, a military whistle called us to gather in front of the office where letters and parcels were handed out. Everyone knew who was receiving mail. Once Reverend Kashiwa received so many letters that he was the object of envy. The Reverend Nisshu Kobayashi of Hokekyo Temple received a good many parcels and, because most of them were from ladies, this became a topic of idle conversation. Letter writing was limited to certain hours during the week. Each of us received paper and an envelope, which were kept at the office, and every ten or so people shared one pencil. Only a few of the men could read and write in English, so they were kept quite busy writing letters for others.

As I mentioned earlier, we had roll call every morning and evening. The guards called us to line up for frivolous reasons as well, sometimes as often as seven to eight times a day. This left us with little time to relax, and it was a constant source of irritation.

Battalion Commander Otani Is Punished

On December 24, our first Christmas Eve since our arrest, Mr. Masaji Marumoto arrived at the camp accompanied by an FBI agent.[3] This was the first time someone from the outside (other than military personnel) had visited us. Mr. Marumoto, a lawyer, had come to write powers of attorney, and I asked to meet with him. We were allowed to speak in Japanese, but of course the FBI agent present was fluent in Japanese. Upon his arrival, Mr. Marumoto's face became deathly pale, perhaps because he saw our surroundings and old friends badly in need of a shave and a change of clothes. I asked Mr. Marumoto to contact my wife about sending me some clothes. Half a month had passed since our arrival at the camp, and Mr. Daizo Sumida, Dr. Takahashi, and I had yet to receive a letter or parcel. We later found out that our letters had crossed with those from home, but at the time we felt somewhat frustrated and suffered from a lack of spare underwear. The day after Mr. Marumoto's visit, all three of us received parcels of clothes from home.

For Christmas, we were treated to turkey at lunch. The Germans and

---

3. Nisei lawyer Marumoto (1906–1995) went on to become a justice on the Surpeme Court of Hawai'i. His life is chronicled in the book *First among Nisei: The Life and Writings of Masaji Marumoto* by Dennis M. Ogawa (Honolulu: University of Hawai'i Press, 2007).

Italians hastily put up a simple Christmas tree in the mess hall. That night one of the German detainees, a lecturer at the University of Hawaii, gave a talk, and many Japanese attended. He said that he would pray for a quick end to the war and everyone's good health and that we be reunited with our families for Christmas next year.

On December 30, when the first year of the war was almost at a close, Battalion Commander "Admiral" Genji Otani, who was often the subject of our conversations, incurred Captain E's displeasure. Apparently he had shown disrespect toward the captain's subordinate, a violation for which he could have been shot. The captain had us assemble outside and called Mr. Otani to the front. He delivered a stiff reprimand and pronounced a harsh punishment. Several guards immediately transported a pale Mr. Otani to the military prison at Fort Shafter, where he was confined for a week and given only hard crackers and water. On January 5, he returned to the camp dejected, displaying long unkempt whiskers. Of course Mr. Otani was deprived of his position as battalion commander. We chose Dr. Kazuo Miyamoto as his successor and Messrs. Fuchino, Hamamoto, Sasaki, and Kimura as commanders. Captain E approved of our new officers, but at the time of the election he made it clear that Mr. Otani should not be elected to any office.

On the first day of 1942, our first New Year's Day since our arrest, we did not get even a piece of *mochi* (rice cake) and did not feel festive at all. We were filled with anxiety, frustration, and hopelessness—not only for ourselves, but also for the families we had left behind. Unless a man was extremely confident and optimistic, it was to be expected that here he might develop "nerves" or begin to display odd behavior. I noticed that men who had been fond of "talking big" outside were now depressed, turning into shadows of their former selves. Still others, refusing to face reality, clung to their prewar social status, which created problems for everyone.

When we are reduced to living at the most basic level, our good and bad points are clearly exposed. On the whole, educators and priests showed themselves to be the worst of the lot. I was not the only one who felt this way. Of course there are always exceptions: There are many respectable teachers and priests. I regret to say, however, that in the camp I was disappointed in most of them.

One Troublesome Incident Happens after Another

While we were detained, our minds grew dissolute. The joyless and dreary life continued day after day. To relieve the boredom, more and more men engaged in filthy talk. Even those who seemed to be men of strict moral character quickly adopted questionable speech or behavior. According to one doctor, these people were already mentally abnormal. The Shinto priest of an Inari shrine in the city was a good man but a little feminine. He became mentally unstable, insisted he was pregnant, and made things very difficult for Dr. Miyamoto. In time he became violent, and once we were forced to take turns watching him for three days and nights. (I was on one of these watches for three hours with Mr. Ryo-u Adachi early one cold morning.) The priest was paroled, and fortunately he recovered.

Our camp was surrounded by a heavy barbed-wire fence. Within ten feet of the fence there was a white line, which we were not allowed to cross. Anyone who did was considered a fugitive and could be shot dead. Despite this, one night a Shinto priest and a Buddhist monk with the nickname "Junior Fifth Rank" crossed the line. The principal of a Japanese school in the city also disregarded the order to pick up some rare seashells. In both cases, the guards overlooked their behavior and all three were returned without incident.

At about this time internees and false rumors seemed to go together. One evening a bookseller with a somewhat wild imagination claimed to have heard that the Japanese air force was ready to attack Hawaii again in the next thirty minutes. We had our doubts, but nevertheless we all became very anxious. Of course it turned out to be false; the man did not seem at all sorry for the trouble he had caused. Trivial as they may seem, such incidents, which occurred with increasing frequency, grated on our nerves.

Once, during an evening roll call, two men were found to be missing. Although their disappearance was later discovered to be a mistake, we worried about the repercussions. Another time, a broken pistol was found on a road in the camp. (Here even a nail was regarded as a weapon; it was impossible for one of us to have had a gun.) Then a metal shaving-soap container disappeared. During a routine body check, guards found one man with a nail and another with a hidden banknote. To deal with these incidents, a court hearing was held with Captain S, head of administration, as chief justice. Someone was appointed prosecutor; Mr. Kango Kawasaki attorney; and Mr. Futoshi Arakawa, the Reverend Himeno, and others jurors. The defendants were found guilty. As punishment, the weekly privilege of purchasing cigarettes was taken away from us for several weeks. The soap container, one of the reasons for the "trial" to begin with, was never found. At the beginning of the trial, Rev. Himeno was appointed prosecutor, but he insisted that he could not serve as one because he was a minister and accepted instead the position of juror. The authorities let us continue this playacting on two other occasions, trying to delude us into thinking that we were settling such matters ourselves.

The Reverend Deme and Old Man Tachibana

I think at least ten people were released from Sand Island Detention Camp due to special circumstances. Two elderly men who were ill, Dr. Iga Mori and Mr. Miyozuchi Komeya, were released at the end of December 1941. Mr. Shinkichi Yamamoto of Ewa and Mr. Kyuichi Hamada were also paroled because of illness, although somewhat belatedly. Rev. Chinpei Goto; Mr. Usuke Seri of Bishop Bank; Mr. Tachibana, a fisherman from Kakaako; Mr. Matsutaro Kamioka, who was affiliated with Mitsukoshi; Mr. Tokuzo Matsuoka, an accountant at Nuuanu Church; and Mr. Isamu Yonemura of Yokohama Specie Bank were all released for other reasons.

There is an interesting story behind the release of the Reverend Josen Deme. I think it was sometime in January 1942 that he was ordered to leave immediately. He believed, as we did, that he was going to be released, so he was very pleased. We also thought that this meant we might all be released soon and asked Rev. Deme to take messages to our families. When there was no news from him, we began to wonder what had happened. A new internee who had just come through the Immigration Office reported that Rev. Deme was being held there. Apparently he had been sent from Sand Island to the Immigration Office and put in with the German detainees there. We later learned that "Deme" is a German name and that "Josen" had been misspelled on the detainee list as "Josef." So Rev. Deme had been mistaken for a German and was being treated as one. Living among Germans was a great inconvenience for him because he could not understand their language. Eventually he was interned on the Mainland. Other Japanese names were mispronounced and mistaken for European names: For example, "Maeda" was pronounced "Meida," a German name. Dr. Ipponsugi's name became "Iponski," and he was mistaken for a Russian.

When the old fisherman from Kakaako, Mr. Tachibana, was released, I was being questioned at the Immigration Office. This man was an honest, good-natured fellow who gladly made straw sandals for everyone in the camp. On the morning of December 7, several Japanese fishermen in Kakaako were killed by U.S. machine-gun fire. Among the victims were two close relatives of Mr. Tachibana, who had been arrested before he heard the news of their deaths. After receiving his parole, Mr. Tachibana was ordered to leave, but he refused to accept his release without first receiving some form of written consent. Without written acknowledgment, he was afraid he might be arrested again. The immigration officials tried to put him in a car under guard, but Mr. Tachibana maintained that once they were gone, he would walk right back. (The Immigration Office was within hailing distance of his home.) He argued that once in the car, he might be taken away to some other place and detained. He gave the authorities quite a bit of trouble.

As I mentioned before, we lived in tents during our first six months on Sand Island. I think the barracks were completed at the end of May 1942. In our tent-living days, we were moved from Tent A to Tent B to Tent C. I was once told to change tents three times in three days. Although we did not have many belongings and it may have been a simple matter, we could not relax. The military's way of doing things seemed irresponsible. As soon as a decision was made, it was changed: Time and labor were often wasted. On top of that, there was no uniformity. I wondered if this was how the military functioned in general.

Many People, Many Personalities

During this period—particularly early on when we faced innumerable challenges at Sand Island—a few men struck me as exceptional: Doctors Tokue Takahashi and Kazuo Miyamoto, who were always composed and dignified; the Reverends Gendo Okawa and Kyokujo Kubokawa; Mr. Kango Kawasaki; Mr. Futoshi Arakawa; and Mr. Hiroshi and Mr. Tatsuo Motoshige, two brothers who were the embodiment of youthful spirit. I was also deeply impressed by the sincerity and cooperative spirit of many ordinary fishermen. Rev. Kubokawa, respectfully called "His Lordship" by the Jodo sect ministers, was always dressed in priestly robes. Pushing his sleeves up high, he volunteered to help tend the vegetable garden the men started. From morning to night, he recited *"Namuamidabutsu"* (I put my faith in Amida Buddha) in a whisper. In his prime, Rev. Kubokawa was known as a "new" Buddhist and served as executive officer at Shiba Zojo Temple in Tokyo. His credentials reflected his unwavering mettle, unlike that of some Zen monks at the Immigration Office.

It was the pretentious braggarts who easily fell apart in the camp, but Mr. Tamotsu Matsumura was somewhat of an exception. The intense questioning by naval intelligence personnel infuriated him, and he continued to make bold statements, acting as though he were the spokesman for Japan's military. Mr. Charlie Hasebe's case was unique in that everyone thought he had been shot dead: When he showed up at Sand Island, we thought he was a ghost.

On January 5, 1942, Dr. Motokazu Mori was brought to Sand Island. Since December 7 he had been detained first at a police station and then at the Immigration Office. When he arrived, his hair was completely white and bristled, his cheeks pitifully hollow. He seemed a completely different man. On the morning of the Pearl Harbor attack, before he even knew war had been declared, he was arrested by the FBI, detained without food or water, and cross-examined until midnight. He spent three days in solitary confinement at the Honolulu Police Station. That his countenance had changed so much was not surprising.

Dr. Mori's wife, Ishiko, was a correspondent for the *Yomiuri Shimbun* in Tokyo. On December 3, the couple received an international call from the newspaper's head office. The doctor answered the phone and reported on various matters. The military charged Dr. Mori with using a secret code during this telephone conversation to help plan the attack on Pearl Harbor. Ishiko and Jiro, their second son, were also arrested and placed in solitary confinement. Dr. and Mrs. Mori were interned directly after their arrest, while Jiro remained in custody for ten days and was then released due to some oversight. After being interrogated as suspected spies, Dr. and Mrs. Mori were cleared and declared internees. The interview between Dr. Mori and the FBI agent, known as "The Mori Report," serves as a reference to this day. Later submitted to the Inquiry Commission on the Pearl Harbor Incident convened in Washington, the document made Dr. Mori an instant "newspaper hero." The story of the Moris is not unique: During the war fathers, sons, and brothers and husbands and wives were arrested and detained.

Companies with the highest numbers of employees detained were my own *Hawaii Times* and the *Nippu Jiji* (Japan-Hawaii News). About thirty of our employees were arrested. In the case of the *Hawaii Hochi,* another Japanese-language newspaper, only three or four staff members were arrested a few months after war broke out.[4] In addition to Japanese

---

4. Soga's *Nippu Jiji* (renamed the *Hawaii Times* during World War II) and the *Hawaii Hochi* were the two most widely read Japanese newspapers in Hawai'i and bitter rivals. See Masayo Umezawa Duus, *The Japanese Conspiracy: The Oahu Sugar Strike of 1920,* trans. Beth Cary and adapted by Peter Duus (Berkeley: University of California Press, 1999), and Tom Brislin, "Weep into Silence/Cries of Rage: Bitter Divisions in Hawaii's Japanese Press" (*Journalism & Mass Communication Monographs* 154 (December 1995): 1–32).

detainees, violators of the Presidential Order of War and other felons convicted of serious crimes were imprisoned at Sand Island.

At a Crossroads

Several incidents in the camp came close to ending tragically. Mr. Shin Yoshida, superintendent of a pineapple company in Wahiawa, and Mr. Zensuke Kurosawa, a coworker, were arrested on February 10, 1942, and then locked up in solitary confinement at the Honolulu Police Station for four days. They were sent to the Immigration Office at around six o'clock on the evening of the fourteenth. Both were accused of being Japanese commissioned officers and were searched at gunpoint. Mr. Yoshida's elder brother had been killed in the Sino-Japanese War and his younger brother was a naval pilot hero. The FBI obtained this information from the *Nippu Jiji* and treated it as "evidence." One of the sergeants at the Immigration Office said, "Let me shoot them." His superior, a second lieutenant, replied, "OK, but do it tomorrow." Hearing this, both men were prepared to die.

It was later discovered that the soldiers were only joking, but of course the two detained men had taken their remarks seriously. That night Mr. Yoshida hung a leather belt in a corner of his cell, and the next morning he waited behind the door for a soldier to bring his breakfast. He intended to seize the soldier's bayonet and kill him, then commit suicide. To his surprise, while hiding, he heard an old woman say to the soldier, "Let me take in that breakfast. I want to ask them to clean the cell." His taut nerves relaxed at once, and he felt disheartened, unable to carry out his plan. If this old part-Hawaiian woman had not taken the soldier's place, a terrible thing might have happened. Because their dinner on the previous night had been especially good, the two men thought it was their last. They agreed that if they were going to be executed, they would kill themselves first by setting fire to their mattresses. Needless to say they did not sleep a wink that night. In the end a tragedy was averted but by a very slim margin. The incident made me realize that for people under great stress, any careless joke can have disastrous results.

Both Mr. Yoshida and Mr. Kurosawa were quickly interned and sent to the Mainland. Later it was learned that the lieutenant who had seemed to agree to have them shot had once worked at the same Wahiawa pineapple company. When he later heard Mr. Yoshida's story, he expressed regret for the poor joke. Life is truly unpredictable. This episode illustrates how a quirk of fate can make all the difference.

At around this time, we began to hold meetings after dark to pass the time. The blackout started at six o'clock and no matches were allowed. We could not go out except to the toilet. Of course meetings were prohibited. From around seven o'clock, people began gathering quietly in Dr. Mori's tent. Reverend Deme served as secretary. People from various fields and backgrounds spoke, and this went on for many nights. Neither the speaker nor the audience could see faces clearly in the dark, which was awkward, but the talks proved interesting. The Reverend Kuchiba talked about his visits to South China and the South Pacific islands in the company of Abbot Kozui Otani and about his experience being shipwrecked off Taiwan, where he narrowly escaped death.[5] His stories were very entertaining. Because he rarely spoke to anyone outside his immediate circle, his stories were new to many of us, and I was impressed with his excellent skills as a narrator. He was originally scheduled to deliver one lecture but wound up giving three by popular demand.

I still remember a talk on airplanes given by Mr. Hiroshi Honda, a pilot and a former teacher at the Hawaii Chuo Gakuin. He was an expert on airplanes, so what he had to say was extremely interesting. A sensitive youth, he was an art school graduate and well known for his Japanese-style paintings. After his parole on the Mainland, he reportedly moved to New York.[6]

Inquiry Commission at the Immigration Office

In early January 1942, an inquiry commission was set up at the Immigration Office, and we were called one by one from Sand Island for questioning. The commission, divided into three groups, was composed of civilians and military personnel. Each of us was assigned to one group. For some, the investigation took three to four days, but for others it was over in fifteen to twenty minutes. I was summoned at the end of January. I stayed at the Immigration Office for two weeks until the middle of February, during which time I was interrogated for two days. On the first day, I was asked routine questions such as name, address, family, profession, date and place of birth, education, date of arrival in Hawaii, and frequency of travel to

---

5. Abbot Kozui Otani was head of Nishi Hongwanji Temple headquartered in Kyoto.

6. Honda was subsequently interned at Camp McCoy, Wisconsin, and in Tule Lake, California. His watercolor paintings of life in these camps were featured in a 1994 exhibition at the Honolulu Academy of Arts titled *Reflections of Internment: The Art of Hawaii's Hiroshi Honda*. The catalog to this exhibition includes reproductions of many of the paintings and a short biographical essay on Honda by curator Marcia Morse.

Japan. Then the chairman, an elderly judge, pointed out that I was being questioned because of a report identifying me as pro-Japanese. My initial reaction was, of course I am . . . I'm a Japanese citizen, but I kept silent. At hearings like these we were entitled to a lawyer's services and three character witnesses, but in my case nothing was said. When I requested these, I was told that I could have a lawyer but witnesses would not be necessary. I insisted on at least one witness. We agreed on Mr. Masaji Marumoto for my attorney and Dr. Sidney L. Gulick for my witness.[7]

The next morning, after I had arrived for the meeting, Mr. Marumoto came in. Dr. Gulick, who was hard of hearing and carried a long rubber ear trumpet, followed and announced cheerfully, "Good morning, gentlemen. I am deaf." Immediately the commission began asking questions, which the doctor answered. He said that he had known me since 1915 and that in the last few years we had been on quite friendly terms. Asked if he could say I was pro-Japanese but not anti-American, Dr. Gulick replied smilingly: "Of course I can. As a Japanese subject, Mr. Soga is denied U.S. citizenship. It stands to reason that he is pro-Japanese, but that does not make him anti-American." I could not tell if this answer helped my case, but I was very pleased with what Dr. Gulick said. After giving his testimony, he shook my hand firmly and left.

Next I was questioned by the commissioners and the attorney. Their biggest concern was my opinion of the Great East Asia Co-Prosperity Sphere. I told them I believed that Japan had the right to secure its independence. A commissioner questioned me further: Did I think it was right to achieve this purpose militarily? I said that was another issue and that I was against the use of force in resolving any problem. Japanese military leaders had viewed me with suspicion because I am a liberal.

During the inquiry, Mr. Marumoto took out a thick file containing clippings of my Saturday column, "On Occasion," which I had written for the *Nippu Jiji* both in English and Japanese for a year. After receiving permission, Mr. Marumoto read a number of pieces that clearly showed my attitude toward the military, my opposition to the triple alliance of Japan, Germany, and Italy, and so on. One commissioner pointed out that these writings did indeed put me in a favorable light, but what about those in which I voiced an opinion against the United States? Mr. Marumoto

---

7. Sidney Gulick (1860–1945) was an educator, author, and missionary who, among other things, was one of the staunchest supporters of Japanese Americans in the midst of the anti-Japanese movement in California dating back to the 1910s. He retired to Hawai'i in 1934. See Sandra C. Taylor's *Advocate of Understanding: Sidney Gulick and the Search for Peace with Japan* (Kent, Ohio: Kent State University Press, 1985).

replied that I sometimes attacked American policies from the standpoint of a journalist. He asked the commissioners themselves to pick an essay. After looking through the file for a few minutes, they made their choice and ordered Mr. Marumoto to read it.

They had chosen a piece I had written on April 19, 1941, entitled "American Women: Where Are You Going?" In it, I wrote: "In the United States, far more women than men attend cultural events and read new books. If this trend continues, the day will come when women will exceed men in intelligence. Consequently they will lose their gracefulness and their minds will grow coarse. What will this do to American society? I am afraid it will do no good." When Mr. Marumoto read what I had said about women exceeding men, the commissioners roared with laughter. The investigation that day ended there. I was told I would be summoned the next day, but for some reason I was not.

At the inquiry a few military policemen were present, but it felt more like a group meeting than a court session. All of us, including the commission's four civilians and one military officer, sat at a round table with a stenographer. Cigarettes and candy were handed around to create a friendly atmosphere. However, the prosecutor, a young military man, quickly got down to business. "Did you buy Japanese government bonds?" "No." "Did you buy American bonds?" "No." "Why didn't you buy them?" "I intended to buy them, but I had no money at the time." At this point, the prosecutor suddenly stood over me and thundered, "You could have bought them if you had wanted to!"

Quite sometime afterward I was formally questioned again at Sand Island. This time the commissioners were all military officers, and they did not ask any new questions. The prosecutor who had interrogated me before was present. When I began answering through Mrs. Hanako Suehiro, the interpreter, he said, "You understand English, so you do not need an interpreter." Here, as at the Immigration Office inquiry, I was forced to answer in my poor English. Among the questions I was asked were: Are you a Buddhist? (No.) A Christian? (No.) And this, in a slightly raised voice, A Shintoist? (No.) I was saying that I did not belong to any church. My records clearly stated that I spoke Japanese and some English and that I had no religious preference.

An Attempted Suicide

During my two-week stay at the Immigration Office, Mr. Takeo Kagawa of Mitsukoshi and others were questioned daily until late at night. They became edgy and I felt sorry for them. One of the men slit his left wrist with a razor early one morning, but fortunately he was saved. He fell from the upper bunk across from mine, so I was awakened by the sound. I was surprised to see him lying in a pool of blood like a dead chicken. All of us were moved to another room and ordered to strip to see if we were hiding any sharp-edged objects. The man did not injure himself seriously, but after his suicide attempt, he was separated from the rest of us. During these same two weeks, Rev. Zenkyo Komagata of the Soto sect, Dr. Yukihide Kohatsu, Rev. Jikai Yamasato, Mr. Koichiro Nakamura, and Mr. George Russell were among those arrested and brought to the Immigration Office. Both the Reverend Komagata and Mr. Russell were immediately released.[8] Dr. Akio Kimura had also been arrested and was at the Immigration Office. It was a while before he could get a haircut, and he had a long, unkempt mustache. Dr. Kimura was not sent to Sand Island but was among the first to be directly transferred to the Mainland, together with Dr. Kohatsu and Rev. Yamasato. He took very good care of all the internees. Mr. Otto Kuehn, the only spy arrested in Hawaii, was kept in a solitary cell in the Immigration Office. His wife and a daughter were in a separate room, which I was once ordered to clean.

Internees from Other Islands and Identification Numbers

While I was staying at the Immigration Office, possibly on February 15, a spoon disappeared from the mess hall. Everyone was ordered out of the tents and told to strip while the guards conducted a body check, which lasted for three hours. Fortunately I was not involved.

Internees from other islands first went to the Immigration Office before coming to Sand Island. On March 3, 45 people arrived at Sand Island from Kauai. The next day, more were brought from the Big Island and Maui. They had been taken first to the Immigration Office on February 22. In all, there were 106 people from the Big Island and 36 people from Maui. On May 12, 28 more people from the Big Island arrived. On June 6, a second group from Kauai entered the camp, among them a woman. Some people on the outer islands were arrested and released without ever coming to Sand Island. Mr. Junokichi Senda, a photographer from Lihue, was incarcerated at the end of 1942 for three months in a camp deep in the

8. George Russell was an Issei businessman and farmer. Born in Yokohama, he was of mixed race descent, with a European father and a Japanese mother.

Kalaheo mountains on Kauai. Supposedly a primary school graduate, he and many others with similar backgrounds were detained there.

All internees were assigned a number. (Numbering people never bodes well.) Those from Oahu were given numbers 1 through 1,000. This did not mean there were 1,000 of us but that these numbers were reserved for internees from Oahu. Numbers 1,001 to 1,500 were assigned to the Big Island; 1,501 to 1,750 to Maui, Molokai, and Lanai; and 1,751 to 2,000 to Kauai. Thus we could easily tell who came from which island. For example, my number was ISN-HJ-385-CI. ISN stood for "internee number," HJ for "Hawaii Japanese," CI for "civilian internee." While at Sand Island, we were told to write this number in indelible ink on our shirts and underwear to prevent mix-ups.

Two numbers drew snickers: 711 and 606. (In the game of craps, 7 and 11 are winning throws, and 6 is also favorable.) The number 1 was said to have been given to Ensign Kazuo Sakamaki. It would seem strange that he was included with the rest of us Oahu civilians, but then the military authorities in Honolulu may have simply assumed that we were all POWs. At any rate, upon arriving on the Mainland, Hawaii internees were assigned new numbers. We received ours at Angel Island in San Francisco. We painted our numbers in white on 12 x 6-inch pieces of denim cloth, which we stitched to the back of our shirts. I did not like this at first. Later I found that all of our clothes, including coats and pants, the new and the old, were stamped with our numbers in white paint. For prisoners of war, a big white "PW" was painted on the back of their denim jumpers and on the kneecaps of their pants. The letters were so large they could be read from quite a distance. I did not know why, but Japanese internees from Alaska had especially conspicuous PWs on their backs and kneecaps.

Novel People from Other Islands and Women Internees

According to the stories of those interned on the outer islands, camp life was generally better outside Oahu, where one was farther removed from the war. Treatment on Maui was the most relaxed. The families of internees went to the camps every day, bringing good food and turning visits into picnics. In our camp there were some unusual internees from the other islands, among them someone whose wife was a public school teacher. When questioned in Hilo and asked what he would do if the Japanese army invaded the island, he replied sarcastically, "I would run away—with the American soldiers." This response earned him a reprimand dotted with colorful language. At Sand Island he criticized one of the group commanders for catering to camp supervisors. When the commander scolded him, saying, "Who do you think you are?" he retorted, "I'm a Japanese. Don't get smart with me, you scum."

Mr. Ichiroji Hara, who had a service station in Hilo, knew a great deal about machines. Twelve years before the war began, he volunteered to repair airplanes for the U.S. Army and Navy. One day a U.S. cruiser was docked in Hilo, and a crew member dropped a jackknife between the engines by mistake: Everything came to a standstill. The ship had orders to leave the port within twenty-four hours, but it would have taken several days to disassemble and repair the engines. Mr. Hara was given special permission to board the ship blindfolded. Within twelve hours, he had the engines running, having retrieved the knife by using an ingenious method. The ecstatic crew lifted him up and carried him on their shoulders. Even this exceptional person was interned in Hilo when war broke out. (Mr. Hara's assistant also shared the same fate.) However, I heard that both of them were released soon afterward.

Female internees were also taken to the Immigration Office before being moved into the women's barracks at Sand Island, which was located some distance away from the men's tents. There were quite a few of them in the beginning, but more than half were paroled because they were citizens or for other reasons. Only eight were sent to the Mainland: Mrs. Kosaku Horibe of Konko-kyo, Waimea, Kauai; Mrs. Miyuki Kawasaki of Tenri-kyo, Waipahu; Mrs. Yoshie Miyao and Mrs. Yukiko Miyao of Izumo Taisha; Miss Haru Tanaka, a Japanese-language schoolteacher from Wahiawa; and Mrs. Tsuta Yamane of Honolulu. They all left on the fourth ship on June 21, 1942. On October 10, Kanzen Ito of Mantoku Temple, Paia, Maui, and Mrs. Ishiko Mori departed on the seventh ship.

Mrs. Mori, as I mentioned earlier, was a correspondent for the *Yomiuri Shimbun*. Most of the other female internees were either nuns or connected with schools. At Izumo Taisha, Mrs. Yukiko Miyao was mistaken for Mrs. Yoshie Miyao and arrested, and eventually both were interned. Mrs. Shizuyo Yoshioka, née Takechi, of the *Nippu Jiji*, who was connected with Tenri-kyo, was arrested but released because she was pregnant. She gave birth to a baby girl on April 1, 1942. She named the baby Sandra, after Sand Island, thanks to a suggestion from an acquaintance. Among the other women arrested were a reputed "lady of the night," who was the topic of lively discussion in the men's tents; a young Nisei *naniwabushi* artist (storyteller trained to sing narrative ballads); and a tall, regal nun who reminded me of a European and was known in the women's barracks as "Miss Takeko Kujo" (a poet and daughter of a Buddhist bishop, who was considered one of the three most beautiful women in Japan during the Taisho period). I must not forget to mention Mrs. Umeno Harada, the heroine of the tragedy on Niihau, which occurred the day of the Pearl Harbor attack.[9] Apparently she was fluent in English and strong in character. Several German and Italian women were also interned. The wife of Captain E served as matron over them all. She was a warmhearted person and took very good care of them.

Of the eight women who were sent to the Mainland, only Mrs. Mori and the nun, Miss Ito, were sent to Sharp Park Center, California, for ten months. The others remained in California for a short period before being sent to Seagoville Center, Texas. They were eventually moved to Crystal City, Texas, where they joined their husbands, who were sent to join them from other camps. Sharp Park was beautiful when its many flowers bloomed. Madam Hirao of Nikko-ro, well known in Seattle's red-light district, was interned there. Some said they heard the elegant sound of her *samisen* (three-stringed musical instrument) in the camp.

Family Tents and Tear Gas

Sand Island Detention Camp had no church, so every religion and sect gathered in a tent on Sundays. In the morning an American minister visited the women's barracks, where he led a gathering of German, Italian, and Japanese women and gave sermons in English. Men wishing to attend were told to apply for permission before each service because the women's barracks was normally off-limits. Twenty to thirty men with ulterior motives put on their best clothes, shaved, and hurried to the women's barracks on Sunday mornings. Shaving was quite a nuisance because razor blades were banned. Once a week at a predetermined time, barracks commanders received blades for the men in their group. Each blade was in an envelope

---

9. A Japanese plane piloted by Shigenori Nishikaichi crashed on the isolated island of Ni'ihau on December 7, 1941. Yoshio Harada, a Nisei caretaker on the Ni'ihau Robinson ranch, decided to guard Nishikaichi until the scheduled boat [the only means of communication and transportation] arrived from Kauai. While Nishikaichi was asleep, a map and some documents were stolen by one of the Ni'ihau residents. Later, while searching for the materials with Harada's assistance, Nishikaichi tried to set fire to houses. An altercation developed in which Nishikaichi was killed and Harada shot himself. Mr. Robinson ordered Harada's wife, Umeno Harada, to leave the island. She was jailed on Kauai and then interned for the duration of the war. [Brian Niiya, ed., *Japanese American History: An A-to-Z Reference from 1868 to the Present* (New York: Facts on File, 1993), p. 255.]

with a name on it. After using the blades, we had to put them back in the envelopes and give them to the commander, who checked the number of blades and returned them to the office. After going to all this trouble, the men were forced to listen to long sermons in incomprehensible English under strict surveillance. After the service, if they were fortunate, they managed to shake hands with women they knew.

In time, eight family tents were built next to the women's barracks, and German and Italian couples moved in. (However, husbands and wives still had to take most of their meals separately.) A German woman had demanded that she be allowed to live with her husband and became hysterical: This may be the reason the family tents were built in the first place. Dr. and Mrs. Mori were also offered this privilege, but for some reason they were too modest to accept. Mrs. E, the matron, let married couples take lunch together on Wednesdays in the women's mess hall, which was very considerate.

Dr. Mori composed this poem at the time:

> While I look at the house beyond the barbed wire, where my wife is confined,
> I pluck a leaf of grass and chew on it.

It is somewhat sentimental but expresses his feelings well.

We did not know if or when Japan would attack Hawaii again, but we were convinced it would bomb Sand Island. The camp office issued gas masks and taught us how to use them. We were also ordered to dig trenches around the camp. Air-raid sirens would sound unexpectedly as a signal for us to jump into the trenches. This often made us feel like sewer rats. We never knew if a real attack was imminent, so we were terror-struck whenever we heard the sirens. Once we had tear gas practice with everyone routed from the men's and women's barracks. With a sizable group of soldiers in attendance, we were led to one side of the field. The siren blew and gas was released downwind. Quickly we put on our masks and ran through the smoke. With women participating, there was obviously much commotion, but the soldiers found it all amusing. Those who did not put on their masks correctly suffered eye and throat irritation. Many had tears flowing from both eyes continuously for two to three days. Doctors had warned us earlier not to rub our eyes once we had been exposed. According to rumors, the authorities reasoned that if the Japanese landed and released poisoned gas, the Americans would counter with a similar weapon. It was powerful enough to ulcerate exposed skin. We were all the more terrified.

German and Italian Internees

As I mentioned before, about seventy to eighty Germans and Italians were interned in one corner of Sand Island. Their living quarters were next to the Japanese mess hall, and beyond that stood the women's barracks. Among them were company men, brewing technicians, doctors, laborers, and a young engineer whom I knew from the Waikiki Rotary Club. I spoke occasionally with an old man who had been arrested on Molokai. There were also Dr. Zimmerman, who made news when a petition for a writ of habeas corpus was filed on his behalf, and the dashing young son of the minister of the interior of a northern European country who had cruised around the world in a speedboat. We were envious of those, like Professor Tower of the University of Hawaii, who were released early from Sand Island. Mr. Liebricht, a violinist, was paroled later.

Those in charge at the camps did not seem to discriminate in their treatment of Europeans and Japanese. Generally speaking, Germans and Italians gave them much more trouble than Japanese. They often quarreled among themselves, tattling to the authorities like children. In the end, they were ignored. As for cleanliness, Japanese were far superior. Apparently the toilets and bathrooms in the European barracks were very dirty.

At the beginning of 1942, Germans and Italians were also sent to the Mainland. Thirteen men who were American citizens returned to Sand Island on April 28, 1942; a new rule stipulated that citizens could no longer be sent to the Mainland. Those who returned reported on the conditions of various camps and on the Mainland in general, which led me to feel I would be better off going there as soon as possible. Around this time, Captain S became our commander at Sand Island. Once when I was talking to two or three Germans in violation of camp rules, Captain S approached us and asked, "What are you talking about?" I answered, "I was asking about friends who went to the Mainland." He said calmly, "It's against the rules, so you should avoid talking to one another." I replied courteously, "I understand." If it had been Captain E, I would have gotten a verbal thrashing.

Of the German prisoners, Mr. Otto Kuehn was the most famous. While he was imprisoned in a solitary cell, his wife and beautiful daughter (the wife of a U.S. army officer) were kept in a small cottage in front of the women's barracks. I do not know what Mr. Kuehn did for a living, but because he had an ongoing relationship with the Japanese Consulate he was indicted as a spy and sentenced to death. Later his sentence was reduced to fifty years imprisonment. After Mr. Kuehn was transferred to a prison on the Mainland his wife and daughter followed. He was the only spy arrested in Hawaii. Once, the first son of Prince Konoye stopped in Hawaii on his way back from Princeton University after failing the entrance examination. It was reported that Mr. Kuehn's daughter was on board his ship, and many rumors circulated about them.

The European with whom we had a close relationship was Mr. George Krielman, the mess hall cook. A huge man, bald and tanned, he was always shirtless. He was our only cook for some time, until menu problems surfaced and it was decided that he and a Japanese cook would alternate and share the task. The problem was resolved just before one of the so-called Judo men (Buddhist priests with judo training), the Reverend Hirayama, was about to demonstrate his skill in a confrontation.

Meals at Sand Island and the Japanese POWs

It was not unusual for the meals at Sand Island to reek of butter since Japanese ingredients were unavailable and our cook was German. However, coffee with every meal and the military standard fare, pork and beans, served on a regular basis, were simply intolerable. Worse, the coffee was coffee in name only, smelling like medicine at times. Some said it was added to control a young soldier's hormones. We could not abide coffee with every meal, so we asked for tea at least at dinnertime. The reply was, "No use asking for luxuries. Can't get it."

At the end of 1941, soon after the war began, we did have a good supply of foodstuffs for a while. Information on the boxes delivered to the mess hall indicated that they had been rerouted because the Philippines were now occupied by Japan. Vegetables and fruits, however, remained scarce, especially on Sand Island. Vegetable gardens sprouted outside the fences and volunteer workers tended them every day under guard. Once the vegetables began to appear, workers were prohibited from taking them back to the tents. Nevertheless, small radishes or a few greens were hidden in hats and smuggled in. We were so starved for fresh food, we devoured them. You see, eating was our only pastime, so whenever there was anything left over, young people took turns finishing it off. There was a brave young man who ate three lunches one day.

There were about fifty Japanese POWs at Sand Island. Ensign Kazuo Sakamaki, known as "POW No. 1," was incarcerated in front of the women's barracks and was completely shut off from everyone. Second Lieutenant S, head of the office, delivered his meals three times a day accompanied by a guard. Later, Mr. Aisuke Shigekuni of Windward Oahu volunteered to tend to his needs, but no conversation was permitted. Ensign Saka-maki was the lone survivor of the two-man midget submarine attack on a Kaneohe naval base on December 7. The name "Kazuo Sakamaki" was clearly inscribed on the *senninbari*.[10]

News from the outside world seldom reached us. Once in a while newly arrived internees brought word of a Japanese victory. We were eager to inform Ensign Sakamaki, but had no way of doing so until some brave volunteers who worked outside the barbed wire began relaying news to him in the form of songs sung in a loud voice outside his shack. This prac-tice made all of us nervous. Ensign Sakamaki was sent to the Mainland on the first internee ship on February 21, 1942. Of the Japanese POWs who had been brought to Sand Island, nine went to the Mainland on the fourth ship and forty-three on the sixth ship.

Ensign Sakamaki caused no trouble while he was incarcerated on Sand Island. However, when the authorities began assigning work to POWs who arrived after Ensign Sakamaki, they met with resistance. POWs were required to stand still when the flag was taken down in the evening, but the Japanese prisoners would often run into their tents as soon as they heard the bugle. Speaking of the bugle, its sound was always accompanied by that of a howling dog whenever the flag was hoisted in the morning or taken down in the evening in front of the Thirty-fifth Regimental Head-quarters. We wondered why, and later learned that the dog had been left behind by a bugler who was said to have died honorably in battle. This is one of the tragic tales of the war.

The Order Is Issued

On the afternoon of February 17, 1942, a whistle sounded as usual and we were all ordered to line up in front of the office. We waited expectantly. Captain E announced: "We will now call names. Those called should take their belongings and gather at one corner of the camp." We thought we were going to be released and grew excited. Names were called in alpha-betical order. As this continued, those left behind became uneasy. My sus-

---

10. A *senninbari* was a stomach band decorated with a thousand French knots, each one embroi-dered by a different woman; it was a talisman to ensure a Japanese soldier's safe return. [Source: Naoko Shibusawa.]

picions were raised when I noticed that a good number of the men selected were those who were least likely to be released. A total of 172 names were called, but mine was not one of them.

Generally speaking, those left standing were rather gentle in character compared with those who had moved to the corner. At any rate, because they assumed they were leaving, those called looked very happy. The rest of us looked glum, and some of the fainthearted began to cry. We asked the chosen ones to convey messages to friends and family. They left many of their things behind because they thought they were going home. I did not have a soap case, which was inconvenient, so I asked a friend to leave me his. I heard later that when Mr. Genji Otani shook hands with Dr. Motokazu Mori, he looked pale as he said, "I may not be able to see you again." It seems he had a premonition.

Of the more than 200 men interned at Sand Island, 172 had left, so the camp was very quiet. Those of us who remained felt pretty lonely. Days passed, but we still did not receive any news of them. Then the rumor spread that they had not been released but had been sent to the Mainland. When this was confirmed, we were dumbfounded. We learned later that when the men left Sand Island on February 17, they were taken directly to the Immigration Office. They guessed they were going to be either released or sent elsewhere on Oahu. On the afternoon of the eighteenth, Messrs. Katsumi Kometani, Isao Murai, Yasuo Goto, Masatoshi Katagiri, Shigeo Yoshida, and Masaji Marumoto arrived at the office. All of them were on the Emergency Service Committee, which had been established by the Japanese American Citizens Association after the war had begun.[11] Mr. Marumoto announced: "I am very sorry, but the military authorities have decided to send all of you to the Mainland. Our committee has already informed your families of this. You are allowed one suitcase each. Your family may send you up to fifty dollars, so we will arrange for remittance

11. The Emergency Service Committee was one of the morale committees appointed by the Morale Section of the Office of the Military Governor in the months after the war began. The Morale Section was essentially charged with keeping a lid on what we would today call race relations in wartime Hawai'i and set up various ethnic morale committees on each island. The Emergency Service Committee was the Japanese morale committee on Oahu, formed on February 8, 1942 and made up of prominent Nisei. They held community meetings promoting loyalty and support of the war effort among local Japanese and also took the lead in eradicating Japanese language and culture in the islands. Though formed under the auspices of the military government, members of the Emergency Service Committee had been active in various Japanese American civic organizations before the war, perhaps leading to Soga's apparent belief that their origins came from within the Japanese community. See the *Final Report of the Emergency Service Committee* (Honolulu, Hawai'i, May 1946) and Andrew W. Lind's *Hawaii's Japanese: An Experiment in Democracy* (Princeton: Princeton University Press, 1946).

later. If you have any message for your family, we will give it to them." When the men heard this, they felt as if a bomb had been dropped on them.

That night, they were inoculated. They had their fingerprints taken as well as their pictures with their internee ID numbers. All this activity went on until the early dawn, so no one slept a wink. On the nineteenth, one thick military overcoat and half a dozen socks were distributed to each of them. Their destination was not announced and the Emergency Service Committee members had no information. They said it could be Wisconsin or Montana or New Mexico. Many of the men grew desperate and felt that no one cared if they lived or died. One man, who had been so brazen and such a troublemaker before the war, broke down in tears. On the night of the nineteenth, at the Immigration Office, some men sang, some cried, and some fell deep into thought.

The next morning their hopes of meeting with their families were dashed. At nine o'clock they were taken to military trucks at the back gate, facing the sea, and were driven away at full speed under heavy guard to Pier 27, where the military ship USS *Grant* was waiting. About five hundred family members who had gathered at the front entrance to the Immigration Office were unable to get a glimpse of their loved ones. My newspaper's general manager, Mr. Kawamoto, who was among those leaving, was at the Immigration Office when he saw his eldest son, Takuji, also an internee, in another room. They exchanged looks but were not permitted to exchange a single word.

Itinerary of the First Group

The men were placed in the hold of the *Grant*. Mr. Matsujiro Otani, who was ill, and Mr. Yoshihiko Ozu, whose father was ill, were taken off the ship and sent back to Sand Island. The ship remained in port on the twentieth; it finally weighed anchor at five o'clock on February 21. The *Grant*, together with a huge Empress-class steamship and several cruisers, formed a convoy, and a total of eight ships headed north on a zigzag course. The temperature dropped fairly quickly. The ship's commander was Lieutenant Baker, and Dr. Akio Kimura served as spokesman for the internees.

Twice on the night of February 24 or 25, the ship encountered a Japanese submarine. Some internees gave up all hope of living and stared silently at family pictures, while others put on life jackets and waited for the impending attack. Some of the younger men continued to play chess calmly, saying, "If we're attacked, that's it." Throughout the voyage, the men remained in the hold and were not allowed on deck. They could not take showers and barely managed to wash their faces in the morning. They did go to a dining room three times a day, however, and the food was fairly good. The biggest headache was the toilet. Every three hours they were lined up and went to the latrine, but oftentimes they could not wait. They urinated in a can and tried to empty it into the sea with the other garbage, but throwing even a cigarette overboard was strictly prohibited because it could alert enemy submarines. The younger men managed to carry the can to a toilet on the upper floor, but it was hard and very dirty work.

At four o'clock on the afternoon of March 1, the *Grant* finally arrived at San Francisco's Pier 7, the military wharf. When the men stepped off the ship, they nearly fainted at their first glimpse of the sun since leaving Honolulu. They disembarked along with Ensign Sakamaki, several American families, and many wounded soldiers. Quite a few of the soldiers were carried away on stretchers. That evening the internees, each carrying a blue barracks bag containing his belongings, were transferred by boat to Angel Island in San Francisco Bay. Formerly the site of the Immigration Office, the island was now being used to barrack soldiers awaiting combat duty. The men were searched and had their fingerprints and ID pictures taken again. Germans and Italians were also being held on Angel Island, as well as two Japanese: Mr. Kikuzo Ichimaru, general manager of the *San Francisco New World Times,* and Mr. Sho Tominaga, who was born in Kagoshima prefecture and lived in Samoa. He was married to a Samoan woman and worked for the Dollar Steamship Company.

The internees remained on Angel Island until March 5. During their short stay, they gathered on a small hill and did calisthenics to maintain their strength. The resounding voice of the Reverend Kabashima as he led the exercises jolted the American soldiers on the other side of the island. At noon, on March 6, they left for Oakland, and an hour later headed for an unknown destination by train. Although it was a passenger train, all the windows were covered with wire netting, which made the cars look like cages for criminals . The group spent four days and three nights going through Nevada, Utah, and Nebraska before arriving at Camp McCoy in Sparta, Wisconsin, on March 9.

In the middle of the snowy and coldest season of the year, many of the internees, with no winter clothing other than the government-issued overcoats, were dressed in straw hats and white shoes. The soldiers at Camp McCoy had rarely seen a Japanese, so they were taken by surprise. Lieutenant Colonel Horace I. Rogers, the camp commander, was a Rotarian and a fine gentleman. He treated the internees well and made camp life as bearable as the rules permitted. He regularly attended roll call and immediately after lights-out conducted the bed checks himself with his assistant. One night, after the men had already gone to bed, a famous aurora appeared in the sky, something not often seen even this far north. Mr. Rogers woke all of them up so they would not miss seeing it. That was also the day the Americans surrendered to the Japanese army in Bataan.

Frequent Transfers

Japanese internees from Hawaii were transferred many times and sent to many places after their arrival on the Mainland. The first group of 172 sent to Camp McCoy remained there for two months before leaving on May 25. Lieutenant Colonel Rogers shook each man's hand and bade him farewell. After traveling through Illinois, Indiana, and Kentucky, they arrived at Camp Forrest in Tullahoma, Tennessee, possibly on May 28, and stayed for a month. It was a very hot place. In the meantime, the first exchange ship, the SS *Gripsholm,* left New York for Japan on June 18. On board were Messrs. Motoichi Matsuda of Yokohama Specie Bank, Shigenari Hattori, Genji Otani, Kyoichi Nakano, Kichitaro Sekiya, and many others. Mr. Onoda of Sumitomo and Mr. Kimura of Nippon Yusen Kaisha arrived too late and missed their chance to return home.

On June 29, the first group left Tennessee and arrived the next day at Camp Livingston, Louisiana, where they settled for a while. The second group from Hawaii had already arrived there a month earlier from Oklahoma, so the two groups enjoyed a reunion. In August, Dr. Miyamoto and eighteen other Japanese American citizens were sent back to Hawaii, and several scores of Japanese POWs were brought in. The second group remained at Camp Livingston for a year, the first group for eleven months.

Camp Livingston was situated only a hundred feet above sea level. A pine forest grew nearby and large fireflies flew around at night, which was fine, but the humidity was very high and it was unbearable in the summer. With temperatures around a hundred degrees, many internees spent much of their time in their underpants. The camp, with a holding capacity of about five thousand, housed Japanese POWs in the beginning. The hospital buildings were numbered in Japanese alphabetical order, and the building numbers were written in Japanese. Like all institutions under military control, the meals were good, but the camp commander was strict and ran a very tight ship.

The camp was closed in 1943, so internees were divided into two groups and transferred elsewhere. On June 2, 208 people (mainly those from the first Hawaii group and a few internees from the Mainland) were moved to Camp Missoula in Montana. Among them were seventeen Japanese who had been building roads in Kooskia, Idaho. Two days later, on June 4, a second group of 504 internees, including the sick and the elderly, left Livingston for the camp in Santa Fe, New Mexico. They arrived on June 7. This group was mostly comprised of Mainland Japanese and a hundred or so Hawaii Japanese. About forty of them eventually moved to Camp Jerome in Arkansas a year later to be reunited with family members. After a few weeks, they were transferred to Camp Tule Lake in California.

In general, the authorities were quite lenient about what internees took with them when they moved. However, those leaving Camp Livingston were not allowed to take any art or crafts they had made or rare stones they had collected: Instead, they were ordered to discard them when they left. The move to Camp Missoula took them north along the Mississippi River and through St. Louis, Minneapolis, and North Dakota. They reached the camp on June 5. Mr. Onoda and Mr. Kimura, who had missed the first exchange ship in New York, were already there. Eventually they both returned to Japan on the second ship.

Camp Missoula was situated at about forty-eight degrees north, or the same latitude as the Russia-Japan border on Sakhalin Island. Although the area was extremely cold, the camp had been built in the basin of an old lake and was not exposed to the wind. The camp commander, Bart H. Frazer, and his staff were very kind. They understood and trusted Japanese, so the internees lived quite comfortably. When the Livingston group arrived, they encountered 101 Japanese from the Mainland, about a thousand Italians, fifty or so Germans and Czechs, and a general from Nicaragua. Later, more than a hundred Japanese who had been interned in Peru, Bolivia, and other South American countries joined them, making the camp quite lively.

At Missoula, Mr. Iwao Matsushita of Mitsui Bussan acted as spokesman and was called "Mayor." After the arrival of the Hawaii group, first Mr. Takaichi Saiki, then Mr. Totaro Matsui, took over the position. Both had the confidence of the commander and were good administrators. In the case of Mr. Matsui, he was entrusted with nearly everything. Thanks to him, the internees could engage in various sports and were free to fish in a nearby river. They were also permitted to shop in town. Missoula was a small but beautiful place. In the cemetery of this remote little town were the graves of dozens of Japanese laborers who had built the Great Northern Railway and their families. The graves were so well kept that everyone was deeply impressed. Priests gladly agreed to hold a memorial service for those buried here.

On April 2, 1944, the internees were ordered to move again. They left Missoula with great reluctance and were taken to Santa Fe, where they arrived on April 6.

The Second and Third Groups Go to the Mainland

The second Hawaii group to be sent to the Mainland was comprised of 166 internees from various islands. The order was issued on March 17, 1942, and the group departed Sand Island at seven o'clock on the morning of the nineteenth. They boarded the USS *Grant*, the same ship that had transported the first group, leaving Honolulu on the twentieth and arriving in San Francisco on the thirtieth. They arrived at Fort Sill, Oklahoma, on April 9. Two days later, about 350 Mainland Japanese arrived at Fort Sill from Missoula. This group included many important figures from New York, Chicago, and other large cities: Mr. Ichiro Matsudaira, the elder brother of Setsuko, Princess Chichibu; Mr. Yahei Taoka, branch manager of Nippon Yusen Kaisha in San Francisco; Mr. Michio Ito, a dancer; and Mr. Iwajiro Noda of Nippon Menka. On the twelfth, about 170 internees from Panama arrived, including Mr. Yoshitaro Amano, who had been a very active businessman in Central and South America and was an expert on the region as well as a talented writer. Most of the internees from Panama were young and full of energy. There were no trees at Fort Sill and everyone lived in tents.

Unfortunately, at Fort Sill Mr. Kisaburo Oshima from Hawaii regrettably broke under the strain of incarceration and tried to escape over the barbed-wire fence. Before anyone could stop him he was shot dead by a guard. Many people witnessed it and were deeply affected. That night a mentally disturbed internee from the Mainland died from shock as a result of Mr. Oshima's death. The camp grew even more melancholy. Within a month, the internees were ordered to Camp Livingston. As noted earlier, here they joined the first Hawaii group arriving from Camp Forrest in Tennessee. A year later, about forty people, including Dr. Takahashi from Hawaii and my newspaper's chief editor, Mr. Asami, were transferred from Livingston to the family camp in Crystal City, Texas.

The 109 men of the third Hawaii group ordered to the Mainland left Sand Island on May 23, 1942, and boarded the SS *Maui* at Pier 6. They left Honolulu at eleven o'clock in the morning on May 24 and arrived at Pier 37 in San Francisco at one o'clock in the afternoon on June 1,

1942. They were taken to Angel Island, and seven days later they found themselves in Houston, Texas. Internees from Alaska and California joined them there. At two o'clock in the afternoon on June 18, they arrived at Lordsburg, New Mexico. Among them was Mr. Ryosaku Kawasaki, who later moved to the family camp in Crystal City in March 1943.

The Rest of Us Are Sent Away

The fourth group, consisting of thirty-nine men, departed Sand Island on June 21, 1942, and arrived at Angel Island on the twenty-ninth. They left Oakland on July 3 and arrived at Lordsburg on the fifth. Nine Japanese POWs were included in this group. Two days before their arrival at San Francisco, all nine tried to commit suicide. Two jumped overboard, but prompt and efficient rescue efforts saved them. Mr. Hatsuichi Toishigawa, the spokesman for the internees, served as interpreter for the POWs. He later said he was deeply moved by their attitude and unwavering determination.

The fifth group left on the SS *Matsonia* on the afternoon of August 7, 1942. Forty-nine men arrived at Angel Island on the fifteenth, and after twelve days, they boarded a train in Oakland. Around August 22, they were moving along the Santa Barbara coast, which had been bombed by Japanese submarines, on to the Imperial Valley, arriving in Lordsburg on the twenty-ninth.[12] I belonged to this group. (My experiences aboard ship and on the way to Lordsburg follow in the next chapter.)

The sixth group of twenty-eight internees left Sand Island on September 16, 1942. Their journey took them to San Francisco on the twenty-fourth, Angel Island on October 26, Lordsburg on the twenty-eighth. Forty-three Japanese POWs and thirty-nine mainland Japanese accompanied them. The twenty-three people in group seven left Sand Island on October 11, 1942. They joined the sixth group on the way to Lordsburg, arriving there on October 28. The eighth group of forty-three left Sand Island on March 2, 1943, the day the detention camp closed, and were sent to Sharp Park after arriving in San Francisco on March 12. After five months they left for Santa Fe, arriving there three days later. On July 1, 1943, the thirty-five internees of group nine left Honouliuli Detention Camp for San Francisco

---

12. On February 23, 1942, a lone Japanese submarine surfaced off the coast of Goleta, California, and began a fifteen-minute attack on an oil refinery. Though little damage resulted, the incident jangled local nerves and led to sensationalized press accounts. See Audrie Girdner and Anne Loftis, *The Great Betrayal: The Evacuation of the Japanese-Americans during World War II* (New York: Macmillan, 1969).

and were taken to Sharp Park on the ninth. They reached Santa Fe on August 15. The final group of twenty-nine left Honouliuli on December 2, 1943, and arrived in Santa Fe on January 9, 1944.

The ten groups totaled 1,693 men and 8 women. At this point, the transfer of Hawaii internees to the Mainland was terminated, and thereafter those interned in Hawaii, both Issei and Nisei, were kept at Honouliuli Detention Camp in Ewa, Oahu.

The First Internee Death

I will now return to events on Sand Island after the first group had been transferred to the Mainland. One of the first and saddest of these was the death of Mr. Hisahiko Kokubo, born in Kumamoto prefecture, who had a shop in Pakala in Waimea, Kauai. He was sixty-five years old when he died suddenly of a heart attack on the evening of March 9, 1942. At that time, internees were being inoculated, and Mr. Kokubo was given two injections on March 9, with no apparent reaction. He had dinner at the mess hall with his friends, then said he did not feel well and went back to his tent to lie down. His condition worsened unexpectedly. Dr. Mori had him taken to a temporary sickroom and did everything possible, but to no avail. (After receiving injections, a couple of internees often came down with a fever and were allowed to rest for a few days. Once Mr. Ryo-u Adachi became very ill and was sent to a military hospital outside. He fortunately recovered, but lost most of his hearing in one ear.)

Mr. Kokubo's death, the first in the camp, was most distressing. An emergency vehicle with the Red Cross symbol took the body to Honolulu. We solemnly lined up in the yard in front of the sickroom to pay our respects and send him off. There was just one tree with little red flowers in front of the sickroom. We wanted to offer our sympathy with some flowers, but we could do nothing. Sergeant Moran, our warden, was very thoughtful. He brought a big bunch of beautiful red bougainvillea blossoms from somewhere outside the camp and put it in the Red Cross vehicle, which made us feel much better.

On the seventh night, we quietly gathered for a memorial service. We were given permission to withdraw ten cents from each of our accounts kept at the office and sent the money to Mr. Kokubo's family with our condolences. In accordance with family wishes, the body was respectfully returned to Kauai on March 30 despite some delay due to shipping problems. The funeral was held at the Waimea Higashi Hongwanji Mission on the morning of April 2. The Reverend Chikai Odate, interned in a camp on the island, was granted special leave in order to officiate. Memorial pictures were taken. Rev. Odate relayed all of this to us when he was transferred to Sand Island some months later. Rev. Donald Fujiyoshi kindly sent letters to the office, thanking everyone on behalf of Mr. Kokubo's family.

When we first arrived at the camp, only a few of us became ill, perhaps because our defenses were up. In contrast, it seemed as though more Italians and Germans were affected. There were, however, some dishonest ones among us who feigned illness to escape work. One rascal, who was something of a troublemaker, stayed in the infirmary and played at being sick. Another man who claimed to be blind took off at a run whenever he heard the air-raid siren.

Fortunately I was in good health, although I once suffered from intercostal neuralgia for two nights. We lived in tents with dirt floors, so I presumed the dampness had affected me. After being examined by Dr. Mori, I discovered that I was suffering from a lack of vitamins, specifically vitamin C. The modest sickroom at Sand Island was not stocked with vitamins and ordering from the outside was difficult. Luckily I was able to get a few tablets of vitamin C from a German internee, a close acquaintance of Dr. Mori. I took half a tablet and the pain disappeared like magic. My illness had been caused by a diet lacking in vegetables and fruits. Thereafter I became a believer in the importance of vitamins.

Welcome News from the Outside

At Sand Island we were shut off from all communication with the outside world. We received no news of the war or of Honolulu, although the city was clearly visible. We caught only a glimpse of what was going on from the heavily censored letters we received from our families. When new internees arrived, we welcomed them eagerly, anxious to hear any news, good or bad. Many people on the outside got their news from Japan directly or indirectly from shortwave radios. Most of the time their information was accurate, but sometimes it was not, which led to many false rumors within the camp.

According to the news we received, Japan was victorious at the battle on Midway Island. Of course we later learned this was false and that this decisive battle turned the tide in favor of the United States. From May 15, 1942, the two English newspapers published in Honolulu were allowed in the camp for the first time. The *Honolulu Star-Bulletin* began arriving for me on the seventeenth and the *Honolulu Advertiser* the next day. Other people began to subscribe as well. The malicious rumors that had distorted our understanding of what was happening in the world gradually disappeared. Around that time, as I recall, we were allowed to keep fountain pens and paper, for which I was very thankful. After my favorite fountain pen had been returned to me, I patted it fondly many times. In May 1942, six months after the outbreak of war, a ray of light began to shine into our world of darkness.

On May 25 it was announced that our families would be allowed to visit us twice a month. This was a tremendous blessing. A building in front of Regimental Headquarters, outside the barbed wire, was designated as the meeting place. A certain number of internees were permitted to meet with their families each day for about two hours under the watchful eyes of Lieutenant S and several guards. Both English and Japanese could be spoken. (Long after my transfer to the Mainland, the rule was apparently tightened so that only English was allowed.) Of course, exchanging letters and packages was prohibited during visits. In the beginning we were given permission to buy candy and chewing gum for our children at the camp's small canteen, but everyone bought so much candy that this privilege was withdrawn. As I mentioned earlier, we could not carry even a penny of our own money. Whenever we bought something at the canteen, the expense was deducted from the amount of cash we had brought with us, which was kept at the office.

We all welcomed newcomers and anything they could tell us of the outside world, but we were also cautious. Many new arrivals held grudges, blaming their arrests on others and calling them "dogs" for collaborating with the FBI. We heard many such allegations. Those of us arrested on December 7, the day the war began, had no such complaints. From the outset we had been listed as persons to be interned if war broke out between the United States and Japan. Some people who should have been listed were not, which of course did not sit well with most of us. A colleague of mine from another island was in Honolulu on business when war was declared. Desperate to return home, he asked a prominent Japanese to speak to the military authorities. When he returned to his hotel, however, an FBI agent was there to arrest him. Both men were in newspaper-related work, so they were prime candidates for internment anyway, but the prominent one escaped incarceration. Similar examples of perceived discrepancies led to suspicion and malicious gossip.

Among the newer arrivals was a minister from Honolulu who joined us at Sand Island about six months later. He gave a lecture one evening, saying: "Quite a few of you who arrived here early on have grown timid. You must be strong! Japan is now waging a sacred war of *hachigen ichi-*

u!" (The correct phrase is *hakko ichi-u,* meaning "the whole world under one roof.") Disgusted by his pretentious exhortation, a half-dozen listeners walked out. They ridiculed the priest, saying, "Humph—what nerve! He talks big now, but before his arrest he was running scared. He doesn't even know his Japanese!"

Most internees worked inside the barbed-wire fence. Even the authorities could not force us to work beyond the fence. The vegetable gardens were located outside the camp, so only volunteers could work there. One Sunday, defense workers at a nearby site took the day off, so some internees were recruited to take their place. The camp authorities got into trouble when the labor union protested.

An Embarrassing Gift

Six months after we arrived at Sand Island, four barracks were hastily built. They were two-story buildings, thirty feet wide and eighty feet high, made of rough lumber. They had no ceilings. Internees who had been contractors before the war estimated their cost at a whopping $15,000 each. (In peacetime they would have been built for about $3,000 to $4,000.) On July 21, 1942, a big radio was placed in the small infirmary and speakers were installed in each of our barracks. We were grateful for the chance to hear current news and music, but the problem was that the key to the radio room was kept in the office, so sometimes jazz would be blaring long after we had had enough. Worse, the speakers in our barracks also worked as microphones, so now the office staff could hear our conversations whenever they wished. Although we had nothing to hide, we were uneasy knowing we were constantly being "watched." The new equipment was very convenient for the staff, in that it could be used to summon any internee to the office. The PA system covered every corner of the camp, which was convenient but also a nuisance.

Sand Island is near Pearl Harbor, so all incoming and outgoing battleships passed right in front of the camp. Once in a while, badly damaged aircraft carriers or battleships had to be towed in. We could clearly tell how many ships left Honolulu Harbor, how many were in the convoy accompanying them, and so on. Mr. Matsujiro Otani was our unofficial "ship spotter" because he spent much of his time in the infirmary, which faced the sea. Whenever a group was slated to be sent to the Mainland, internees would watch the ships leaving the harbor and speculate on the one that might carry them to their destination.

The Characteristics of Japanese

We Japanese like to be clean, and we were really thankful when we had clean showers. At the Immigration Office, guards watched the shower room while six or seven of us had to wait, naked, for our turn. The shower was limited to three minutes per person. If you were flustered even a little, you could easily find yourself jumping out of the shower with soap bubbles still clinging to your body.

During my four-year camp life I experienced my fill of the shortcomings among us Japanese, but I also rediscovered some characteristic virtues. (Being interned with Germans and Italians also made it easier to draw comparisons.) Generally speaking, Japanese obey rules and their superiors and are clean and diligent. These characteristics were clearly evident in the camps. After ten or so female internees were transferred to Sand Island, the fastidious Captain E gathered us together and announced: "Japanese are cleaner than Germans, and Japanese women even more. Among those recently transferred from the Immigration Office, the German and Italian women failed to tidy up, while the Japanese women put everything in order." When I heard this, I felt very proud. It should be remembered that however difficult our lives were, we Japanese were able to keep our wits about us and make the most of things. Despite our limited circumstances and surroundings, we retained our ability to appreciate beauty. We were not allowed to keep knives and did not have any materials or tools, but we expressed ourselves artistically by using materials which had been discarded or found. These aspects of the Japanese character are especially praiseworthy.

Sand Island is basically a coral reef. Small pieces of coral broken by the wind and waves are scattered everywhere and come in many colors and shapes. Someone began collecting these to create beautiful patterns and pictures on the ground along or in front of the tents. Looking at them, I recalled my childhood days when I saw street artists in Asakusa, Tokyo, skillfully spraying colored sand on the ground to form pictures, patterns, and letters. Soon coral artwork became popular in the camp. Lieutenant E, who appreciated the artistic expression of Japanese, showed the paintings to the mayor and other government officials as well as military personnel who often visited the camp. The most unforgettable of these works of art was Mr. Shuji Mikami's creation entitled "Dog Show." He used pieces of coral in their natural form to depict dogs in various positions. The result was so pleasing that if I had had a camera, I would certainly have taken a picture of it. Later, shell work became all the rage: Many shells scattered on the ground were used to make ornaments.

It was simple to make *go* and Japanese chess boards with thick surplus cardboard. Although chessmen were also simple to construct, *go* stones were a bit more difficult. At first internees dried orange skins, cut them into round pieces, and used the inner skin for white stones and the outer for black. Later they chiseled out pieces from sheets of tin roofing or used dried mixed cement and painted the pieces with India ink and white paint or flour paste. Anyone was able to make clogs and straw sandals.

Leaving Sand Island

We were not allowed to keep watches because it was feared that we would use them to bribe the guards. However, without a watch, life was very inconvenient—even in the camp. I used to guess the time by looking at the length of the shadow cast by my tent. Finally Dr. Takahashi made a sundial on the ground in front of our area. Although he did not have access to any special materials or tools, he created a highly sophisticated device which everyone found very useful. Dr. Takahashi was an amateur navigator and well versed in astronomy. When the night sky was very clear over Sand Island, we often gathered around him to listen to stories about the stars we could see right above us. With my nearsightedness, I had never seen the Southern Cross before and did not know much about it. Thanks to the doctor I now remember it well.

Having to carry a wet soap bar in one hand is such a bother; many of us did not own a soap case. Someone came up with the idea of drilling a hole in the center of the soap so a thread could be passed through it, making the soap easily portable. Another good idea was simply to use an empty Durham tobacco bag. When inconvenienced, one manages to find a solution. Anything discarded can be useful. As they say, "Necessity is the mother of invention."

Internees discovered hundreds of pieces of old tin roofing from buildings used to house the nearly one thousand contract laborers who had immigrated to Hawaii about forty years before. Some of them were inscribed in black ink with people's names, birthplaces, and even destinations such as the names of other islands and plantations. I thought these would later be invaluable to historians and wanted to take pictures of them, but I could do nothing.

At Sand Island every kind of military aircraft roared over our heads from dawn to midnight. We could hear antiaircraft guns firing at floats being pulled by airplanes and coastal guns blasting at targets at sea. We did not know when Hawaii would again be turned upside down. We often thought that if and when that time came, we all had to be prepared for death.

There was not a single book among us at Sand Island. The office staff loaned us old magazines published six months before the Pearl Harbor attack. Most of them were mediocre, but *Readers' Digest* was very informative, and I never became bored with one of Sinclair Lewis' long novels, which normally I would never have read. Later, pocket books and magazines were sold at the canteen. An English–Japanese dictionary that would have sold for a dollar before the war was priced at an exorbitant two dollars. It was unfortunate for those who read only Japanese that such printed books were prohibited in the camp.

On July 27, 1942, Mr. Yoichi Kagimoto, forty-eight years old, born in Yamaguchi prefecture, died suddenly. He was the second victim. He was the eldest of three brothers, all interned. At this time, conditions in the infirmary were again called into question.

On the morning of August 5, 1942, the fifth group of internees (to which I belonged) was ordered to the Mainland. I immediately wrote letters of farewell to Shigeo and others at home. The day before I left, I asked Dr. Mori to give my wife the ninety poems I had composed while in the camp. I felt like the aimless wanderer in the old Japanese tales. I carried a suitcase in each hand and asked a young man to carry the big barracks bag for me. When we passed in front of the women's barracks, they called out, "Good luck!" I heard Mrs. Mori say, "Mr. Soga, be strong." A tear fell in spite of myself. We boarded ship at four o'clock that afternoon.

3

THE VOYAGE
TO THE MAINLAND

WE REMAINED in port for one night before leaving Honolulu on the SS *Matsonia* at 2:30 on the afternoon of the seventh. The commander in charge of our transportation was Colonel Craig and our spokesman was the Reverend Keizo Miura, a Nisei. Both proved to be responsible and efficient. I understand that the treatment of internees and conditions on board for the first four groups were more or less the same. By the time our group boarded, however, things were more relaxed. We could use the toilets and showers freely—although the water coming through the showerhead was salt water. We were also allowed to walk and smoke on deck for half an hour in the morning and in the afternoon. We were given strict orders to wear a life jacket whenever we went to the dining room or up on deck. To guard against an attack by a Japanese submarine, several cruisers guarded the convoy, and our ship avoided a straight course, zigzagging through the water.

As one who had received a letter from Lieutenant General Emmons notifying me of my internment in the event of war, I had been prepared. I thought if I was going to be interned, I would prefer to be on the Mainland. Anyway, I was fed up with the tedious and shabby living conditions at Sand Island. Now that I was actually being sent away, however, I began to doubt if I would ever return home to Hawaii or see my loving family again. I cannot express the feelings I had at the time here in writing. All my friends aboard ship must have felt the same.

Fortunately the sea was as calm as a lake. This was my third voyage to the Mainland, and I had never before experienced such a serene passage. Even if we had tried to become seasick, we could not. Mr. Ryukei Maeda was the exception, and Mr. Nekketsu Takei, who practiced *ki* health exercises, could not muster his usual energy.

Fresh greens and fruits were served with our meals, and having gone without tea for so long, I found the iced tea delicious. The youthful exuberance of the several dozen mainland MPs was annoying, but there was no prejudice against us. By chance I became friendly with the youngest of them, a handsome soldier from New Jersey. He seemed to favor me and even gave me some novels in English. As the days passed the MPs became more sociable and began joining us for card games with no compunction, an attitude that can be traced to the reduced level of war hysteria and the commendable openhearted nature of Americans. (The Immigration Office MPs at the start of the war had looked as menacing as goblins from hell. At my inquiry in January the following year, however, these same MPs looked completely different, almost gentle. In just two months, circumstances had changed the face of our captors.)

While walking on deck one morning, I met an old acquaintance, the Reverend Robert Spencer, who was born in Fukuoka. He was wearing the uniform of an army colonel. Rev. Spencer was surprised to see me, and we talked about many things, including his reason for being on the ship. He would only say that he was on his way to the East Coast to teach Japanese to military personnel. He did not mention the circumstances. That Sunday, August 9, he came below to see us and delivered a sermon in Japanese entitled "The Grace of Suffering." In it he cited the example of Mr. Taro Uchiyama, a patient with a unique skin disease that had forced him to spend many years in a special bath at Fukuoka University Hospital. The story deeply affected us because of our own situation. The Reverend Spencer concluded with words of comfort and encouragement. Those who had never heard him speak were amazed at the fluency of his Japanese.

Graffiti at Angel Island

The ship headed north and in three days the air grew colder.

I often overheard the conversation among the MPs, who swore after every word. I was surprised to hear "goddamn" or "Jesus Christ" used continuously. The only two who did not swear were the amiable young man from New Jersey and his friend.

I asked Rev. Spencer to cable my family after he reached San Francisco. He said the commander would not permit that, but he would be able to send something to newspapers in Hawaii via clipper mail. Another internee, Mr. Tokuji Onodera, had been a reporter for the *Hawaii Hochi*, so on behalf of both of us, I requested permission to write the newspaper articles. The next day we were each allowed to send both newspapers four-to five-page articles in either Japanese or English. Mr. Onodera and I wrote them immediately and they were sent off. It was some time after my arrival at Lordsburg when I finally saw my article in the *Hawaii Times*. To my amusement, the entire piece was printed, in English and Japanese, except for the part about the MPs and their constant swearing.

The day before we arrived in San Francisco, our ship pitched and rolled. We entered San Francisco Bay on Saturday afternoon, August 15, 1942. The first thing that caught our attention was the magnificent, snake-like Golden Gate Bridge.[1] We were quickly transferred to a barge and then taken to Angel Island under heavy guard. I had not seen San Francisco in more than twenty years and had never been to Angel Island. The body and baggage checks were strict but businesslike. A young military doctor ordered us to strip. My usual weight, including clothes and shoes, was 135 pounds, so I was surprised to learn that I was now only 113 pounds.

Living quarters for all forty-nine of us were two rooms measuring about thirty-six feet by seventy feet on the second floor of an old building that had once been the Immigration Bureau office. Because there were about ninety internees from California already housed there, space was very tight. The beds were trilevel bunks with barely enough walking space in the aisles. There were about ten windows and one ventilator, but with 140 occupants, air circulation was poor. That night I had difficulty breathing and had a headache. The place reminded me of the Honolulu Immigration Office soon after my arrest.

A spacious vacant room occupied the ground floor, but we were not allowed to use it. Besides Japanese, about twenty-five Germans and Italians were being held on the island. As befits its name, Angel Island was a pleasant place. The distant window view of Richmond and the surrounding area beyond the sea reminded me of the Hira Mountains as seen from Lake Biwa. The meals were good, but the living quarters were very unsanitary. I was selected, along with Mr. Nagaoka and Mr. Honma from California and Mr. Miura from Hawaii, to petition for better conditions. The authorities sympathized with our situation but asked us to be patient since these were temporary accommodations. (Mr. Eimu Miake had become one of my closest friends since our internment together at Sand Island. He was a cheerful and physically very strong man who had developed stomach problems during the crossing and was now so weak that I was very con-

---

1. The original text reads "Golden Gate Bay."

cerned. Fortunately he recovered in the two weeks he spent enduring those "temporary" conditions.)

Graffiti covered the walls of our rooms. From the messages written, I knew Japanese POWs had been here, too.

> "Father said to die bravely in battle. Mother did not say to be a POW, but here I am now . . ."
>
> "For the whole world under one roof, I go to sea under a blue sky."

I found the graffiti interesting, so I read on: "Arrived San Francisco August 5, will leave for Honolulu August 7. Takeo Akizaki, Kazuma Araki, Tokumei Atsumi, Kenkichi Fujimoto, Shigeo Fujino, Hiroshi Honda, Tamotsu Iwohara, Masao Ishimoto, Takeo Kagawa, Kazuo Miyamoto, Tokuichi Niimi, Shunichi Odo, Seiichi Sugimoto, Masao Sakamoto, Sanji Sakamoto, Shinzaburo Sumida, Manabu Tashiro, Kenjitsu Tsuha, Kouji Kawahara." [2] (The order of the names is different in the original. These are the nineteen Japanese American citizens who returned to Hawaii in August 1942. They sailed from San Francisco on the seventh, so our paths crossed somewhere in the Pacific Ocean. All were interned at Camp Livingston except for Mr. Kawahara, the last one listed, who joined the group from Lordsburg.)

I do not condone graffiti, especially the kind that disfigure nature or historical sites. However, after reading the graffiti at Angel Island, I realized there is a place for it. One horrifying message written by a Chinese, "We should kill all white men under the sun," was probably written when our rooms were used by the Immigration Bureau.

Once a day we were allowed to walk and socialize on a small hill behind our quarters. I talked with many people there: Mr. Shigehiko Nagaoka of the *Chuka Nippo* (Central California Daily) in Fresno; Mr. Fukuzo Nakahara of McKay Wireless Station; Mr. Ko Arai, principal of a Japanese-language school and our spokesman on the island; Mr. Shigeru Nagata, an office worker at Osaka Hirabayashi-gumi (he once visited Hawaii, and his wife was the second daughter of Mr. Tsurukichi Tanaka, the San Francisco adventurer whose exploits thrilled us when we were young); Mr. Motomu Kambara, owner of a shoe shop in Sacramento and an admirer of Dr. Tasuku Harada, professor of Japanese literature, history, and language at the University of Hawaii; the Reverend Joshin Motoyoshi of the

---

2. The correct name should be "Toraji" Kawahara.

Hongwanji Mission; Mr. Chitose Hotta, a laundry owner from Gilroy and brother-in-law of the late Mr. Naoto Nakajima, one of my good friends; Mr. Kitoji Honma, a businessman; Mr. Taro Kuroi of the *Rafu Sangyo Nippo* (Los Angeles Business Daily), reportedly a Mexican army officer and a younger brother of Japanese Navy Admiral Teijiro Kuroi; and Mr. Toyojiro Inaki of California, who lectured on various alternative health programs. I became especially friendly with these people. Among those representing the high-spirited European group were a young German lawyer and a German brewing technician.

4

SCENERY SEEN
FROM A TRAIN WINDOW

ABOUT ONE HUNDRED and forty of us left Angel Island at four o'clock in the afternoon on August 27, 1942. As usual we were not told of our destination. I felt I did not care where I went. Following the example of those before me, I left my graffito mark in a corner of the room before leaving: "So we are Japs. Let us stomp defiant over sea and mountain."

At Sand Island the bed next to mine had been occupied by a dangerous-looking tattooed man of about fifty. When I had hesitantly asked what part of the Mainland he was from, he had sneered, "Nowhere." I learned later that he was indeed from nowhere. When he was young, he had signed on as a cook's helper on a Yusen Company ship bound for Europe.[1] He jumped ship at some point, then worked as a sailor again on various ships. Twenty years ago he arrived on the Mainland, where he remained, without a fixed address or family. He was a homeless gambler in America, but here he was part of our group. We got on well and became friends. I discovered there were quite a few people like him from the Mainland.

We had a long, tiring wait in Oakland before we finally began moving at eleven o'clock that evening. The train had three cars that were at least thirty years old. One of them resembled a bamboo cage used to transport a criminal in feudal Japan. The view was limited, but the windows were open. The others were observation cars, where one could get a good view but the windows could not be opened, so it was hot. (For every positive there is a negative. In that sense, the military authorities are quite fair.) The meals were really superb—what one would expect while traveling on

---

1. "Yusen" is short for Nippon Yusen Kaisha Shipping Company.

the Southern Pacific Rail. Black porters brought them to our seats. The train ran along the coast and passed through Santa Barbara and Old Mission. Oranges, lemons, and walnuts grew in clusters on the various fruit farms along the way. Thick forests, their lines of trees disappearing into the distance, came and went one after another. Seeing the size and beauty of these forests made me feel I was really on the Mainland. I managed to get through the very cold night with my overcoat, but I could not sleep well.

A Mirage in the Desert

We arrived in Los Angeles at noon on August 28. We passed a number of aircraft factories, operating on a large scale and at full speed. Mountains of scrap parts were piled high. A battle mood prevailed everywhere. Later, several Italians and nineteen Japanese internees from Glendale boarded our train, the Reverends Daisuke Hori and Kiyoshi Ishikawa among them. I was surprised to see their ID numbers stamped in white on the backs of their coats and pants. Those of us from Angel Island had our numbers pinned to the back of our coats. That evening we reached Imperial Valley and passed through it during the night. I was tired and fell asleep in my aloha shirt. Lying on a coach seat like a cooked shrimp, I ached all over.

On Saturday, the twenty-ninth, we traveled through the vast desert of the Arizona highland at full speed. As expected, the air was crisp and comfortable. At 10:20 in the morning, we adjusted our watches to Mountain Time, advancing them by one hour. At 11:20 we saw water from a river gushing down amid the red mountains of the New Mexico desert. It seemed strange, because what we were in fact seeing was a famous mirage that occurs once in a while in this area. I had never seen a mirage before. At noon we passed through Tucson, a fairly large town.

We arrived at a small, dirty station in the afternoon. All the Germans and Italians were taken off the train and driven away. After an hour, we were suddenly ordered off and told to form a line. The sick were taken away in cars. Guarded by soldiers with machine guns, we were marched two and a half miles with our baggage to a large barracks. We could not tell where we were. Some guessed we were in Texas, others New Mexico, which later proved to be the case. The small, dirty station we had pulled into was Lordsburg, and we were now standing in front of Lordsburg Barracks, fifteen hundred miles from San Francisco.

5

LORDSBURG CAMP

AS WE APPROACHED the camp gate, the third and fourth groups from Hawaii, having arrived earlier, gathered to greet us. I nearly wept for joy at being reunited with the following old friends: Mr. Kango Kawasaki, Mr. Sadato Morifuji, Mr. Tokuji Adachi, Rev. Shunsei Shiratori, Mr. Shin Yoshida, Rev. Sutekichi Osumi, Mr. Ryoichi Tanaka, Mr. Takegoro Kusao, Dr. Ryuichi Ipponsugi, Mr. Sutematsu Endo, Mr. Yoshio Koike, Mr. Riichi Togawa, Mr. Shogo Miwa, and Mr. Matsujiro Otani. That night I took a shower and felt like a new man. Although the camp was four thousand feet above sea level, it was hot. I was excited and did not sleep well.

The next night after dinner, the third and fourth groups held a welcoming party for us in the dining room. The fare was very simple, each man receiving an orange, a piece of cake, and a bottle of soda. They could not afford anything more. There were more than two hundred internees in all. Mr. Sadato Morifuji led the toasts. Mr. Kanji Fujikawa welcomed us formally. On behalf of the guests, I expressed our appreciation. After a short speech by Mr. Teiichiro Maehara of Maui, Mr. Sotaro Kawabe, a successful businessman from Alaska and leader of the second battalion's fifth regiment, led a cheer. (We new arrivals had been designated the sixth regiment of the second battalion.) The latter half of the party, with Mr. Shigeo Shigenaga as toastmaster, featured the hidden talents of internees from various islands, which lasted until nine o'clock. It was a warm and very memorable gathering.

September 1 was very hot. In a partial reshuffling of the Japanese Cabinet, Foreign Affairs Minister Togo resigned. I sent my first letter, permitted only in English, to my family in Honolulu via clipper registered mail. The next day, at around 2:30 in the afternoon, the thermometer read 104 degrees Fahrenheit. I sang the *noh* song "Chikubushima" with the *noh*

Hoshoryu group from the Mainland. This was the first time I had sung since I was interned. That night a whirlwind whipped through the camp. We heard the howling of coyotes; they sounded like wolves.

Lordsburg, which means "village of God," is located in southern New Mexico. It is a small, desolate village with a population of about four thousand. "The Southwest" generally refers to three states: Texas, Arizona, and New Mexico. Located in the middle of a huge, barren desert, Lordsburg is 25 miles from Arizona and 100 miles from Texas. Other states in the vicinity are Colorado, Oklahoma, and California. The area of 400 miles between Lordsburg and the Rocky Mountain watershed is composed of alkali soil and limestone. Cattle ranching is the main industry; agriculture is insignificant. Mining, forestry, and oil drilling are conducted 150 to 200 miles away. The Lordsburg Dam is one of several built on the Rio Grande River.[1] In the last ten years, the highest recorded temperature here was 104 degrees and the lowest minus 4 degrees. In the Southwest, only sandstorms are dangerous. I wondered why we had been brought all the way from Hawaii to a place like this.

New Mexico covers about 123,000 square miles. Its population, mostly Catholic, is only 600,000. The remains of old Indian sites and Indian reservations, with schools from the primary to college level, are abundant. More than ten tribes live in New Mexico. Eighty percent of the population are of Mexican (*Mexi,* in Japanese) descent, which is to be expected, as the state was originally part of Mexico and later annexed to the United States. (Mexicans yielded political and economic power to the Americans just as Hawaiians did.) Spanish-language newspapers are available, but Mexicans generally do not read newspapers or listen to the radio. Like the Indians, they are skilled in native craftwork, but one cannot detect any modern cultural influence. I do not think I am guilty of overstatement if I say that they lack any knowledge of modern sanitary practices. Education and standard of living levels in New Mexico are low.

The immigration of Japanese to the Southwest occurred quite late. Only a few hundred Japanese lived here before the war, engaged primarily in agriculture. About eighty had grocery businesses on the Mexican side of the border. Unlike California, where foreigners are not allowed to buy land freely, here Japanese could own land. Although their businesses were small, they were well established. Chinese owned the important part of town. Mr. Wong, a gambling boss of some repute, lived there, as well as a nephew of

---

1. Lordsburg Dam; the original text says "Rose-velt Dam." Closest dam appears to be the Leesburg on the Rio Grande River.

Mr. Wang Ching-wei who drummed up anti-Japanese sentiment in a town where no Japanese lived. Wherever I went, I saw the impressive footprints of the Chinese presence. Lordsburg may have looked like a ghost town, but it had casinos and houses of ill repute. These catered to the workers from the many iron, copper, gold, and silver mines nearby who came to town on holidays. Besides the working mines, there were quite a few that had been abandoned because they were unpredictable. However, some of these began operating again to meet the wartime demand for metal.

Organizing the Camp

Our barracks and the surrounding camp for Japanese internees were about two and a half miles from town. The camp, surrounded by barbed wire and several watchtowers, was divided into three battalion areas, each housing about a thousand people. A battalion was in turn divided into four regiments of 250. The second battalion was comprised of the fifth, sixth, seventh, and eighth regiments; the third of the ninth, tenth, eleventh, and twelfth regiments. Each regiment had about sixteen barracks. (All the barracks in the first battalion area remained empty and unused until we left.) The total number of internees at the time was about fifteen hundred. As was the case at other camps, internees were responsible for governing themselves.

Each battalion had a governor, vice-governor, chief secretary, public welfare manager, work manager, postmaster, accounting manager, store manager, medical manager, sports manager, service manager, and supply manager. Each regiment had a mayor, vice-mayor, and secretary. Battalions and regiments had their own offices, communicated by telephone, and negotiated with the military office staff. Each battalion elected its own barracks chief and vice-chief. All officers served without pay. However, doctors, orderlies, some of the cooks and KP staff, barbers, and sales clerks at the camp store were paid a flat sum of eighty cents a day, or twenty-four dollars a month.

To the west of us was the soldiers' barracks and to the south a magnificent hospital that seemed out of place. Besides offices for battalion and regiment administrators, each regiment had four dining rooms with kitchens, an infirmary, two bath-and-shower buildings, a supply room, a meeting room, a library, a store, a recreation room, and a woodshop. Inside the camp were a newspaper center, softball field, tennis court, volleyball court, golf course, and vegetable garden. Water was brought in through a small canal from a faraway dam, and natural gas supplied us with fuel. Although we lived in a desert, water was abundant and the quality fairly good. We could use the showers as often and whenever we pleased, for which we were grateful beyond words. In general, the facilities at Lordsburg were nearly perfect and the autonomous system worked well. Some complained about the meals, but I thought they were fairly good.

From the beginning the military authorities were generally liberal in the way they treated us, giving us a greater sense of freedom. There was never any lining up or roll call as at Sand Island. The authorities did a count of all the internees only twice. All battalion gates were closed at the same time and the soldiers began counting, but sometimes, for some reason, the head counts did not tally.

Our biggest problems were the hot weather and the sandstorms that came and went several times a day. When I arrived at Lordsburg, I noticed that each corner of the barracks was tied down with thick wire. I was told this would keep the building from being blown away by strong winds, but that in Texas it would never work. When a sandstorm came, the air became so dense with sand we could see nothing more than an inch in front of us, and we could do nothing. Columns of sand would pile up, then collapse. Once, on a train traveling south from Washington, a sandstorm held us up in Arizona. I was also exposed to sandstorms in Manchuria and Beijing. Wherever I go, sand seems to follow.

Work beyond the Barbed Wire and a Strike

The 247 internees of the third Hawaii group entered Lordsburg on June 18, 1942, before the facilities were completed. They arrived with internees from Alaska and California who had come from Sam Houston Barracks in Texas. Then the following groups arrived: thirty-nine internees of the fourth Hawaii group on July 5; forty-nine of the fifth group on August 29; twenty-eight of the sixth group on October 28, accompanied by forty-three Japanese POWs and thirty-five internees from the Mainland; and twenty-three of the seventh group on October 28. The internees of the eighth through tenth groups were sent to Santa Fe Camp. Before the arrival of our group on August 29, there were two serious incidents. The first was an internee strike against forced labor outside the camp; the second, the violent deaths of Mr. Kobata and Mr. Hirota Isomura, which later resulted in a hearing. The aftertaste of these two incidents was still lingering when we arrived a few months later.

Chronology of events leading up to the strike:

June 18	Third Hawaii group and Alaska-California group arrive and form Third Battalion Tenth Regiment with Mr. Sotaro Kawabe as mayor
Jun 19	Work order issued
June 20	140 internees arrive and form Third Battalion Ninth Regiment with Mr. Yaeju Sugimachi as mayor
June 20–26	Two mayors submit protest letter; no response. Two mayors submit second letter; no response
June 26	177 internees arrive and form Third Battalion Eleventh Regiment with Mr. Geji Mihara as mayor.

Mr. Mihara claimed that, based on his experience at a previous camp and his knowledge of the Geneva Convention, internees did not have to work beyond the barbed wire. The military authorities and internees began to discuss the matter. In the meantime, the internees of the ninth and tenth regiments continued to work on both sides of the fence.

On July 14, the authorities ordered the newspaper office shut down and radio broadcasts stopped. All internees were given a physical and divided into three groups: L, O, and H. Those designated "L" were fit for light work, "O" were too old, "H" were healthy. On July 23, so-called antimilitary internees, including Mayors Kawabe, Sugimachi, and Mihara, and Chief Secretary Yano, were placed under double confinement. Guards were placed at the entrance of their barracks and they were prohibited from leaving.

A request for help to the Spanish embassy in Washington, which represented Japanese interests in the United States during the war, brought Spanish consul Garay and State Department representative Young to the camp. They met and talked with the mayors and those in confinement. Consul Garay assured the internees that he would inform the State Department of their interpretation of the Geneva Convention and asked that, pending the former's decision, they follow the commander's order to the extent their health would allow. The internees accepted the consul's offer, the strike was called off, and the confined internees were released on August 15.

The Violent Deaths of Mr. Kobata and Mr. Isomura

On July 27, 1942, at 1:40 P.M., 147 internees from Bismarck Temporary Camp in North Dakota arrived on a special train under heavy guard.

Among them were Mr. Kobata and Mr. Isomura. Both were ill, so they were left behind at the station to wait for a car to take them to the camp. After the group had arrived at Lordsburg, it was learned that someone had shot the two men dead. This triggered an uproar. On the twenty-eighth, Dr. Teiichi Furugouchi of the medical department explained to the internees that both men had been shot early the previous evening after trying to escape. Everyone was shocked and surprised. Barracks chiefs immediately held a meeting and asked the commander's office to let Dr. Furugouchi, Dr. Akimoto, and the mayors examine the bodies and conduct an autopsy. The request was denied; instead an order was issued for funeral services to be held at four o'clock that day. The internees felt it was an unreasonable order and refused to comply, opting to pay their respects in their own barracks.

Both victims had been from the Mainland. Mr. Kobata was born in Takou-mura, Futami-gun, Hiroshima prefecture. He was a gentle man and worked in behalf of a Buddhist group. He had been nominated to serve on a school committee and as a director of the Japanese Society. He understood everyday English. Mr. Hirota Isomura was born in Kotani Ibu, Higashi Asai-gun, Shiga prefecture, and was about fifty-seven years old. He was from Terminal Island, California, and had owned a fishing boat. He was a trustworthy man of good character. Such were the testimonies of old friends at the barracks chiefs' meeting. All agreed that the two men had been ill for a long time and would never have resisted the guards or tried to escape.

Lieutenant Colonel Hankatta, the investigating officer, and his group from division headquarters visited the camp and held a pretrial. The following internees appeared in court: Kajuro Yasutake, Rev. Sutekichi Osumi, Senmatsu Ishizaki, Fukujiro Hoshitani, Hiroshi Aizawa, Masahiro Konomi, Bigi Okita, Shokichi Nishizaki, and Yoshiaki Fukuda. Mayor Mihara and former Mayor Sugimachi were also questioned. Later, Mayor Yasutake, Rev. Osumi, Mr. Ishizaki, Mr. Aizawa, and Mr. Hoshitani appeared as witnesses on September 9 at a court-martial hearing at Fort Briggs. They did their best and came back to Lordsburg on the eleventh. It was said that the court found the soldier suspected of shooting both men not guilty based on insufficient evidence, but we received no official word.[2]

---

2. Tetsuden Kashima, author of *Judgment without Trial: Japanese American Imprisonment during World War II*, was able to obtain the official court-martial transcript, and the person tried was Private First Class Clarence A. Burleson. According to the transcript, he was twenty-nine years old. Burleson was found not guilty.

Our mayors, advisers, and more than ten people who had given testimony at the pretrial met with Lieutenant Mitchell, who was in charge of internees at the camp, on the afternoon of November 18. They listened to the military's interpretation of the events on the early morning of July 27. Lieutenant Mitchell explained that, while he was counting the newly arrived internees, Sergeant Everett reported hearing two gunshots. Lieutenant Mitchell did not hear them but ran immediately to the spot and found one of the men already dead and the other badly injured but still breathing. He called for an ambulance. He said he believed the injured man died at around 5:30 that morning.

Lieutenant Mitchell then answered the internees' questions. There was no commissioned officer present at the time, but Master Sergeant Packham was on duty and in charge. The name of the soldier who had been on trial was a Private Poston, about twenty-eight years old and married. Lieutenant Mitchell did not know the private's ethnicity or personal history. He avoided answering whether or not the soldier had been found guilty, saying, "If I had to give an opinion, I'd say the two men committed suicide." He added that he had instructed his subordinates to be sure such an incident never happened again. And so the case of these two men was resolved.

Thoughts about the War

I now have in my hand "The List of Japanese from Hawaii at Lordsburg Camp." This mimeographed document was compiled by the internees who arrived in the fifth, sixth, and seventh groups. I believe its preface clearly reveals our thoughts about the war at the time:

> December 7, 1941! Black smoke rose and explosive sounds reverberated over Pearl Harbor in the early morning. They not only woke the people of Hawaii but also announced the arrival of a new age. The memory of this day is deeply ingrained in the minds of many. It was the first day of the great leap into a new world. It was the day when a bright light began to shine on the futures of one billion Asians.
>
> In the year that has passed since then we have had joy and sorrow in quick succession in this foreign land. In the meantime, the blood and tears of the hundred million people in our native land have forged a sacred fire that liberates the Asian races in the southeast. Like a great storm blowing through young grass, it carries before it the many splendid deeds performed in this sacred war.
>
> Now we are destined to spend our days behind barbed wire in desolate New Mexico because the Japanese blood runs through our veins. Whenever we see the sun rising silently over these barren fields, we send Japan our best

wishes for victory. Whenever we see the sun sinking slowly, we think of the old country and tearfully give thanks that we were born in Japan. Whenever we see the bright moon shining over a hill in the cloudless night sky, we lose ourselves in fond memories of Hawaii. We have compiled a list of all those who were destined to dine together at one table and sleep side by side under the shade of trees and alongside a river among sand-swept hills. In doing so we honor the friendships that have developed among us and give thanks to those who came here before us. We wish to express here our gratitude for their boundless goodwill.

All members of the fifth, sixth, and seventh groups
January 1943

I do not remember who wrote this preface. Although it now seems shameful when we think of the war and its outcome, many of us at the time agreed with its sentiments. Both Japanese from Hawaii and the Mainland shared this kind of thinking, and it undeniably influenced our behavior.

The total number of Hawaii Japanese listed was 244. They were tallied by prefecture as follows: Hiroshima, 74; Yamaguchi, 38; Kumamoto, 34; Fukuoka, 19; Fukushima, 12; Okinawa, 11; Niigata, 8; Tokyo, 6; Shimane, 6; Nagano, 4; Ehime, 4; Kagoshima, 3; Wakayama, 3; Fukui, 3; Tochigi, 2; Chiba, 2; Nara, 2; Kanagawa, 2; Kochi, 2; Yamanashi, 1; Toyama, 1; Tottori, 1; Shizuoka, 1; Kyoto, 1; Hyogo, 1; Aichi, 1; Hokkaido, 1; Mie, 1; Shiga, 1. They were also tallied by island: Honolulu, 84; Oahu (outside Honolulu), 35; Hawaii (the Big Island), 64; Maui, 35; Kauai, 19; Lanai, 4; Molokai, 3.

Wherever there are Japanese, there are *kenjinkai* (prefectural people's associations). Sometimes these become too exclusive, but it is only natural for people who have something in common to form a group—especially those who have been removed from their usual circumstances and surroundings. At the camp there were *kenjinkai* for nearly every prefecture; these brought people from Hawaii and the Mainland together. People from Tokyo and its surrounding area established *Edokai,* to which Dr. Mori and I both belonged. There was a San Francisco *kai,* which had a membership of about fifty. We talked about establishing a Hawaii *kai,* but this did not materialize at either Lordsburg or Santa Fe.

The Heavy Burden of Mainland Japanese

After living with Mainland Japanese, I noticed their backgrounds and circumstances were very different from ours. Of course there were exceptions but, generally speaking, those of us from Hawaii were firmly established in our new country and were well settled, while for the most part Mainland Japanese worked seasonally as agricultural laborers and moved from place to place. In dealing with Americans, Hawaii Japanese were friendly and cooperative, while those from the Mainland were not. The living standard for Japanese in Hawaii improved considerably before the war. This was not the case for Japanese elsewhere: I understand that many living in the more rural parts of the Mainland could not afford curtains for their windows. I found this difficult to believe, but it seems to be true. I once overheard a conversation between two prominent internees from the Mainland. I doubted my ears when I heard one of them ask, "Were you ever invited to dinner at the home of an American?" To someone from Hawaii, hearing such things was quite a shock.

In March 1942, four months after the war had begun, 119,000 Issei and Nisei living in California, Oregon, and Washington were forced to move inland by order of Lieutenant General Dewitt, commander of the Western Defense Area. Rumors had been circulating that Japanese living on the West Coast were very active in espionage. In Los Angeles alone there were six thousand members of the Nippon Butoku-kai (Japan Martial Arts Association). According to some, the 1,600 Japanese fishermen living in San Pedro were poised for military action against the United States. After the attack on Pearl Harbor, anti-Japanese factions persuaded military and judicial authorities to order people from their homes and businesses. The hardship and injustice they suffered during the sudden evacuation were beyond our imagination. Quite a few Jews took advantage of unlucky Japanese and secretly paid next to nothing for furniture and other goods. Items stored in warehouses and other assets were either broken or stolen. The wickedness of these people became apparent.

Japanese were chased from their land and their homes and herded like sheep into ten relocation camps in states beyond or near the foot of the Rocky Mountains. They were first lodged at fifteen temporary assembly centers built on horse racetracks in California and neighboring states. The resulting confusion was disastrous. After hearing the many tragic stories of mainland Japanese, I felt that we in Hawaii had a comparatively easy burden to bear.

Internees from the Mainland were more rebellious than those from Hawaii. From the point of view of Americans, this kind of behavior was seen as extremely disloyal but, given the pitiful circumstances under which mainland Japanese were placed, it was to be expected. I would not be exaggerating if I said that part of the responsibility for the recalcitrance of these internees rested on the United States government. Japanese in Hawaii were very lucky in comparison. Throughout the war, most were allowed to live comfortably and keep their businesses. For this we must thank Lieutenant General Emmons, a fair and intelligent man, who was commander in Hawaii when the war broke out.[3]

The Relationship between Internees from the Mainland and Those from Hawaii

When the first and second Hawaii groups came into contact with internees from the Mainland, they were generally considered inferior. (By the time I arrived at Lordsburg, this was no longer the case.) Japanese from Panama and South America were also held in low esteem, so they felt much closer to internees from Hawaii. Japanese resent being discriminated against, but they themselves are prone to "closing ranks" to exclude others. Few ethnic groups exhibit this kind of behavior: It is definitely one of the shortcomings of Japanese. Those from the Mainland had suffered greatly under anti-Japanese policies and regulations, so they tried, consciously or unconsciously, to gain satisfaction by excluding those whom they considered to be "outsiders"—Japanese from Hawaii, Panama, and South America.

After we had lived together for a while, the Mainlanders began to think better of us. Hawaii people often took the lead in promoting events and participated in many camp activities: theatricals, exhibitions, and sports, including sumo and softball. They began to realize we were fairly strong in not only number but also character. We received monthly remittances of fixed amounts from home and were the best customers at the canteen (camp store), which gave us a certain amount of clout. What we hated most was being blamed by Mainlanders whenever something went wrong. But in general we were not reproached and maintained a good reputation in the camps. I think this was due to our strong willpower.

Internees from the Mainland were often paroled early, especially those from the eastern United States. Mr. Kiyoshi Kawakami of Washington, D.C., and Mr. Ryusaku Tsunoda of New York were interned at the start of the war and paroled in March of the following year. Others were released one after another during my time at Lordsburg through the beginning of my internment at Santa Fe. Several Mainland internees were moved to other centers or to free zones under special permission or with guarantors. Mainlanders greeted one another daily with "Haven't you had your

---

3. Lieutenant General Delos C. Emmons became commander shortly after the outbreak of World War II. He replaced Lieutenant General Walter C. Short on December 17, 1941.

hearing yet?" or "When are you going to be paroled?" Those of us from
Hawaii were somewhat jealous and grew disgusted after hearing these conversations over and over. The only men from Hawaii who were paroled
from Lordsburg were Mr. Seiei Wakukawa, who had appealed directly to
President Roosevelt, and Rev. Sutekichi Osumi, who was given permission
to leave the camp to do missionary work.

Among Mainland Japanese were quite a number of illegal immigrants
who had jumped ship in the San Diego area in southern California to
work as fishermen or had smuggled themselves into the United States from
Mexico. Lured to this land of Canaan, where honey and milk were said to
be flowing, hundreds of Japanese and Chinese attempted the crossing. All
along the vast, barren border lie the bones of many adventurers who failed.
Swindlers offering transport to the United States for several hundred dollars would open their cargo doors while flying and dump their "shipment"
in the middle of the desert without a second thought. I heard all of this
from a man who lived in Mexico.

As I mentioned before, some Jews took advantage of helpless Japanese
who had been ordered to evacuate. A man was forced to sell a new $200
refrigerator for a mere $2.50 because the Jew who bought it said he had
to take into consideration the money he was going to spend transporting
it. Another man sold a bureau for $5.00. Later his wife tried to retrieve
the $350 in cash that had been left in the bureau by mistake. The buyer,
a Jew, refused to help her, saying the deal had been closed. Pianos valued
at $400 were sold for $30.00. I was told there were many such cases just
like these.

Japanese from Alaska

When I first arrived it seemed odd that the Alaska internees were wearing government-issued denim clothing labeled "PW" in large white letters
painted on the back and both knees. I guess they were considered prisoners
when the war began.

Alaska is incredibly vast; it is larger than Germany, France, and Eng-
land combined, and larger than Manchuria. Its population of 28,000
whites and 30,000 Indians and Eskimos is only 58,000. Japanese in Alaska
(including those who have Indian or Eskimo blood) aged sixteen years
and older were evacuated at the start of the war. From December 8, 1941,
through March 6, 1942, most of them were ordered to leave Alaska permanently. The first ship left the port of Ketchikan on April 27, 1942; the
second on May 4. A total of eighty-six Alaska Japanese were transferred to

Seattle and sent to a temporary camp at Fort Lewis, Tacoma, where five other Japanese were already interned. They left the camp on May 19 and were joined by an internee from Seattle and four from Portland. They were sent to Sam Houston Barracks in Texas for several weeks before coming to Lordsburg on June 18. Most of the Alaska Japanese were bachelors. Native women married to Japanese men were not interned. However, Japanese women, including Mrs. Sotaro Kawabe and Mrs. Shonosuke Tanaka, were taken to Seagoville, Texas, where several women from Hawaii, including Mrs. Haru Tanaka and Mrs. Miyao, had been placed. They were later transferred to the family camp in Crystal City.

At Lordsburg I became acquainted with Japanese from Alaska for the first time. I found their stories very interesting and informative. I had always thought Alaska was much too cold for the average person, but one of the first things I learned was that it is not, thanks to a warm ocean current. When this Pacific current moves up along the south shore of Alaska, a tremendous volume of humid air hits the mountains, creating clouds and snow in quantities rarely found anywhere else.

The second thing I learned was that Eskimos and Indians are as simple and honest as they were in ancient times. They like Japanese people. Their faces and physiques are similar to ours. Young bachelors are so welcomed in Alaska that, once settled there, they cannot tear themselves away and move elsewhere. Most of the internees agreed that no place in the world could match Alaska for easy living.

Another surprise was transportation in Alaska. With few roads covering a wide area I thought travel would be inconvenient. I was told that, because the land is covered in snow for most of the year, dog sleds are used everywhere, providing a fast and efficient means of getting around. There are also sixty-two commercial airfields in Alaska, and the airline network is so well organized that traveling long distances is no problem at all.

Strange Stories of the Snow Country

Alaska was originally occupied by Russia, which had coveted this part of the world since the days of Peter the Great and made huge profits from the fur business. In the nineteenth century the Russians encountered a large colony of Indians in Sitka in southern Alaska and eventually conquered them. Later, in 1867, the United States purchased Alaska from Russia for a mere $7,500,000. At the time, many Americans thought there was nothing to be gained from this snow-covered land and they opposed the purchase.

In the end, Secretary of State William H. Seward succeeded in negotiating the purchase. I greatly admire his foresight and ability.

While I was at Lordsburg, I got to know a few of the eighty or so Alaska Japanese quite well and learned a great deal about their fairy-tale land and its people. Mr. Sotaro Kawabe was one of those I befriended. He was born in Sakata-gun in Shiga prefecture and was fifty-two years old. He served as a mayor and governor in the camp. A man of good character, he had been a successful businessman in Alaska and lived on the Kenai Peninsula in Seward, a small seaport with a population of about two thousand. This port was the terminus of the Seattle–Seward Sea Route. During his twenty-five years in Alaska, he was involved in many businesses, including laundering, banking, and mining. He was especially knowledgeable about mining, emphasizing it was not a risky business and that, depending on the management, there was nothing more stable.

A man whom I thought was especially outstanding was Mr. Frank Yasusuke Yasuda. A segment of his life story had appeared in a Japanese magazine along with that of Mr. Jujiro Wada, a successful businessman who had made his fortune at the Klondike gold mine. (Mr. Wada's last years, however, were miserable. When he was found dead in a San Diego alley in 1940, he had only fifty cents in his pockets.) Mr. Yasuda was already seventy-five years old when I met him. He had rheumatism in one leg but was otherwise in good health and seemed youthful and full of vigor. His mind was sharp and his character impeccable. Dr. U and I became especially friendly with him. Mr. Yasuda had lived in Beaver, Alaska, for the past fifty years and had a wife of Eskimo descent. He had two well-educated daughters, one a public schoolteacher and the other a postmaster. He was born in Ishimaki, Miyagi prefecture, and had traveled to the United States on the same boat as Mr. Yurei Mori, who later became Japan's minister of education. He had many friends among politicians in Japan. At their suggestion he had thought of returning to Japan, but his love and affection for Alaska kept him from leaving. Because he had not been in the company of Japanese for fifty years, Mr. Yasuda had difficulty speaking Japanese when he arrived at Lordsburg. However, being a well-educated man, he quickly rediscovered his mother tongue and was listening eagerly to a news broadcast when I met him. Generally speaking, Japanese from Alaska (including Mr. Yasuda) are fluent in English and their pronunciation is good.

Mr. Yasuda's main business had been mining, but he said laughingly that he had had eight different careers. He had been a doctor, a minister, a funeral director, an interpreter, and even a midwife, although he admitted that for native women, childbearing is very easy. When labor pains begin, the pregnant woman moves into a "birthing shack," where she remains alone until the delivery, cleans up, then returns home carrying the baby.

Sailors on whaling ships and those shipwrecked often suffer from scurvy due to a lack of vegetables and fruit in their diet. The natives and Japanese in Alaska almost never eat vegetables or fruit, but they do not suffer from scurvy. Dr. U wondered how they avoided the disease without taking vitamin C supplements. The blood of fresh fish is rich in vitamin C, and Alaskans drink it as part of their diet. Anyone living in Alaska for a long time becomes very sensitive to the smell of blood. He is able to smell a wild hare some distance away. Fish blood may not appeal to us, but the Alaskan begins to crave it because his body is aware of the vitamin deficiency. Nature works in very strange ways.

A Rough-and-Tumble Life

I heard many stories of the rough and sometimes violent lives of men in Alaska that corresponded with Jack London's tales of wine, women, and gambling. Prices of goods in Alaska are the highest in the world, but wages are also high. A large number of the Japanese seasonal laborers from around Seattle work in the Alaska canning factories every year, but most of them gamble away their pay. Even if they manage to keep some of their money, they eventually lose it gambling on the voyage home.

One of my Alaska friends was Mr. Chiyozo Kamimura. He was not very tall and his stomach protruded, but he was a strong man and often participated in sumo matches at the camp. I once saw him wrestle a big POW and carry him effortlessly out of the ring. During the match, Mr. Kamimura lost a toenail. Later he casually smeared salt on the wound. A likable character, he was forty-six years old but looked younger than his age. He was married and had a family in Alaska, where he was also known as a scoundrel. Mr. Kamimura had arrived in Alaska when he was a boy. He went to school and later opened a restaurant. The sale of liquor to natives was prohibited, but he sold it to them "under the counter." He would kick drunkards out of his restaurant and take their money. He went around with Eskimo girls, who were loose and free for the taking. He gambled openly, but after coming to this camp, Mr. Kamimura began attending sermons regularly and turned honest.

I heard many interesting stories from this man who loved the outdoors. Once, after the trout fishing season had ended, Mr. Kamimura made his way to a waterfall where he knew trout were jumping. Some of them could not scale the falls and fell into his boat. After a while, so many had fallen in that the boat nearly sank. It sounds incredible, but the fact is that there is an abundance of trout. Upon his return, a patrol officer stopped him. Mr. Kamimura calmly explained that the fish had simply fallen into his boat. There were no fishhooks in the boat and no scars on the trout, so he was released.

Mr. Hiroo Shiihara of Kagoshima prefecture was in our second battalion. He was not a resident of Alaska but a newspaper reporter from Seattle. As a graduate of a Japanese fisheries college, he had been commissioned by the Ministry of Agriculture and Industry to travel to Alaska every year and send reports back to Japan. Mr. Shiihara knew Alaska very well and often gave interesting lectures on the Aleutian Islands. One of the many things I learned from him was that you can tell the age of a salmon by dipping a fish scale in ammonia water, which makes it transparent, then using a magnifier and counting the rings, the way it is done with trees. At Imperial University in Tokyo you can still find the Alaskan salmon scales sent by Mr. Shiihara.

Another point he made was the lack of public morals. According to Mr. Shiihara, Catholic priests traveled by airplane to preach throughout Alaska. When a priest presided over the wedding of a native couple he had the prerogative of spending the first night with the bride. Another example was the report filed by an expedition party sponsored by Hochi Newspaper Company. During the trek across Alaska, the reporters were set upon by a band of women in a surprise attack. Popular morals were quite disordered. This was one aspect of Alaska related in Mr. Shiihara's lectures.

There was also an internee nicknamed "Quarreling Saito," who was said to have been quite violent in Alaska but was known in camp to have some lovable qualities. I knew him only indirectly.

Thirty of the Alaska internees (including Mr. Yasuda) were paroled on the night of December 4, 1943, after they were moved to Santa Fe. They were sent first to relocation centers and were eventually allowed to return to Alaska. All other remaining internees from Alaska were sent home before we were returned to Hawaii in October 1945.

Japanese Newspaper Reporters

At Lordsburg there were thirty-one journalists, including Mr. Sei Fujii, president of the *Rafu Kashu Mainichi* (California Daily of Los Angeles) and an old friend of mine; Mr. Toyoji Abe, president of the *Soko Shinsekai Asahi* (New World Asahi of San Francisco); Mr. Sumio Arima, president of the *Seattle Hokubei Jiji* (North America News of Seattle); Mr. Keitaro Kawajiri, adviser to the *Seattle Hokubei Jiji;* Mr. Masaru Akabori, chief of the Northwest Bureau of Seattle's *Nichibei Shimbun* (Japan America News); Mr. Ayao Tahara, acting president of the *Taihoku Nippo* (Great North Daily) in Seattle; Mr. Toshiharu Kanbe, editor-in-chief of Seattle's *Nichibei Koron* (Japan America Public Opinion); Mr. Ten-you Yazaki of Los Angeles' *Rafu Nichibei* (Japan America News); and Mr. Iwao Oyama, president of Portland's *Oshu Nippo* (Oregon Daily). Here, gathered in one place, was an array of talent.

I was the second most senior journalist, the oldest being Mr. Kawajiri, who was also known as Hokumei. Mr. Akabori, known by his literary name, Hyoroku Oishi, was a good speaker as well as a journalist and widely known throughout the camp for his comments on current affairs. Mr. Kanbe was an enthusiastic Christian; Mr. Yazaki, a one-legged poet. Mr. Deiso Takayama was not in the newspaper business but was famous on the Mainland for his Japanese verse.

On the night of September 27, 1942, we held the first meeting of newspapermen in the social room of the sixth regiment. Thirteen attendees were served Japanese tea and snails (Danish pastry) provided by the chief cook. It was an extremely pleasant and friendly meeting.

I discovered that Mr. Kawajiri (born in 1868) was not only older than I by five years but also had come to the United States in 1895, a year before me. He outdid me on these two points, but in newspaper work I was his senior by three years, having begun my career in 1899.

Wherever there are Japanese, there is a Japanese newspaper. The first issue of the *Lordsburg Jiho* (Lordsburg News) was printed on August 26, 1942, four days before my arrival. It was written largely in Japanese, with a short column in English. The four-page paper measured fourteen inches by eight and half inches and was mimeographed on both sides. It was published twice a week.

About two weeks earlier, Dr. Fischer, a representative from the International Chamber of Youth, an organization dedicated to helping POWs, had visited the camp for the first time and met with Japanese internees. After discussing equipment and supplies for education, recreation, and sports, he had asked the internees if they published a camp newspaper. This sparked our interest. The military authorities agreed to the publication of a newspaper on the condition that the circulation would be restricted to the camp. Unfortunately we had neither equipment nor funds. At first the authorities agreed to supply the paper, but there was a slip-up the day before the first issue was to be printed. Other problems arose, but they were finally overcome. Originally the plan was to distribute the newspaper free of charge, but the policy was later changed to a ten-cent-a-month subscription fee.

The newspaper staff was as follows: Mr. Keitaro Kawajiri, editor-in-chief; Mr. Masaru Akabori, editor; Mr. Kenji Kasai, general manager; Mr. Kiyoshi Nozaki, English news; Mr. Shukichi Nagasawa,[4] Hawaii news; Mr. Ichiji Sugiyama, Internment Center news; Mr. Teizo Takayama, miscellaneous news; Mr. Bigi Okita, stencil; Mr. Toshio Tsunoda, design cut; Mr. Kenji Kasai and Mr. Kiyoshi Nozaki, printing; Messrs. Toyoji Abe, Sumio Arima, Sei Fujii, Iwao Oyama, Yasutaro Soga, and Ayao Tahara, advisers. The central power behind it all was Mr. Kenji Kasai, a younger brother of Mr. Choji Kasai, a representative in the Diet. He was very capable and honest.

News Broadcasts and Comments on Current Affairs

From the start, internees were hungry for news of the world outside. We had our own modest newspaper; newspapers and magazines in English were allowed. We could listen to any domestic radio broadcast (shortwave radios were prohibited), but we generally enjoyed the news broadcast in the camp. The main announcers at Lordsburg were Mr. Iwao Oyama and Mr. Toshio Sakaguchi for the second battalion, and Mr. Yasumasa Yoshizumi and Mr. Masaru Akabori for the third. We listened to the broadcasts in the dining room after dinner or in an empty barracks. Both rooms would fill up so quickly that the walls seemed to bulge and many were forced to listen from the doorway. Mr. Shichitaro Fujii and Mr. Kumemaro Uno also served as announcers for the third battalion, but the most popular ones were Yoshizumi and Sakaguchi. Announcers worked hard. They listened to the radio twenty-four hours a day, read every kind of magazine, and edited the news. In the case of Mr. Sakaguchi, Mr. Kensaku Murata listened to the radio for him and fed him news.

Internees tried hard to be optimistic about whatever they heard; they wanted to hear good news. Announcers who understood this won plaudits from their listeners. Whenever there was good news from the Imperial headquarters, everyone went wild, although what we were hearing at the time was mostly propaganda. Near the end of the broadcast, an announcer would raise his voice and solemnly say, "An announcement from the Imperial headquarters!" and everyone would quiet down and listen with rever-

4. The original text reads "Nagasaki"; "Nagasawa" is correct.

ence. It was amusing that broadcasters sometimes presented conflicting information. In news about Admiral Isoroku Yamamoto, one said the admiral had died while another said he was still alive. Neither announcer would acknowledge an error in his report, so for a while we were more in limbo than the spirit of the deceased admiral.

In addition to his role as a news broadcaster, Mr. Akabori commented on current affairs every Sunday. His commentaries were his own particular interpretation of what was going on, but they were fairly interesting. He always attracted at least three hundred listeners. Even after moving to the camp at Santa Fe, this energetic man would always copy his radio commentaries onto a big blackboard, and many people in turn diligently copied them.

Mr. Shungo Abe translated timely articles from magazines and once in a while held lectures on the war and other topics, which were popular. He was a graduate of the University of Chicago and had practiced law in Los Angeles. A leader among the internees, he was appointed governor of the second battalion and resolved many difficult situations through his gentle character and intelligence. He had the rare gift of eloquence despite his strong northern accent. (I still fondly remember him saying, "The issue of Endo [India] is the issue of *zukan* [*jikan,* or 'time']." After moving to the camp at Santa Fe, he returned to Japan on the second exchange ship and was reportedly active in Manchuria. We were happy to hear that later he was elected to the Lower House of the Diet.

Mr. Kiyoshi Nozaki, a graduate of Waseda University's English department, worked at the *Lordsburg News* office. He had no interest in lecturing or announcing, but he was very good at English and had a light and easy writing style. His bulletin board displays outside the office showed his ingenuity and skill with discarded materials. His creations, accompanied by comments and witty English explanations, were eye-catching. The contributions of all these talented men provided immeasurable solace and comfort to many of us.

Religious Organizations

At Lordsburg there were close to a hundred Buddhist, Shinto, and Christian ministers, pastors, and lecturers—quite an amazing number. Fifty-four Buddhists represented various sects. The twenty-five in the second battalion organized a Buddhist association, and the twenty-nine in the third established a Buddhist ministers' organization. Each organization held study sessions and a service every Sunday. Among the special events were the Bon Festival, equinoctial service, and Buddhahood attainment service. Twenty-three ministers were from Hawaii, thirty-one from the Mainland. Other Buddhist groups included the Jodoshu Mission, the second battalion's Sodoshu Mission, the second and third battalion's Buddhist hymn group, and a Kannon sutra reading group. Key figures among the Buddhists were the Reverends Enryo Shigefuji of Fresno, Jokai Ko of Los Angeles, and Eimu Miake, Kodo Fujitani, and Kogan Yoshizumi of Hawaii.

Shinto associations in the camp included Daijingu and Konko-kyo. Twelve Shinto ministers hailed from the Mainland, two from Hawaii. Mr. Miryo Fukuda of the Konko-kyo San Francisco Mission was said to be a graduate of Tokyo Imperial University, but he was an ultranationalist and a troublemaker. The Tenri-kyo Mission had twenty ministers, including two from Hawaii. Their leader was Mr. Masaji Hashimoto, bishop of the North America Tenri-kyo in Los Angeles. A graduate of Kokugaku-in College and an easygoing, interesting character, he was an authority on *kana* writing and an excellent poet. He established a Tenri-kyo village in Manchuria.

Christians from the Mainland and Hawaii organized the United Church of Christian Sects here. Of the eleven pastors, four were from Hawaii. They held Sunday morning and evening services, Wednesday prayer meetings, bible lectures, special meetings, and hymn study meetings. Rev. Kiyoshi Ishikawa, a graduate of Doshisha University, and Rev. Takashi Kamae, a graduate of Aoyama Gakuin University, were devoted scholars. They were both from California. Rev. Sutekichi Osumi from Hawaii devoted himself not only to the pastors' association but also to his work as the chief secretary of the third battalion, a barracks chief, and an English lecturer. I had the greatest respect for him.

Whenever a funeral was held in the camp, if the deceased happened to be a Buddhist, dozens of clerics would line up at the service in colorful, beautifully decorated surplices. In the outside world one could never expect to see such an assemblage of ministers in such finery. Upon seeing this spectacle, someone joked, "If you have to die, now is the time." I had to agree, and I mean no disrespect, but I question the character of some of these religious leaders. Frankly, many of them disappointed me in that they did not know the way of Buddha or God. Most important of all, they did not know the way of Man, since they knew too little about the world. They could not understand the ever-changing international situation. They secluded themselves in their sect or religion and did not know or care to know about anything beyond it. It seems perfectly clear to me why they failed to enlighten or inspire others.

I knew quite a few Buddhist monks who were greedier than ordinary people—some were no better than professional gamblers or racketeers. I was not the only one who was utterly disgusted with them. To cite an example, there was a minister named Todoroki. Some internees had peeled away the tops of desks stored in an empty barracks in order to make boxes for shelves. Some even dismantled part of the framework of the barracks. When I heard about this, I was indignant and said it was a terrible thing to do. The minister overheard me and said: "What difference does it make? This is a battle of attrition. You are not a Japanese." I answered, "If I'm not a Japanese, you're not a human being." He was silent after that and never talked to me again.

Dissension among Mainland Buddhists

At the outbreak of the war between the United States and Japan, a disagreement divided the Hongwanji Mission on the Mainland into two opposing groups: those ministers who sided with the United States and those who sided with Japan. The Reverend Ryotai Matsukage of the Honpa Hongwanji North America Mission issued a statement early on, saying that Japan's surprise attack on Pearl Harbor was cowardly and dishonorable. He encouraged other ministers on the Mainland to break off their relations with the head temple in Japan and support the United States. His views were published in English-language newspapers and endorsed by the Reverend Okayama, his successor. Whether or not because of this statement, Rev. Matsukage and his supporters were not interned.

Many Japanese accused Rev. Matsukage's group of speaking against Japan and the head temple to save themselves. In mid-March 1943, the minister sent thirty dollars to the Hongwanji ministers interned at Lordsburg. After a heated discussion involving diehards and moderates that nearly led to an exchange of blows, the ministers decided to return the money.

There is no one more despicable or troublesome than a hypocrite. I was surprised to discover so many of them among the religious men and teachers in the camp. A man from the Mainland told me the story of a high-ranking monk who supposedly lived according to Buddha's teachings and was arrested by the FBI. When agents searched him, they found more than a thousand dollars in cash in his coat pockets. Interrogation followed, and when his residence was searched agents discovered a bundle of love letters from a married woman. His followers were shocked by the deception.

Here was a man who had gained their sympathy and respect by appearing to embrace poverty and a strict moral code of behavior. He is not an exception among those of his profession.

Like many ministers, a surprising number of teachers fail to comprehend anything beyond their own limited experience. They lack even the simplest and most basic knowledge of international affairs. They hardly have the will to study. Because they have spent so much of their lives teaching, they feel they can educate anyone—even adults—when they have taught only children. They want to help others to learn, which is admirable, but many of them have lost the humility necessary to learn from others and fail to realize that they are behind the times.

Hospital Facilities and Doctors

In scale and services the hospital at Lordsburg was comparable to those outside the barbed wire. It was opened on August 1, 1942, just one month before we arrived. When the first Hawaii group arrived in June, there were no facilities for the sick. The internees immediately opened an infirmary, where pharmacists Mannosuke Koumu and Sutematsu Endo helped Dr. Bond, the military physician, take on emergency cases. Soon after Dr. Teiichi Furugouchi of El Paso arrived with the second group, he was appointed chief of the medical department and immediately began attending to the internees. He was kept very busy and hardly slept or ate. Fortunately, Dr. Kensuke Akimoto and two dentists, Drs. Ryuichi Ipponsugi and Hideo Inaba, were later transferred to Lordsburg. The second and third battalions each had their own clinic, where patients were examined and treated; those requiring further medical attention were sent to the hospital.

The hospital was of course run by the military authorities. The hospital head was Lieutenant Colonel R. C. Baker; military officers were appointed chiefs of surgery, internal medicine, and dentistry, and heads of the pharmacy and other departments. The chief nurse and her staff were all American. The hospital served both military personnel and internees. At the end of 1942 there were 149 inpatients: 127 internees and 22 soldiers. The internee hospital staff was made up of Dr. Furugouchi (hospital chief), Drs. Ipponsugi and Inaba (dentists), Mr. Endo (pharmacist), Mr. En-ichi Saiki (pathologist), Mr. Sumine Miura (X-ray technician), twenty orderlies, and more than thirty kitchen workers. It was a grand lineup of devoted workers.

In addition to dentistry, Japanese internee doctors specialized in dermatology and venereal disease (Dr. Furugouchi), otolaryngology (Dr. Akimoto), surgery (Dr. Motokazu Mori), and internal medicine (Drs. Yokichi Uehara,[5] Jiro Yoshizawa, and Tokujiro Yanagi). Drs. Furugouchi, Akimoto, Uehara, and Yoshizawa, and Mr. Koumu divided their time between the hospital and the second battalion clinic, while Drs. Mori and Yanagi and Mr. Endo concurrently worked at the hospital and the third battalion clinic. There were also four other staff members at each clinic.

Soon after I arrived at Lordsburg, Mr. Tokuji Adachi, who worked at the second battalion clinic, gave me a tour of the hospital and introduced me to a number of people. I thought the facility was well equipped and comfortable. I met with Dr. Ipponsugi, renewing our old friendship. Until I arrived at the camp, I never realized how many Japanese have problems with their teeth. In the washroom, I saw many thirty- and forty-year-olds with full dentures. They, on the other hand, wondered why I did not have false teeth. Everyone knows that Japanese characteristically have poor eyesight and wear glasses, but I am sure many do not know our teeth are so bad. Dr. Ipponsugi and Dr. Inaba were kept quite busy.

Dr. Kensuke Akimoto was from the Mainland and had been a ship's doctor for the Japan Yusen company. He was an amiable and honest man but pitifully small and thin. Once a dishonest and lazy internee tried to persuade Dr. Akimoto to give him a false diagnosis so he could get out of work. When Dr. Akimoto refused, the man threatened him and shouted, "If you don't do as I tell you, I'm going to throw you around."

A Better TB Sanitarium Than Those in Switzerland

I met Dr. Teiichi Furugouchi at Lordsburg. He arrived in El Paso, Texas, in 1903, and began to practice there the following year. He was a pioneer, had many Mexican and Indian patients, and was well respected for his kindness. An influential man, he was responsible for making various medical facilities available to Japanese and other travelers in the Southwest. He often told me interesting stories about this part of the United States, so I invited him to give a lecture one night. Under the sponsorship of the mayor's public welfare department, Dr. Furugouchi spoke on "The Climate of the Southwestern United States and Sanitation" on September 17, 1942, with me acting as master of ceremonies. In his two-hour lecture, Dr.

---

5. Dr. Yokichi Uehara, a longtime physician who practiced in Waipahu, Oahu, was sent to various internment camps, the last being the Santa Fe Camp. He was a frequent companion of Mr. Soga on morning walks around camp. Dr. Uehara returned to Waipahu to resume his medical practice upon the cessation of World War II.

Furugouchi went over general health conditions in the Southwest, which was very helpful. Here are some of his remarks:

> Most of the outpatients in this area suffer from respiratory diseases or neuralgia. Endemic diseases are malaria, amoebic dysentery, and hookworm. Hookworm, which can be contracted through soil handling, resembles duodenal worms. Its symptoms are glittering nails, diarrhea, and hemafecia.
>
> New Mexico, nicknamed the Sunshine State, is said to be sunny 366 days a year because it receives an extra minute of sunshine per day. The ground absorbs more ultraviolet rays and the air is drier than in Switzerland. This type of climate, very beneficial for those suffering from respiratory diseases and neuralgias, attracts patients from all over the United States. Those from the eastern part of the United States flock to places like Lordsburg, Santa Fe, and Tucson for a change of air. Seventy percent of El Paso's population of 110,000 are tuberculosis patients. Those suffering from TB here at this camp gain two to three pounds a week. The reason is not improved nutrition but the fresh air and sunshine.
>
> When we look at the relationship between war and health, we find that the number of TB patients increased tremendously around the time of the previous world war, in the years 1915 through 1920. Statistics clearly show that this number had decreased by 1940, but then it rapidly increased in 1941. In light of this, one could say it was a lucky break to have been interned here where we can enjoy beautiful sunshine and be safe from contagious diseases.
>
> The increasing number of nervous breakdowns in the camp has many causes, but this disease must be brought under control. It decreases one's resistance and may lead to the contraction of other diseases. Gastroenteric disorders are our biggest problem. These stem from drinking too much cold water and from overeating and eating too quickly. What is shocking is that so many of us wear full dentures which, together with poor eating habits, can only lead to stomach problems.
>
> Most important, we should all be careful not to transmit diseases and do our best to stay healthy. To this end, I propose that "sanitation police" be posted at various places throughout the camp.

Dr. Furugouchi reminded us that we should try to maintain our health while living as a group. This was a very useful lecture. His suggestion for a sanitation police corps was sensible and appropriate, but it never saw the light of day.

Living on the Border between the United States and Mexico

Let me digress a little here and record a few things I learned from Dr. Furugouchi about life on the U.S.–Mexico border. A graduate of Okayama

Medical College, Dr. Furugouchi came to the United States before the great San Francisco earthquake. He sent a letter to every state asking if he could take the medical license examination in Japanese. The Texas medical board consented on condition that he pay for an interpreter, so a friend from Chicago accompanied him to El Paso. After passing the examination and receiving his license, Dr. Furugouchi decided to stay in El Paso, which seemed like a promising place to start a practice. He operated out of his hotel room, and it was soon overrun with mainly Mexican and black patients. After a while the hotel refused to allow him to practice there, but by then Dr. Furugouchi had made up his mind to remain in the city.

Dr. Furugouchi, a kindly man, did not bill his Mexican patients. If he saw sixty patients in a day, only one-third paid in cash; the rest paid when they could. (This is similar to the doctor–patient relationship in China.) The doctor was highly revered; he could not go to the theater because people would recognize him and cause a great uproar. Nevertheless, he enjoyed working in El Paso.

Across from El Paso lies the city of Juárez, named after a Mexican president. At one time there were about eighty Japanese living there. Most of them married Mexican women, raised large families, and worked in the grocery business. Before the war, one dollar equaled five or six pesos; in Mexico you can live a life of luxury on just thirty pesos, or five dollars, a month. People would cross the border to work for U.S. dollars while living in Mexico, thus enjoying the benefits of the United States without having to fulfill any of its obligations. (Many Mexican women simply walked across the bridge from Juárez to El Paso to give birth so the baby would be born a U.S. citizen.) However, since the outbreak of the war, these practices have come under question.

Mexicans are like native Hawaiians in that, if a family is well off, relatives will gather around to share in the wealth. In this way a Japanese married to a Mexican woman can lose his fortune. Among the blacks are also vicious gangs and a high percentage of murders and robberies, yet nothing can be done because of corruption among the police. Even a criminal facing a death sentence can escape his fate by bribing officials. Across the bridge from El Paso there is no order and, for practical purposes, no police. Mexicans say Americans are great but despise them in their hearts. Their warm feelings toward Japanese, however, seem genuine.

I once passed through El Paso on a train from New Orleans. Although it was midnight, immigration officers noisily boarded the train and carefully checked the passports of all the Asian passengers. They were looking for illegal immigrants from Mexico. Many interesting stories and political issues revolve around national borders. This is one of them.

Inside the Tokyo Club

Several Tokyo Club leaders were interned at Lordsburg. Members of this club, headquartered in Los Angeles, were feared by Japanese up and down the West Coast. However, after becoming friendly with them in the camp, I discovered they were not scoundrels; in fact, as is often the case with this type of people, many of them had a high sense of duty and honor. They were always very quiet and cooperative. This was my impression, but according to some Mainland Japanese, they were merely putting up a front.

The Tokyo Club resembles the gambling clubs run by American and Chinese gangs on the Mainland. It asserts its right to a percentage of the income from Japanese-sponsored events. If ignored or rebuffed, members use pressure or take retaliatory actions, sometimes ruining a promoter's fortune. On the other hand, they contribute, financially and otherwise, to Japanese charities and welfare organizations. They play their bad and good roles skillfully.

The Tokyo Club was responsible for many shocking murders that never went to trial. One member was known to have killed five or six people. Several club bosses were in turn assassinated and the perpetrators never found. The Tokyo Club's "methods" were similar to those used by Chinese gangs. A man who knew the workings of the club well told me that initially dead bodies were hidden deep in the mountains. Later they were thrown into the sea so they would never be found. The killers would cover the head, tie eight bricks to each leg, and throw the body overboard to sink to the bottom of the sea and vanish forever without a trace.

One member used this method to get rid of a body and escaped arrest due to lack of evidence. Once free, he brazenly invited a large number of people to a party to celebrate his release. Many Japanese in Los Angeles, aware of the situation, nevertheless sent congratulatory gifts of cash to avoid future problems. The evil influence of this club made its way into various segments of the Japanese community in California. Lawyers and newspaper companies conspired with them. Religious men enjoyed their protection, albeit indirectly. Even the police in some areas may have been a part of their "racket."

Japanese in Hawaii are very lucky. In the days of contract immigration, there were groups like the Isshin Club and the Gikyo Club right in Honolulu that committed crimes and tormented honest citizens. However, a united campaign among the citizens inside and outside the city succeeded in wiping out these groups at the time of the plague-related fire in January 1900. Nothing remains of them now. I earnestly hope that, as a result of this war, the West Coast Tokyo Club and similar organizations will meet the same fate.

The Amateur Entomologist and the Rattlesnake

Mr. Kumemaro Uno, a man with a goatee, is one of the most unforgettable gentlemen with whom I became friends. A florist by trade, he was an amateur entomologist and an expert on Jewish culture. Originally from Tokyo, he often lectured on both topics and broadcasted his comments on current affairs.

While at Lordsburg Mr. Uno collected insects in cigar boxes displayed on narrow shelves. He also had a few bottles containing rattlesnake bones. These reptiles are so venomous that a single bite is enough to kill a man. According to Mr. Uno, the bones are sold in the city as a strong aphrodisiac. Being timid, I kept my distance, but Mr. Gakushi Miake, who was with me, left the barracks with a bottle, looking pleased. There was also the dried skin of a large king snake, all rolled up. The pattern was extremely beautiful. It was interesting to learn that this snake eats rattlesnakes but is not poisonous in itself.

Mr. Uno told us that rattlesnake meat is so delicious that you cannot forget the taste once you have tried it. Hunters go into the mountains and flush the snakes out of the bushes, catching five or six in a day if they are lucky. They sell the skin and bones and eat the meat. If bitten, you must cut into the wound with a sharp knife to keep the poison from circulating in the body. Most people who are bitten nowadays, however, receive an antidote serum injection. Nevertheless, rattlesnake hunting sounds quite thrilling.

There were many snakes at the camp. Sometimes they were seen wriggling out onto the road from under the floor of our barracks. Most of them were nonvenomous, but rattlesnakes appeared once or twice; they were chased by people and dogs and killed. One evening I heard that an unusually large rattlesnake had been caught alive in the third battalion barracks, so I went to see it. The snake had been run over by a guard car outside the barbed-wire fence, so it lay there, a ghastly blue color, half dead and twitching. It was an amazing fifty-one inches long and had thirteen rattles on its tail. When I shook the snake's tail, the rattles buzzed like a toy. This was the first time I had ever seen a rattlesnake up close. Some say the number of rattles corresponds to the snake's age. The next morning I heard that the snake had been eaten. It gave one man a stomachache requiring hospitalization. We also had poisonous insects like spiders and scorpions in the camp. Once in a while someone would be bitten in the shower or toilet and have to be taken to the hospital.

Mr. Uno supported Japan during the war. His eldest son, Kazumaro, was an American citizen, but he worked for the Japanese military in Tokyo and had captured Mr. James Young, the International News Service correspondent in Chungching who had been sending reports attacking the Japanese military since before the war. Mr. Young was pardoned before war broke out between the United States and Japan, and was sent home through Honolulu with his wife. During the war he used his more than ten years of experience in Japan to inspire anti-Japanese feeling.

An American newspaper reported in March 1944 that Mr. Uno was a first lieutenant in the Japanese army. His younger brother, who was an American soldier, wrote a letter to the paper saying that, while he himself had been born and educated in the United States, his brother Kazumaro was an ungrateful wretch who had joined the Japanese army. He also said that he would be willing to go to Japan to kill Kazumaro because he was no longer his brother but the enemy. This was like a story from the old days, but there were many such cases where family members fought on opposite sides.[6]

Among Mr. Uno's lectures that I attended were "The World War as Seen from the Standpoint of Entomology" and "Human Beings, Insects, and the Jews." Extremely beneficial and interesting, these lectures explained how insects are senior to human beings in terms of years on earth; our relationship with insects; the never-ending struggle between humans and insects; and the use of insects to wage war.

The Coyote and the Horned Toad

Among the other animals I learned about were the coyote and the horned toad. I heard the howling of coyotes as soon as I arrived at the camp. It

6. See Yuji Ichioka, *Before Internment: Essays in Prewar Japanese American History*, ed. Gordon H. Chang and Eiichiro Azuma (Stanford, Calif.: Stanford University Press, 2006), which contains a lengthy biographical piece on Kazumaro Buddy Uno titled "The Meaning of Loyalty: The Case of Kazumaro Buddy Uno."

makes one think of wild and vast deserts and evokes feelings of loneliness. Coyotes are like wild dogs or wolves but more ferocious. When they come across a man, they usually run away, but if driven into a corner, they will attack. In winter when food is scarce they enter villages and attack cattle. They have been known to harm children. Being very clever animals, coyotes take advantage of an unguarded moment to bring down cows and horses. They devour even the bones of their prey. Hares often ran into the camp to escape coyotes, and we chased them just for fun.

According to a report published by a New Mexico bird and animal protection officer, in March 1943 a conservative estimate of annual losses attributed to coyotes included 60,000 sheep and lambs, 70,000 calves, and 3,000 antelope. Total annual revenue losses from chickens, eggs, and other livestock eaten by coyotes reached a million dollars. Many states are trying to eradicate the coyote, and everyone is watching to see how Utah's new system, which offers a cash reward for each coyote killed, will fare.

The horned toad is grotesque-looking but extremely gentle and harmless when compared with a rattlesnake. A cross between a frog and a lizard, the horned toad has four horns on its head. Some are gray and red, blending in with the desert surroundings. Feeding mostly on ants, they lay small eggs from which hatch cute little horned toads. As soon as the toad breaks out of its shell, it begins eating ants. The speed with which it eats is amazing. A horned toad is small enough to sit in your hand. When one stayed still and did not try to escape, we called it a "good boy." A *National Geographic* magazine once reported that a rattlesnake had its stomach cut up by a horned toad it had swallowed. Both animals died. The horned toad is found in neither Hawaii nor Japan.

Life Inside the Barracks

I once read *Ukiyo Furo* (Bathhouse of the Floating World). In it the author cleverly describes the various people who gathered at the bathhouse. In many ways our life in the camp resembled scenes from *Ukiyo Furo.* Most of us did not know one another before coming to Lordsburg, and our circumstances and backgrounds differed. My barracks was like a zoo at night. Loud snoring could be heard from one end to the other. At first there were complaints about this—and grinding of teeth—but in time the problems became unimportant. Some talked and others cried out in their sleep. Some had unique voices, such as the man with a loud and gravelly voice, another with a shrill voice, and still another whose high-pitched voice was most irritating. One man from the Mainland had an especially loud voice. It was said that as his wife's hearing grew worse, his voice grew louder. He had my sympathy.

If you were reading or writing quietly, someone was sure to be reading aloud. Those who were playing chess, cards, and other games of chance were so noisy that one would have thought there was a battle going on. Some wanted the windows open, others wanted them closed. In winter the barracks was equipped with automatic heaters powered by natural gas. Because we could adjust the temperature as we wished, some wanted it higher, others lower. Then there were those who made uncalled-for remarks about everything or continually complained, those who pretended to know everything and cut in while others were talking, and those who did not talk at all. Some polished wood or stones with files or sandpaper and scattered dust thoughtlessly. Some sang *noh* songs, played the *shakuhachi* (bamboo clarinet), or walked around indoors in noisy wooden clogs. Others lazed around and did nothing. One man tried to monopolize the milk and sugar in the mess hall, creating a problem.

Many people were ignorant of even basic table manners. They indiscreetly reached over and grabbed salt containers or other things at the far end of their table. Some ate their food like dogs or cats. Two men came to the mess hall in their undershirts and clogs. Who would have imagined that both of them were monks? One day a KP duty helper unintentionally handed out a plate with a slightly broken edge. The recipient became so angry he threw the plate back at the helper. Thereafter, he was given a child's aluminum dish.

Among the Mainlanders were many eccentrics. There was a man from Seattle whom we called "Crow Uncle." He doted on a pair of crows named Jack and Mary, which he had brought with him from another camp. The extent to which the crows obeyed their master's commands was truly surprising. I discovered how clever as well as mischievous they are. One day one of them took my precious fountain pen in its beak, flew up to the roof, and would not come down. Eventually, with the help of "Uncle," I got it back. On the camp golf course, these two—there were no other crows around—often stole golf balls, upsetting players.

A few of these eccentrics made camp life difficult. One man, who had arrived in March 1943 from the Mainland, never took a bath or washed his clothing. He sat quietly on his bed all day except to go to the mess hall, where he made short work of his meal. A man in the eighth regiment of the second battalion, who also never bathed or washed his clothing, became infested with lice. The men in his barracks could not tolerate this, so they asked him to take his bed out and disinfect it. He had been a hobo before the war and lived under a bridge near Los Angeles. These are just some of the types of people we lived with for four years. It really is not surprising that a few internees suffered nervous breakdowns.

Internees called the world beyond the barbed wire *shaba*. Although I did not like this word and did not use it, nearly everyone else did because it was convenient. Another word, *chokuchi,* often used by Mainlanders, was new at first to those of us from Hawaii, but it means to cheat. It probably comes from a Chinese word. Instead of *tekipaki* (quickly), internees said *baribari,* which I think is vernacular from somewhere in Japan. Farmers from the Mainland who grew vegetables at the camp said *kyukanpo* for "cucumber." Japanese often confuse the *p* sound with *b* because there is no *p* sound in the original Japanese language. My friends from Hawaii often say "blantation" for "plantation" and "Poston" for "Boston." I thought this strange at first. As the influence of Hawaii internees grew in the camps, the use of Hawaiian words began to spread among the Mainlanders. Soon everyone was using *kaukau, aikane,* and *moimoi.*

Unfortunate Soldiers and the Rising Sun Incident

At Sand Island, POWs and internees were separated. However, on the Mainland, Ensign Kazuo Sakamaki (POW No. 1) lived among Japanese internees. After I moved to Lordsburg, forty-three Japanese POWs arrived and lived with us for a while. This group was the crew of the submarine *Hiryu,* which was unfortunately sunk during the fighting at Midway Island in June 1942. They were rescued while adrift and came to Lordsburg on October 28, 1942. Among them were five officers, including the captain. We internees deeply sympathized with them and showed these unfortunate men every consideration. As for the sailors themselves, they were ashamed of being POWs. They would not reveal their names or their hometowns and said little, but gradually they became friendly. Although they would not openly admit it, they began talking to us about the war. We were very curious about what they had to say concerning the Pearl Harbor attack. It was a thrilling story recounted by actual participants and the most brilliant accomplishment in this war. The chief engineer, the chief petty officer, and most of the other crew members were young and high-spirited. The captain, however, seemed very reserved and wary, possibly because he was in an unfamiliar situation. While adrift, some men had wanted to sink the lifeboat to avoid being taken prisoner, but the captain would not give the order. His subordinates seemed to disagree with him over other things as well.

On November 3, 1942, the birthday of Emperor Meiji, a large-scale celebration was held at the camp with the permission of the authorities. The POWs participated in a sumo match, which was fine, but they also made a Japanese flag, using white sheets sewn together and a circle cut from red cloth, and they flew it in front of their barracks. The military authorities overlooked most things, but they ordered the flag pulled down immediately. The POWs adamantly refused. Internees who had been watching the altercation added to the problem by urging the soldiers on and pushing them from behind.

Our mayor's office intervened to calm everyone down and removed the flag, thus resolving "The Rising Sun Incident." A little later, however, on November 10, the authorities moved the POWs to Camp Livingston. The internees scrambled to collect donations of clothes and money and scraped up a little more than a hundred dollars. With this we bought cigarettes and candy and gave them to the soldiers as farewell gifts. These tokens of friendship and solidarity brought tears of gratitude to the eyes of the soldiers as they left.

At Camp Livingston they joined Ensign Sakamaki, who had arrived earlier. The captain of the *Hiryu*, along with eighty-nine other naval officers, was sent to San Francisco for investigation. Members of his crew attempted to accompany him, forcing the police to use tear gas to disperse them. In San Francisco about six weeks later, the captain tried to commit suicide by cutting his stomach and neck with a razor blade. After he returned to Livingston, he tried to kill himself again, this time by cutting his wrists. Dr. Masayoshi Tanaka treated him and served as his interpreter during the psychological investigation that followed. He reported that the captain was not behaving normally. Eventually all of the officers were moved to Camp McCoy in Wisconsin, but the captain of the *Hiryu* was said to have been sent to Elizabeth Hospital in Washington, D.C.

Banzai Cheers

After December 7, the lives of Japanese in Hawaii were severely restricted. All meetings were prohibited. Funerals could be attended by close relatives only. Such measures were unavoidable inasmuch as the Islands were the focal point of the attack that unleashed a war of the century. In contrast, those interned on the Mainland, resigned to their fate and despondent over their separation from homes and families, consoled themselves by celebrating Japanese national holidays and events in a grand manner and as often as possible. German and Italian internees on the Mainland did the same, but they were much bolder, displaying with loud enthusiasm pictures of Hitler and Mussolini. Being interned on "enemy soil," we wondered about the propriety of such a display, but the military authorities were relatively generous and tolerant as long as we sought prior approval. They did not encourage these things, however.

November 3, 1942 was cold and windy. On that day, all internees, about fifteen hundred men, gathered for an all-day athletic meet to celebrate the birthday of Emperor Meiji. (This was the day of the Rising Sun Incident mentioned earlier.) On February 21, 1943, we celebrated the 2,603rd anniversary of Emperor Jinmu's accession. Everyone took a holiday and participated in the anniversary ceremony, which began at nine o'clock that morning. We sang the national anthem, and Mayor Abe made a congratulatory speech. There was an exhibition of artwork by internees as part of the entertainment. On April 29 of that year, the emperor's birthday, the second battalion held a ceremony in the religion hall during which we sang the national anthem and bowed in silent prayer in the direction of the Imperial Palace. After Mayor Abe's speech, I led the *banzai* cheers.

At Missoula Camp, the New Year's party was held with Mr. Minoru Murakami as master of ceremonies. I understand this celebration was very lively. Italian internees joined the party in their famous black shirts. A tipsy Mr. Kiyoshi Ichikawa was asked to lead the *banzai* cheers. He led cheers not only for Japan, Germany, and Italy, but also all the Axis powers, including Manchuria, the Nangching government, the Philippines, Thailand, and Independent India. He led twenty cheers in all, each time asking the participants to stand up and join in. In the end, all the participants were very tired. This was a light anecdote from the camp.

Whenever we held prefectural or other meetings in the camp, we would sing a marching song like "Miyo, Tokai no. . . . " You may think we were being childish or foolish. But by doing these things, we were all unconsciously trying to eradicate that interminable sadness hiding somewhere in our hearts. One probably would not understand this feeling unless he had experienced internee life.

Entertainment behind Barbed Wire

Sumo matches were some of the most important events at Lordsburg Camp. There were many sumo lovers, so the matches were always popular. Mr. Naobumi Maehokama did not wrestle often in Honolulu, but at Lordsburg he was an *ozeki* (champion) for the Hawaii group and took on formidable challengers from the Mainland. He had many fans.

We had many good actors, so plays staged at the camp were splendid. We had our own theater company, the "Hinomoto Theatrical Group," managed by Mr. Shinkichi Miyoshi. He was the younger brother of Mrs. Yukichi Ishii, who worked at Ishii Drug Store in Honolulu. Before he went to San Diego and became a Shinto priest, Mr. Miyoshi had been in the theater business in Hawaii. Proficient in choreography, costume design, *gidayu* accompaniment, dressing, and makeup, he was respected as a teacher by everyone. Mr. Keisuke Takahashi of Sacramento, who was an orderly at the hospital, worked as a caretaker for the theatrical group and appeared on stage from time to time. He was also one of our sumo judges.

The players were mostly from the Mainland. Messrs. Tajuro Watanabe, Zenshiro Okubo, Junzo Ideno, and Seishi Okazaki were among the most outstanding. The last two were good female impersonators. As Ishiko, wife of Kuranosuke Ohishi in *Chushingura* (The Story of the Forty-seven Ronin), Mr. Ideno showed grace and dignity. I was especially impressed with Mr. Watanabe's performance as "the fox in the form of Tadanobu." His stage entrance on the *hanamichi* (extended stage runway) after Tadanobu returns to his former self was far beyond that of an amateur.

Because we had no *shamisen,* elderly Mr. Wasaburo Uranaka of Wahiawa used his voice to provide the *gidayu* accompaniment. His imitative *shamisen* was thoroughly convincing. All costumes, wigs, stage props, and scenery were made from whatever was at hand. The effort expended in making them was something to behold. Every piece was so well done that I found renewed respect for Japanese inventiveness and creativity. I watched as one of the wigs was being made. For hair, Manila hemp rope was unwound and combed, then dyed black with ink and made into wigs for various male and female characters. The results were truly amazing.

During the intermission of a play, I went backstage with a friend and talked with Mr. Miyoshi. As I watched him work at fever pace during the performance, I realized that one must really love the theater to work as hard as Mr. Miyoshi. If I remember correctly, three plays were performed at Lordsburg. Each was performed once a day for three days and the cost was covered by small donations from the audience. Plays were staged outdoors or in the empty barracks of the third battalion, which was also used as a recreation room. (The women internees at Seagoville Camp in Texas heard about our theatricals and sent us a beautiful stage curtain.) Some of the famous scenes performed were: "The Pine Corridor," "Teahouse Scene," and "Quiet Life in Yamashina" from *Chushingura;* "Heisaku's House at the Iga Pass," "Benkei, the Messenger," "Tamazo," "The Walk among a Thousand Cherry Trees," "Miyagino Room in Shiraishi Stories," and "Father Returns," which was turned into a parody.

The entertainment division, under the umbrella of the public welfare department of the third battalion, organized evening programs, ensembles, and *naniwabushi* (narrative song) story meetings, which were received with enthusiastic applause. I fondly recall that on New Year's Day, 1943, lively groups performed the lion dance and other festive dances, reminding us of the old Japan. The performers visited the barracks and clinics of both battalions. It goes without saying that the services provided by the public welfare department and these men brightened the entire camp atmosphere.

Returning to Japan and Anti-American Sentiment

From the latter half of 1942 through the autumn of 1943, U.S. policy on the future of internees was not clearly defined. We internees certainly had no way of knowing what was going to happen to us. We felt insecure and constantly speculated on our fate. Our thinking was blurred and we were most vulnerable at this time. When I arrived at Lordsburg, those who were already there from Hawaii were eager to return to Japan. They recommended I do the same. Many from the Mainland shared their feelings. Adding to our anxiety were concerns over the possible conscription of our American-born children and reunification with loved ones in family camps, for which negotiations were still ongoing. Mainland Japanese were especially opposed to their sons being drafted into the U.S. military and brought lawsuits in various places. Some Japanese lawyers in the United States supported and encouraged them, arguing that the U.S. government had discriminated against Japanese American citizens by forcing them into camps in violation of the Constitution; thus Japanese Americans were under no obligation to comply with the conscription. Of course, this argument would not hold up in court, but it was applauded by many Japanese.

On September 26, 1942, under the guise of a lecture on Shintoism, the Reverend Yoshiaki Fukuda of the Konko (Golden Light) Mission denounced American policies. He argued that all Japanese in the United States should move to the South Pacific after the war. Of course he said this because he firmly believed that Japan would win the war. However, I thought it was unfair and irresponsible of him to make such a sweeping statement before so many naive internees. One day a discussion was held to exchange opinions about the future of the Japanese (including the Nisei) in the United States after the war. At that meeting, too, Mr. Fukuda argued against the conscription of Nisei and made a case for all Japanese to move to the South Pacific. I countered by saying: "Such things should be decided by the individual based on his circumstances. Japanese in Hawaii are in an entirely different situation. The Nisei conscription issue is not something new. As long as they are American citizens, the Nisei are obliged to serve their country, and it is a mistake for Issei to try to hinder the process."

At the time no one said anything, but later I was criticized and branded pro-American. My position, however, has not changed since then. Of course I sympathize with Mainland Japanese, who were illegally removed from their homes, and understand that many difficult concerns would arise because of the forced relocation, including compensation. It was also to be expected that any sentiments that seemed the least bit anti-American would find favor among the internees.

Details of the Family Cohabitation Issue

Internees from the Mainland worked hard to petition the authorities to allow them to live with their families who had been placed elsewhere. Mr. Edward J. Ennis, chief of the Department of Justice's Enemy Aliens Section in Washington, made it clear that cohabitation for interned families was his intention: Husbands and wives and parents and children would be allowed to live together as soon as the family camps were ready. However, there were a few restrictions. If both parties (husband and family) were internees, permission could be granted quickly. If the family was in a war relocation center the husband first needed to apply for parole. The family at the relocation center could initiate the application procedure for family camp, but members had to agree to be classified as internees.

The same rules applied to those of us from Hawaii. However, Hawaii internees planning to return to Japan requested cohabitation so their families would be sent to the Mainland and they could all leave for Japan together. According to a report that came from Hawaii to Lordsburg in the middle of September 1942, forty families left Honolulu at the end of August. Internees soon began receiving cables or letters telling them that their families had arrived on the Mainland. Most came by their own consent, but a few seemed to have been forced to leave Hawaii. It is not clear if it was the intention of the authorities, but families of those interned on the Mainland were advised to leave almost by force. Rumors circulated that they would have been compelled to go to the Mainland sooner or later. They prepared for the cold Mainland weather by purchasing heavier clothing, and soon all the stores in Honolulu were sold out of winter clothes. Fortunately, not all of them eventually went to the Mainland.

The wives and children of Hawaii internees were told they would be able to live with their husbands and fathers as soon as they arrived on the Mainland. But this proved not to be the case and they became quite frustrated. In the worst cases, families spent more than a year apart before they were reunited at the family camp in Crystal City. (In the meantime, many Mainland Japanese internees were paroled one after another after their cases were reviewed, and they joined their families at the various centers.)

Morale at the relocation centers was often low. Lonely young wives and girls found themselves entangled in unfortunate relationships. Some men who were paroled and sent to join their families found themselves drinking from an unexpectedly bitter cup. One internee had just been reunited with his wife at a relocation center when one of his close friends visited him to offer his congratulations. As the friend was leaving, the internee's little daughter asked him, "Aren't you going to stay over tonight?" This remark made all three of them extremely uncomfortable, to say the least.

Cultural Activities and Meetings

Life behind barbed wire can be boring and dry. Many events were planned to add a bit of charm and warmth to our lives and to give us opportunities to make good use of our time. This was the task of the public welfare department. It organized all cultural events, lectures, classes, exhibitions, sports, entertainment, and games. The second battalion department staff consisted of Mr. Joshin Motoyoshi, Mr. Kodo Fujitani, and me, and we supervised the broadcasting, library, music, drilling, entertainment, and sports divisions. Mr. Takuritsu Morita served as the third battalion's public welfare director.

Here are some of the major lectures that were given and their speakers: "The Climate of the Southwestern United States and Sanitation," Teiichi Furugouchi; "The World War as Seen from the Standpoint of Entomology," Kumemaro Uno; "The Civilization of Ancient India," Eimu Miake; "The Dawn of Japan from a Scientific Perspective," Kiyoshi Ishikawa; "A Story of Alaska and Its Mining," Sotaro Kawabe; "Alaska and the Aleutian Islands," Hiroo Shiihara; "A Story of the American Indian," Toshiharu Kobe; "Expeditions to India, Burma, and Tibet," Kodo Fujitani; "Geopolitics," Motokazu Mori; "The Importance of Rubber in U.S. Military Goods," Kango Kawasaki. I lectured for two evenings on "The Past, Present, and Future of Hawaii." "Geopolitics" by Dr. Mori was a series that consisted of more than ten lectures. They were very popular, because the subject was a new field of study and timely.

Among the many classes held at the camp, the most important were: English (Rev. Sutekichi Osumi), calligraphy (Rev. Kogan Yoshizumi), Japanese grammar (Rev. Eimu Miake), watercolor painting (Messrs. Deiso Takayama and Taichi Tsuyuki), Japanese painting (Mr. Shingetsu Akaboshi), painting (Mr. Yoshio Hoshida), and *tanka* poetry (Mr. Ten-yo Yasaki). Messrs. Isao Yano, Kango Kawasaki, and Koshiro Nakabayashi also taught English. Internees who had a mind to study benefited a great deal from these classes.

The camp had three *tanka* groups. Two were study groups consisting of poets from the Mainland, led by Mr. Deiso Takayama and Mr. Ten-yo Yasaki. The third one was called Sakyu Shi Sha (Sand Hill Poem Group), comprised of members from Hawaii's Cho-on Shi Sha (Wave Sound Poem Group). All three groups held meetings biweekly. Poets from the Mainland were ranked according to the number of poems each individual had in the *New Man-yo* (Myriad Leaves) *Collection*. Kaizo-sha had called for entries for this collection before the war. Because the poets of Cho-on Shi Sha had not been a part of the Kaizo-sha project, they did not get along with the Mainland poets. Needless to say, there were no joint meetings between the Hawaii and Mainland poetry groups.

As for *haiku*, Yutsuka Gin Sha (Yutsuka Poem Group) of the Hototogisu Sect had more than forty members, with Mr. Shukei Miyata at the center. Nisshokyo Gin Sha (Sunshine Country Poem Group) included internees from Hawaii. The Senryu Sand Dust Club had about forty members. Their name was most suitable under our present circumstances.

These *senryu* poems were presented at a club meeting:[7]

In this Paradise
Exchange of New Year greetings
In a public bathhouse. (Harusame)

Dawn of a new year
Image of the Rising Sun
An internee's perception. (Kamiyama)

Flutes accompany lion dance
Visions of my child
I leap out of bed. (Shiohito)

---

7. *Senryu* are three-line poems, similar in structure to haiku, that typically deal with human nature, often in an ironic or satirical manner.

Mr. Masaji Hashimoto, North American president of Tenri-kyo, gave an impressive speech in the neighboring barracks on his establishment of the Tenri-kyo Village in Manchuria. He also performed *kodan* (storytelling), which was his hobby, for several consecutive nights at the third battalion mess hall. It was very popular. On one of these nights I happened to be strolling by the mess hall. I found Mr. Hashimoto's performance an unexpected treasure. He squatted firmly on a cushion onstage, just as the storytellers did in old Tokyo. Two candles flickered on either side of his small table while he recited "Musashi Miyamoto" by Eiji Yoshikawa. How skillfully he told the story to make each part come alive before my eyes—an old woman, a young girl, a child. Each part was done so convincingly I felt as though I were watching a play. His performances were always very well received. Mr. Hashimoto was a graduate of Kokugakuin University and a good poet. However, his specialty was *kana* calligraphy, which he had studied for twenty-five years under the guidance of Mr. Haruno Haneda, a former priest for the Imperial Court.

If I remember correctly, we had two handicraft exhibitions at the camp. An exhibition to commemorate our confinement was held in the social hall of the fifth regiment, second battalion, on Sunday, September 20, 1942. Nearly seven hundred items reflected the intelligence and skill of Japanese. These included collections, handicrafts, calligraphy, paintings, and literary works. The picture of a yacht by Mr. Kippei Ishikawa, a fisherman from San Pedro, was outstanding. There were collections of rare stones from Missoula, insects, and grasses; various woodcrafts, walking sticks, and inkstones with cases. I was particularly struck by a *zushi* (miniature Buddhist shrine often encasing a deity) constructed by Mr. Keiichi Okamura, a *haiden* (Shinto shrine worship hall) by Mr. Genko Banba, a big drum made from an empty keg covered with duck by Mr. Kinai Ikuma, and caricatures of internees drawn in ink by Mr. Yoshio Hoshida. All of these had been made with the simplest tools and materials. The third battalion decided to hold its own handicraft exhibition on the twenty-fifth and twenty-sixth of the same month. Many of the items were made from stone and wood. Mr. Hashimoto of Tenri-kyo exhibited more than ten small inkstones. Their colors and shapes showed great artistry. Both events attracted the attention of the military authorities, who were so impressed that they sponsored a joint exhibition of work from the two battalions. This was held at the recreation hall of the military barracks outside the camp on the afternoon of October 4. Many Americans came to see it, not only from Lordsburg and the surrounding area, but from as far away as El Paso. They were quite impressed, and many newspapers and magazines reported on the exhibition.

As for sports, softball was the most popular, followed by golf, tennis, and table tennis. For recreation everyone played *go* and Japanese chess. Mahjong was also popular. There were clubs for each of these.

The camp boasted no less than three *noh* clubs: the Kita Club, the Kanze Club, and the Hosho Club. Each member practiced with intensity. Joint performances of the three clubs were held two or three times. The Hosho-ryu Noh Lovers Club was formed by the second battalion under the guidance of Mr. Hisashi Imamura, who was from the Mainland. Many internees from Hawaii joined in the singing, and the number of *noh* club members reached more than eighty. *Noh* was so popular and the singing so powerful that they were dubbed "the coyote group."

Postal Rules and Inspectors

A letter from one's family was the greatest source of happiness for an internee. We jokingly referred to all of them as "love letters." However, for various reasons these did not come and go as often as we would have liked. Rules for handling mail differed slightly among centers and were routinely changed without advance notice. Mail was seldom lost but always delayed. Once a cablegram took 60 days to arrive and a letter 150 days. My family sent me at least one letter a week, but at Lordsburg there was a time when I received nothing for two months.

The mail rules were roughly as follows:

1. The sender must include his signature. If an amanuensis is used, he must also sign.
2. Correspondence between internees is prohibited except in the case of relatives. The sender must indicate his relationship to the recipient on the envelope.
3. Only one addressee is permitted per envelope.
4. Letters with portions crossed out will not be sent.
5. The total length of a letter must be less than twenty-four lines.
6. Letters containing ambiguous remarks will not be sent.
7. Written descriptions or drawings of the camp are prohibited.
8. Providing an itinerary or details of an internee's move is prohibited.
9. Two letters and one postcard may be sent per week.
10. Only one piece of mail may be sent per day.
11. All correspondence must be written in ink.
12. Registered mail is prohibited.
13. The letter *J* (Japanese) or *E* (English) should be written accordingly in the lower-lefthand corner of the envelope.

14. Only letter paper supplied by the authorities is permitted. It has been treated so invisible ink cannot be used.

15. Surface postage is free. Airmail delivery must be paid for by the sender.

16. Packages must be within 42 inches in circumference and 11 pounds in weight. Postage is free up to 4 pounds. Only one package may be sent per month.

At first only English was allowed, which had also been the case at Sand Island, but soon both English and Japanese were permitted. Although not listed in the published rules, writing about the illness, hospitalization, death, or funeral of another internee was prohibited. If someone was seriously ill and could not write for himself or had died, his family would not know what had happened until they were contacted by the camp commander. As for events in the camp, we could write about theatrical performances and exhibitions, but we could not mention anything that might meet with the disapproval of the authorities. Any letters that violated these rules were mercilessly returned by the inspectors. One was still fortunate if his letter was returned right away. If it was delayed at the central inspection office in New York, several days passed before one learned of its fate. It was enough to make a man cry. Letters of even fairly well-known Americans were inspected. The correspondence of Governor Ernest Gruening of Alaska was handled in the same way.

The letters of POWs and internees were checked closely. Camp inspectors were responsible for scrutinizing the thoughts of internees, and inspectors at the central office in New York examined them from a military point of view. Unlike a few German and Italian internees who had to be watched carefully, Japanese internees never posed a serious threat. We suffered because of the suspicious behavior of others.

Other Postal Matters

At Lordsburg, the main post office was just outside the barbed-wire fence. It handled the collection, delivery, and inspection of all mail, including packages from the two battalion post offices on the opposite side of the fence. We were given special permission to go to the main post office to pick up registered mail or to send or receive packages. At one corner of the main post office was a meeting area, where families of Mainland internees were allowed to visit their loved ones. Only English was permitted and a guard was posted nearby. A wire net separated the internees and their families, which made the place look like a chicken coop. The net was set up to prevent the exchange of money and letters.

All mail to and from Lordsburg went through the main inspection office in New York, where photocopies of letters were made, then sent to the FBI and other intelligence agencies. About four thousand people were said to have been employed at this office during the war. Many were the girlfriends of congressmen and high-level officials; the actual working staff numbered only a thousand or so. This shameful situation was brought to light by one of the workers. Mail from Hawaii was inspected there before it was sent to the Mainland, so any letters and packages I received from home had been inspected a total of three times before I opened them at Lordsburg.

At first internees were allowed to send letters by registered mail, but this privilege was later withdrawn without advance notice. Even registered mail that had already arrived at the inspection office in New York was returned to the camp. It was quite distressing to see all that mail returned forty or fifty days after it had been sent out. The same thing happened at other camps. Internees received notices to pick up their mail, but when they arrived at the post office, happy and expectant, they received cards and letters they themselves had written. Some of the internees had sent letters by registered mail, but no one was reimbursed for the cost of the stamps.

Surface mail to and from Hawaii ordinarily took one month, so we used airmail most of the time. In the beginning, the cost was 20 cents per ounce, later reduced to 15 cents. Airmail usually took about nine to ten days between Lordsburg and Hawaii. Once in a while, it arrived in five to six days, or in two to three months. If I added up all the money that internees and their families paid for airmail postage during the four-year internment, the total amount would be substantial. There was no restriction on how often we could receive packages from Hawaii. Japanese foodstuffs and books were allowed but later prohibited. (After we moved to Santa Fe, the restriction on Japanese books was lifted.) I received a set of *noh* songbooks and a copy of the *Hawaii Yearbook,* 1941 edition, as soon as I arrived at Lordsburg at the end of August 1942. The *Yearbook* proved very useful to all in the camp. As I mentioned earlier, the "coyote group" was growing in number, so books on *noh* were always in demand. Many people conscientiously copied my songbooks. I think my service in promoting interest in *noh* was good enough to rate an award from the grand master of my school.

As I said before, letters from home were our greatest comfort. We often greeted each other with "Did you receive a letter?" Close friends talked about the letters they had received from their families or shared them to exchange news and information. Everyone was interested in discussing the number of letters everyone received.

Mess Hall Disputes and Dangerous Weapons

Every camp had at least two mess halls. There were four at Lordsburg. Meals followed predetermined menus. Kitchen departments sometimes ran into problems when the amount of food was less than expected or menus were suddenly changed. Of course, occasional mistakes in the meal plans or preparation were to be expected, but many of us wondered if middlemen were "*chokuchi*-ing" our food supplies on a regular basis. All the commissioned and petty officers, governors, mayors, and heads of kitchen departments gathered at the ninth regiment's social hall on January 16, 1943, to discuss the problem. The military authorities had this to say:

> We estimate the cost of foodstuffs at 40 cents per head per day, or $100.00 for a regiment of 250 internees or military servicemen. Servicemen get butter and eggs once a week. Fresh milk is not available now. The method of food distribution here is the same as on the battlefield. We distribute today what you need tomorrow. There is no need to save food for the next day. We will replace what you do not use with other things. Hereafter, when we distribute food, we will send an invoice signed by the officer in charge to each governor. If there is a problem, you must solve it among yourselves and not disturb the commanding officer.

The glutinous rice for the New Year's rice cakes had cost about $780.00. We asked whether this amount had been deducted from our daily expenses and were told that the rice had not been included in the daily budget because it was a gift from the camp commander. Some internees had been using the kitchens to prepare their own late night snacks, which accounted for some of the food shortages. The authorities ordered that in future only cooks on duty be allowed in the kitchens at night.

A mess hall dispute occurred in my regiment, the sixth. It happened for many reasons, but money was at the root of it. Cooks and KP chiefs received an allowance of eighty cents a day. However, there were other people working in the mess hall who were not paid, and these workers claimed they were being treated unfairly. The situation came to a head on May 4, 1943, and a meeting of barracks representatives was held. Those from the Mainland could not come to an agreement, so the matter was left to a seven-man committee, which I was forced to chair. The problem was a fairly complicated one, but a temporary solution was finally agreed upon four days later on May 7, and the committee was dissolved.

Ten days later, this problem flared up again, aggravated by the beer sold at the canteen. A drunken playboy from the Mainland and a couple of high-spirited internees from Hawaii clashed with a KP chief and others. They went on a rampage with knives and chisels. A conceited florist from Los Angeles joined in and was physically attacked. Mr. Tomita, a Tokyo Club boss, got in the picture and put on a show of his own. The original troublemakers were left holding the bag.

We decided not to say anything about the identities of the knife-wielding men who had gotten carried away, but the authorities had already been alerted so the details of the incident would soon surface. We quickly convinced Mayor Abe to persuade the unruly internees to shake hands with the KP chief and his crew, which placated the camp commander. Then we asked the governors to sponsor a reconciliation party with tea and cake for all concerned. The problem was finally resolved. For the troublemakers, it was a bitter experience.

Delicious Food

While I am on the subject of mess halls, let me say a little about the food at the camp. Readers would generally sympathize with us on the quality of our meals. Yes, we were forced once in a while to eat sand with our rice, or pork and beans day after day. However, considering the wartime conditions, I think the food in general was quite good—especially if you compared it with our clothing and housing. If our clothes were too natty, we attracted attention, so we wore the drab clothes issued to us. As for housing, we lived in shabby barracks like refugees taking shelter from an earthquake or flood. But the food we were served was neither better nor worse than what most people had to eat outside the barbed-wire fence. Of course there are those who would disagree. As one who quietly eats whatever is placed in front of him, I may not be qualified to comment on food. Strange as it seems, however, the taste of certain foods that I enjoyed during my four years on the Mainland still lingers somewhere in my mind.

Although I am usually not particular about what I eat, I did not drink the powdered milk we were given at the camp. However, the milk on the Southern Pacific train was like nectar. After I returned to Honolulu, I began drinking a glass every morning. I remember the dish of delicious rice cakes boiled with vegetables served at Lordsburg on New Year's Day, 1943. The night before I had newly pounded rice cakes with grated radish. One night the cook treated Mr. S, Dr. M, and me to steak and coffee. Dr. U prepared his specialty, an Okinawan dish of roast pork preserved in miso. There was also that dish of smelt boiled in soy sauce with a bowl of rice. These memorable meals prove that not all of the food we ate while interned can be written off as bad.

Throughout the war, a variety of fruit was available on the Mainland, as you might expect. We had grapefruit at breakfast once or twice a week, which I especially enjoyed. Some internees did not like this heavenly fruit, so they offered me theirs. Sometimes I received three or four of them. Alabama grapefruit is the tastiest. According to people from Imperial Valley, if you have two grapefruit trees in your backyard, your whole family will be able to enjoy grapefruit all year round. The trees begin bearing fruit after three years. I was surprised to learn that you can buy a grapefruit for a penny in that part of California. Around Sacramento, you can buy three or four for a quarter, an entire box for about three dollars. How I envied them.

As for apples, I thought the Delicious variety was best. According to people from California, there are many others. Everyone seemed to like Jenneting. There is also a delicious green apple, but Americans use it only in cooking and not as a fresh fruit.

Green asparagus is delicious. The plant, which produces its first crop after three years, can yield up to ten harvests.

Hidden Efforts and Services

At Lordsburg Camp more than a thousand men were interned while the outside world was at war. It was a time when we were often irritable, but unlike German and Italian internees we seldom quarreled, which I thought was commendable. Once the canteen began selling beer, however, the situation changed somewhat. The fracas in the mess hall, which I described earlier, fortunately ended without bloodshed, but six months later a drunken American soldier attacked an internee with a knife. Both incidents were attributed to alcohol.

November 26, 1942, was Thanksgiving Day. Several military deserters were being held in a neighboring barracks. The soldiers got drunk and one of them attacked a group of internees out on a stroll. A Hawaii man narrowly escaped, but a Mainland internee was stabbed in the back. If the knife had penetrated an inch farther, it would have punctured his lung. It was a mistake to keep deserters with us. In the past, they had stolen goods from the canteen and hidden them. Other complaints were lodged against them. The mayor's office demanded that the deserters be moved and the guilty soldier punished. Fortunately the victim of the attack was not seriously injured, and he was released from the hospital soon after.

In general, the attitude of the guards toward us was good and we had no serious complaints. However, one of them fired a gun without warning on several occasions, nearly causing a few accidents. Our two mayors had the guard reprimanded and reassigned to an unarmed position. The other guards received a stern warning. The major representing the commanding officer and Governors Abe and Yoshizumi issued a joint statement, which maintained that internees were free to play and walk anywhere on the golf course despite the rule that prohibited them from coming within twelve feet of the barbed-wire fence.

The fact remains that problems always cropped up in the camp. We solved most of them ourselves, but in cases involving Americans, governors and mayors were called on to represent us. Often they were criticized or hampered by trivial misunderstandings while trying to handle complex as well as annoying situations. But they did whatever they could to uphold the honor of Japanese internees and worked diligently for our benefit. We should be deeply grateful for their unselfish service.

As I mentioned earlier, the consul general of Spain in Washington, D.C., was in charge of protecting the rights of Japanese in America during the war. Internees were always sending petitions to his office and making demands. Representatives of the International Red Cross and the International Young Christians also visited Lordsburg twice to listen to our requests and provided what help they could. Dr. Fischer, an International Young Christians representative, donated cultural, religious, recreational, and educational materials that were needed in the camp, including sports and art supplies, books, and magazines. All of these things greatly enriched our lives. There was even a piano among Dr. Fischer's donations, which was somehow replaced by an older model while in transit. We received the original piano eventually.

The Climate

I lived in the wild desert of Lordsburg from the end of August 1942 through the middle of June 1943. During this period the climate was a problem for me. Although I was from Hawaii, I preferred cold weather, so the scorching desert heat was difficult to bear. The camp was four thousand feet above sea level and the humidity comfortably low, but we had sandstorms nearly every day. When they were severe, I could not distinguish the faces of people a few feet in front of me. I could not open my eyes or mouth. It reminded me of the Japanese phrase "like chewing sand" (meaning "tasteless"). My mouth was gritty and the feeling was terrible. Everyone conceded defeat to the sandstorms.

The climate at Lordsburg is continental, and in general the range of temperatures is wide. There is almost no spring or autumn. The seasons jump from summer to winter and winter to summer. The differences in temperature can be like night and day. Lordsburg is comparatively hotter than the rest of New Mexico, and it seldom snows in winter. In consulting my diary, I noticed that the temperatures were highest when I arrived there at the end of August. At the beginning of September, we suddenly had a few cool days. The weather was mostly fine every day, becoming cloudy for only a few days and turning chilly. It did not rain often, but when it rained, it poured. The average temperature at the beginning of September was about 60 degrees in the morning, 80 to 90 at noon, and 85 to 86 in the evening. On September 22, the temperature was 56 in the morning and 94 in the afternoon, a difference of about 40 degrees. After three or four hot days, uncomfortable chilly weather suddenly returned. Then there was a cycle of three cold days and four warm days. In this way a natural balance was maintained.

Winter arrived in October. The famous sandstorms gradually grew worse. It was very cold in the early morning and evening of October 18, but it was very hot during the day. There was ice on the ground on November 1, but the weather turned hot again on the sixth, seventh, and eighth. We were having an Indian summer. There was an especially fierce sandstorm on the eleventh before the cold returned the following day. The outdoor thermometer read 22 degrees in the early morning of the twenty-ninth. Winter came in earnest in December. We had a magnificent view of distant mountains covered in snow on the sixth. The temperature stood at 28 degrees on the morning of the seventh, the first anniversary of the attack on Pearl Harbor. The frost was so thick that the roofs of barracks where heaters had not been turned on looked as if they were covered with white sheets. The grassland glistened with sunshine. The next day the ice was an inch thick. It snowed and hailed once in a while from January through the middle of February. The wind kicked up, so I could not go out walking with friends, my only form of exercise. When I summoned up enough courage for a short walk one morning, I felt as if my face and ears were being sheared.

Laundry work was easy in summer. Clothing hung outside dried in an hour. However, in winter, clothes froze stiff as boards while being hung. Our fingertips became crimson and stiff, our hands chapped. At night it was especially difficult to go to the outside toilet just a few steps away. At the end of February, the temperature was around 30 degrees in the morning, but it shot up to 80 degrees during the day. It was already summer. Sandstorms raged. We also had thunderstorms once in a while. At the beginning of April, everyone already began to unpack their summer clothes. On May 3, the temperature rose to 100 degrees. Then it suddenly became cold on the ninth and tenth. The temperature on the eleventh was 40 degrees in the morning and 90 at noon, a difference of 50 degrees in half a day. When June came, the temperature was always more than 100 degrees. It was unbearable.

I do not think there is any place in the world where the climate is so changeable throughout the year as Lordsburg. Winter was bitter, but summer was even more agonizing. The lingering summer heat in the early evenings was especially uncomfortable, and the barracks offered no haven. We finally got relief at night and in the early morning, when it turned as cool as autumn. The fact that more of us did not become ill in such an unforgiving place is puzzling.

A Lonely Graveyard in the Desert

Ten internees died at Lordsburg Camp, all of them from the Mainland: Jinsaku Saito (Shizuoka), Toshiro Obata (Hiroshima), Hirota Isomura (Shiga), Yahei Shioda (Kumamoto), Zenshiro Nakayama (Fukuoka), Torao Kanazawa (Yamagata), Masato Yamasaki (Fukushima), Takeo Takehara (Wakayama), Ayao Tahara (Hiroshima), and an internee who belonged to the twelfth regiment. He died suddenly due to a heart attack on the evening prior to our moving to Santa Fe. I cannot ascertain whether his name was Mukai or Mukuno.

Mr. Obata and Mr. Isomura died tragically at the hands of a soldier as I reported earlier. The funeral of Mr. Nakayama was held at the mess hall of the eleventh regiment on October 10, about a month after I arrived at the camp. Internees from Alaska and Hawaii in both battalions packed the hall. Thirty-five ministers of various sects held a religious service. The deceased had been suffering from stomach cancer while interned in Seattle and had come to Lordsburg through Missoula. He had been miserable there because at that time there was neither a hospital nor doctors. After he was pronounced terminally ill, his son, Tadashi, was allowed to remain at his bedside for a month. On the night of the funeral, Tadashi accompanied his father's remains to Seattle by train. According to the internal rules of the camp, all mourners gave five cents each in incense money. Although I did not know Mr. Nakayama at all, I attended his funeral. When I looked at his young, disheartened son, tears streamed down my cheeks.

Mr. Ayao Tahara, acting president of the *Taihoku Nippo Sha* of Seattle, died on March 31, 1943, and a Christian funeral was held on the morning of April 1. His remains were buried in the camp graveyard beyond the barbed-wire fence. I did not attend the burial, but about a hundred others did after receiving special permission. During his six-month stay at the camp hospital, Mr. Tahara was given oxygen two hundred times: This of course was a record. Before the war this treatment cost five dollars, so Mr. Tahara's bill would have been a thousand dollars. After his death, Dr. Furugouchi took care of the remains himself. Later I joined some other internees and made the thirty-minute walk to the camp graveyard for the memorial service. More than ten guards, holding their guns conspicuously, came with us. The graveyard consisted of three lone wooden posts, each about three feet high, surrounded by pebbles. From left to right, the names of Hirota Isomura, Ayao Tahara, and Yahei Shiota were inscribed on the posts in Japanese *romanji* (roman characters), together with their birth and death dates in English and their internee ID numbers.

Nine internees had died up to that point. The remains of all but the three mentioned above were returned to their families through the auspices of friends. Mr. Kobata was buried at the camp graveyard at first, but later his remains were transferred elsewhere. The Catholic churches in the area allowed only burials, so bodies had to be sent elsewhere for cremation. Graveside memorial services for Mr. Tahara were both Buddhist and Christian. The Reverends Sei Odate and Seitetsu Ono recited a sutra, Pastor Iken Kouno led us in a hymn, and Mayor Abe gave a memorial speech. The service lasted thirty minutes. We all brought with us small wild chrysanthemums or artificial flowers to pay our respects. In all, the trip to and from the graveyard and the service took an hour, and everyone returned covered in sand. In time we will all forget the lonely little graveyard and all traces of it will be obliterated. Whenever I think of this, I feel sorry for those buried there.

Moving Begins

Every internee camp had a canteen where nearly all the daily necessities, as well as magazines, canned goods, fruit, candy, cigarettes, and beer were sold. The canteen did not need to turn a profit to remain open, so prices could have been lower, but they were not. Everyone received a beer ticket for a bottle a day, which was the rule, but this was hardly enough. It was no secret that some internees drank ten to fifteen bottles a day. Too much drinking led to problems.

People tend to buy unnecessary things when they have access to a canteen. At first, each internee received a dollar a month in coupons, but this was later increased to three dollars. The coupons could be used only at the canteen. In addition, everyone was allowed to withdraw ten dollars a month from his "bank account." Internees gradually began to purchase items from the Sears Roebuck or Montgomery Ward catalogs.

Because it was wartime, labor was in short supply everywhere. Businesses were very busy and shorthanded, so once in a while they would turn to the internee camps for a supply of eager young laborers. The Lordsburg authorities agreed to the hiring of internees as cotton pickers and put out a call for thirty-five workers at the beginning of October 1942. The compensation was 1.75 cents per pound of picked cotton, out of which the laborer was to give 80 cents to the government. We discussed the terms among ourselves, but there were no takers. We were told that in Arizona even 3 cents per pound was not an attractive offer. Picking cotton was such backbreaking work that most people could not do it.

Since March 1943 a rumor had been spreading that we were all going to be moved to Santa Fe. Ninety-four people from the Mainland, including Mr. Sotaro Kawabe, a former mayor, were taken by truck in the early morning of March 22 to the family camp in Crystal City. It was a very cold morning. We later heard that they had arrived at their destination earlier than expected—at five o'clock the following morning after a twenty-two hour trip.

The first group of 357 internees (including more than 20 from Hawaii) left for Santa Fe at five o'clock on the morning of March 23. It was not so cold that morning, so they walked to the station. Trucks carried the sick and elderly and lunch boxes for midday and evening meals. They all took the eleven-car train leaving at nine that morning for Santa Fe. Among them were my friends Messrs. Sei Fujii, Hisashi Imamura, Tetsusho Matsumoto, Enryo Shigefuji, Seimoku Kosaka, Teisuke Takahashi, Seizo Takahashi, and Sutematsu Endo. Messrs. Kinai Ikuma, Shu Nakayama, and Kaichi Miyamasa, all from Hawaii, were also in this group.

At the end of May, a request was received by the authorities for internee laborers to build roads in Kooskia, Idaho. Kooskia is to the north near the Montana border. The conditions were "No fences, no guards,

$45.00 per month, meals paid." Only seventeen internees signed on. At least twenty-five laborers were needed, so the campaign was stepped up. They were unsuccessful, however, for the following reasons: First, we were convinced by then that all of us were going to be sent to Santa Fe; and second, many internees felt that by working for Americans, they were helping the enemy.

6

SANTA FE CAMP

THE OFFICIAL ORDER to move to Santa Fe Camp was issued on June 10, 1943. The first group was comprised of 350 internees, all of the second battalion's fifth through seventh regiments and several members of the eighth. They left on Monday the fourteenth. The second group of 350 included the remaining members of the eighth regiment and all of the third battalion's eleventh and twelfth regiments. They left on Wednesday the sixteenth. The last group, consisting of the third battalion's ninth and tenth regiments, followed soon afterward. The rumor was that three thousand Italian POWs would be taking our place at Lordsburg. We gathered our luggage and made storage boxes. Many farewell meetings were held, and everyone was quite busy. The vegetables and melons that internees had been growing behind the barbed wire were ripe, but they could not harvest and enjoy them.

I was among the 350 in the first group. We rose at three o'clock on June 14, had breakfast at four, and left the camp at five. Everyone except those who were sickly made the fifty-minute trek to the station. Fifty guards accompanied us. The commander of the camp came to the station with his assistant and bade us farewell. The authorities were very attentive to the details of our transport. The train left at 7:40 A.M. The cars were old, but at least they were not the bamboo-type cages used for transporting criminals in feudal Japan.

It was a journey from one camp to another, but the trip promised to be enjoyable. We were leaving Lordsburg in the southern part of New Mexico and traveling 165 miles to El Paso, Texas. From there we would head north 250 miles to Santa Fe, the capital of New Mexico. At the end of the day, we were to have traveled 415 miles.

We arrived at Deming at 8:40 A.M. Green trees, houses, farms, and an airfield with hangars caught our eye. We turned left at 10:00 A.M. and   *123* saw a muddy tributary of the Rio Grande River. We moved uphill slowly and passed through a tunnel. Large factories and a mining town appeared on our right. We arrived in El Paso at 11:15 A.M. With a population of 120,000, it was a metropolis of considerable size with a large train station. We saw many black soldiers boarding a train. We left at 11:30 A.M. An hour later we ate the sandwiches we had been given for lunch.

After El Paso, we felt uncomfortably hot. The temperature was over 110 degrees. We stopped for a while at Rincon at 1:25 P.M. A little later, lakes, rivers, and green trees appeared on both sides of the train. We saw Indian adobe houses built of sun-dried clay bricks here and there. We looked for schools and churches as well but did not see any. After passing Belen, we arrived at Albuquerque, New Mexico, five thousand feet above sea level, at 5:50 P.M. Although its population was only about thirty-five thousand, it was the largest and most modern city as well as a thriving commercial center. Spelling "Albuquerque" is a bit tricky; it is pronounced "Albakahki."

The heat aboard the train was terrible. The fans in my car did not work and we could open the windows only a few inches. Cigarette smoke filled the air. The dinner sandwiches would not go down my throat, so I just drank iced water. The train left Albuquerque at 6:25 P.M., climbed two thousand feet, and went on for another eighty-six miles before arriving at the Santa Fe station, our final destination, at 9:30 P.M. Santa Fe, at seven thousand feet above sea level, looked beautiful at night, with streetlights flickering and a few neon signs adding color. I suddenly felt like leaving the desert and jumping into civilization.

We were all sent to the camp in buses, trucks, and cars. It was only a five-minute ride. After I took my first breath of fresh air, I felt as if I had been reborn. Although my body was dead tired, I was pleased when we were greeted by the many internees already at the camp. I was especially surprised to see Mr. Kawamoto, the general manager of my newspaper, who had arrived the week before from Livingston. We were escorted to our barracks and treated to tea and cakes in a big mess hall. There was no hot water at that hour, so I took a cold shower, changed, and jumped into bed. I slept soundly because it was cold and I was exhausted. So ended my first night at Santa Fe. It was Monday, June 14, 1943.

Comparisons with Lordsburg

Santa Fe Camp was located two miles from the city. Unlike at Lordsburg, there were many trees on our side of the barbed wire. We could see the steep Rocky Mountains on one side and the whole distant town of Santa

Fe on the other. The domes of government buildings and the spires of churches were visible. If I had to compare Santa Fe to a place in Honolulu, I would say the city resembled sections of Kaimuki. Our eyes were hungry for the sight of greenery, so we were pleased to see many trees. The climate in Santa Fe is exceptionally good. There were only a few sandstorms, which had troubled us so much in the past. However, given the high altitude, many of us did not feel well early on. When we worked, even for a short time, we tired easily. *Noh* chanting was difficult because I was often short of breath. It took about a month to get accustomed to our new surroundings.

If I continue on like this, I will give my readers the impression that Santa Fe was a paradise on earth. It was not. As they say, "Heaven never gives us two good things." The camp facilities were very poor. In the beginning, there were only a few bathrooms and toilets. Most important, water and electricity were unreliable. The hospital facilities were especially bad. In many ways, the administration of Lordsburg Camp was superior. One barracks housed sixty-two people, so it was very crowded. However, by the time I arrived, eleven cabins had been built, each measuring sixteen square feet and large enough for five people. I was lucky to be assigned to one of these.

Our luggage had accompanied us on the train. The bags and boxes of 350 internees required thirty-six trucks (or one truck for every ten internees), and everything was crammed into two freight cars. After unloading, the mass of luggage resembled a small mountain. The Lordsburg authorities had generously given us permission to take everything, including shelves and desks. The second and third groups were allowed to do the same. According to internees from Camp Livingston in Louisiana, before moving out they were obliged to throw out all their handicrafts and collections.

The second group of 350 from Lordsburg arrived after midnight on June 16, completely exhausted. Among them were my friends Dr. Mori, Dr. Uehara, and Mr. Konosuke Iwakami. It was a very cold night. Other old and new Mainland acquaintances I met as soon as I arrived at Santa Fe were journalists Mr. Ko (Hihutsu) Murai of the *Rafu Sangyo Nippo* (Los Angeles Industry Daily), Mr. Sei Fujii of the *Kashu Mainichi* (California Mainichi), and Mr. Hiroshi Suzuki and Mr. Toyosaku Komai of the *Rafu Shimpo* (Los Angeles News); lawyers Messrs. Gongoro Nakamura, Katsuma Mukaida, Dotatsu (Shonan) Kimura, and Shuichi Watanabe; Revs. Hisanori Kano, Takeshi Ban, and Ikugoro Nagamatsu; the dancer Mr. Michio Ito; Dr. Masayoshi Tanaka; and agriculturalists Mr. Yaemon Minami and Mr. Ichikuro Kondo.

A group of internees from Hawaii, the Mainland, and South America who had been transferred from Livingston to Missoula, Montana, eventually joined us at Santa Fe in April 1944. The camp now included Japanese from both American continents. In the end, I decided that Lordsburg and Santa Fe had both good and bad points. Despite the heavy snow and a few troublesome incidents, I have fonder memories of Santa Fe, probably because I was there longer, and because I so enjoyed walking with good friends in that sunshine rich in ultraviolet rays.

The City of Santa Fe

Santa Fe is the capital of New Mexico and the oldest town in all of North America. Named by a Catholic priest from Mexico, "Santa Fe" means "sacred faith." In 1536 four shipwrecked Spanish sailors arrived here from the Texas coast. They were later routed by Indians and escaped to Mexico City, the capital of Mexico. Here they spread rumors of mountains of treasure and seven villages of gold in the north, which triggered a military expedition of three hundred men. Led by Francisco Coronado, the group reached Santa Fe in the summer of 1540 and established the town with headquarters from which they began to expand their territory and conquer the Indians. General Coronado pushed west and east; he invaded California and traveled as far north as Kansas. Bloody battles against the Indians were fought for the next three hundred years.

Mexico won its independence from Spain in 1822. While the United States was gaining in strength and prosperity, Mexico was in chaos. When the United States invaded Mexico, the Mexicans could do nothing and lost California, Arizona, New Mexico, and Texas. The U.S. army, led by General Stephen W. Kearney, faced almost no resistance when it occupied Santa Fe and raised the U.S. flag there for the first time in 1846. During the Civil War, New Mexico fought on the side of the South. In one incident, they intercepted a gold shipment from California to the East in order to lend support to the Southern army. Troops from New Mexico also fought fiercely against the Indians, gradually pushing the Apache tribe into the Sacramento Mountains and the Navajo tribe to Fort Sumner. Thus the early history of the state of New Mexico is defined by a series of wars among Americans, Mexicans, and Indians, which continued into the twentieth century. General Via of Mexico staged an unsuccessful invasion of New Mexico on March 9, 1916. This would prove to be Mexico's last attempt to regain its former power and glory.

Santa Fe is located halfway up the Sangre de Cristo Mountains, which

are a part of the great Rocky Mountains. It is the oldest (and highest) capital in the United States and has a population of twenty thousand. Among its famous spots are the Chapel of San Miguel, built in 1620; the Museum of Navajo Ceremonial Art, which houses the weapons and outfits of the Spanish invaders and Indian stone and clay crafts now coveted by historians; and the Monument of Martyr Las Cass, located on a hill northwest of the city, where a large expedition was surrounded and killed by Indians in the covered wagon days. Of equal interest are the Indian adobe houses built of sun-dried clay bricks, which I mentioned before, and the remains of collective dwellings of the native tribes, who skillfully used the slopes of hills for shelter. Blessed with a temperate climate and abundant sunshine, Santa Fe is regarded as one of the healthiest places in the United States. Those suffering from lung diseases come here from all over the country. Historians and archeologists are frequent visitors as well. The summer visitor count is especially high, making tourism an important source of revenue for the state.

New Mexico has an almost unlimited number of minerals and fossils. Gold, silver, copper, lead, zinc, and platinum can be found lying in the sand. The estimated amount of coal reserves is said to be 192 billion tons, and of gypsum, 3,300 tons. The variety of fossils found here is unparalleled; the remains of dinosaurs and sea creatures ("sea stones") from New Mexico are famous.

The Publishing Office

A few days after I arrived at Santa Fe, all the newspapermen gathered and decided to publish the *Santa Fe Times* as soon as possible. Messrs. Kasai, Ogawa, Kawajiri, Akabori, and Kusao were in charge and Messrs. Abe, Komai, Murai, Fujii, and I served as advisers. Using a mimeograph machine that we had brought from Lordsburg, we began publishing from July 1. Our publishing office was independent at first, but became a part of the Japanese Internee Administrator's Office after the consolidation of various departments. Mr. Iwao Oyama managed the newspaper for a long time. After he was paroled, Mr. Toshio Sakaguchi served as manager until we left the camp.

Although the department was small, we printed weeklies and other publications for the Buddhist and Christian groups in addition to our daily newspaper. The extent to which this old mimeograph machine contributed to the cultural enrichment of the entire internee population is immeasurable. The newspaper was reviewed by the censors every day prior

to publication. News was limited to what was reported in the English-language newspapers. Sending our paper out beyond the camp was strictly prohibited.

Strangely enough, there was only one mess hall for nearly two thousand people, and it was on the hilly side of our camp. Nearby were a laundry room, library, and meeting hall, which was used by the Japanese office. Beyond that were our pitifully inadequate hospital and twelve barracks. In the middle of the camp were a canteen, post office, immigration office, and shacks for carpentry and the iron works. We called this area "Upper Town." A baseball diamond, tennis courts, and about twenty barracks faced the town of Santa Fe; we called this part of the camp "Lower Town." Between Upper and Lower Town was a gate that was always kept open. In Upper Town, near the gate, was the liaison office of the supervisory bureau. Next to it were the police and fire departments, a shoe repair shop, and the Japanese office. In front of these buildings was a square that was used as an open-air theater. In Lower Town, beyond the gate, were the cabins (including mine), the supply department, and a warehouse.

Unlike Lordsburg, Santa Fe Camp was not under the control of the military but the Department of Justice. The supervisory bureau's office contained radio communication equipment, which was used to communicate with the watchtowers along the barbed-wire fence, the hospital, and the liaison office. The Japanese office was purposely left out of the system, so working without a telephone was a great inconvenience.

The seat of our self-government was the Japanese office. Leaders were elected for the positions of administrator, assistant administrator, head secretary, accountant, and auditors. As at Lordsburg, twenty department chiefs assisted the officers. The administrator was our spokesman. Each barracks elected a leader, who in turn elected the department chiefs. Every official served for three months. Department staff members worked on a volunteer basis, except for cooks and barbers and those working at the hospital, laundry, post office, and newspaper office. A public welfare fund committee was made up of five members elected by the internees. They were responsible for handling donations and profits from the canteen and for determining budgets for various events and occasions.

At a glance, this seems like a perfect system. At Lordsburg, internees were divided into small groups of 250, each governed by a mayor. At Santa Fe, one governing body controlled all 2,000 internees, so matters did not run smoothly. The forty barracks chiefs made the final decision in every matter handled by the Japanese office. As you would expect, there were quite a few barracks chiefs who had something to say about everything.

These people had been like this even when they were in the busy outside world. Here they had nothing to do, so they made even longer and
more tedious speeches. The Japanese office seemed to have been a failure
in many ways, primarily because it was poorly organized.

Fire in the Mess Hall

Accidents occurred one after another from late June through July 1943.
The first, which surprised and troubled us a great deal, was the fire in the
mess hall. At around 2:15 A.M. on June 23, I was awakened by the loud
screeching of sirens. A fire was raging in Upper Town. It started in the mess
hall and soon spread to the meeting hall and second and third barracks.
These buildings were completely destroyed by the fire, but our firefight-
ers performed courageously. The hospital was leeward of the fire, so many
helped to evacuate the patients amid the confusion and fear. The wind fortunately shifted, so the hospital and other buildings were left untouched.
It took about fifty minutes to extinguish the fire. Several internees in the
second and third barracks lost some belongings, but no one was injured,
which was one consolation.

People in the city must have been surprised to see the fairly extensive
fire in the distance. The government supervisory bureau officials were quite
impressed by our quick action and pluck. News of the fire was reported in
newspapers all over the United States, but internees could not even allude
to it in their letters. A cable, which simply read "All Japanese internees
at Santa Fe Camp are safe and sound," was dispatched to newspapers or
government offices in the cities and towns where the families of internees lived. It was signed by Mr. Ichikuro Kondo, our camp administrator.
The Honolulu newspapers printed the news verbatim. I doubt that most
people understood what it was all about.

The cause of the fire seems to have been electrical. With our only
mess hall gone, two thousand internees were greeted the next morning by
rows of tables set up in front of the canteen. The Santa Fe prison trucked
in our meals three times a day. I was on KP duty at the time, so I gave
out the bread. Because so many people had to be served, everyone who
worked with me that day was soon dripping with perspiration. It was a hot
day; lunch was served under a blazing sun. By dinnertime everyone had
adjusted to the heat.

In the midst of the confusion caused by the fire, the remaining 291
internees from Lordsburg arrived sometime after 9:00 P.M. They had left
the camp at around 4:00 A.M. Although they had received news of the

fire along the way, they came to Santa Fe as scheduled. As I mentioned earlier, the day before their departure, an internee who had been seriously ill passed away. His death brought the total number of internees who died at Lordsburg to eleven.

A Fearsome Landslide

On Sunday, June 24, the day after the fire, the water supply was cut off. There was nothing we could do about the long lines of men waiting to be served or the army of flies hovering around the open-air mess hall. If it rained, it was even more miserable. The meals from the prison were very unappetizing. Looking at stew in a feed bucket, I was so repelled that I could not eat it or any of the other meals. On the twenty-seventh we finally decided to set up an army-style kitchen on one side of the square and cook for ourselves. The next morning, we had coffee that smelled like coffee for the first time in a long time. Before the meeting hall burned down, it had been used for religious and social gatherings and as a library. On Sunday, June 27, morning service was held on a hill next to the hospital. The Reverend Kono led the service, Reverend Kano delivered the sermon, and Mr. Michio Ito led the choir.

We were cursed with water as well as fire. At around one o'clock in the afternoon on June 28, there was a roar and a sudden landslide on the northwestern hillside. A bubbling river of mud became a tidal wave, uprooting trees and rocks. I saw the landslide advance toward our camp with a terrible force, as if the veterans of many battles were charging forth. The rainfall around the camp had been minimal, but it must have been heavy in the mountains a few days earlier, developing into a destructive wave of water. Fortunately, the camp did not sustain much damage, although the floors of many barracks in Lower Town were under water. It later began to rain and the weather suddenly turned cold after dinner. The ditches around our cabins (we called them "peace dormitories") were flooded. Soon frogs began croaking so loudly at night that we could not sleep well. I had never seen a landslide before, and it was truly a frightening experience. Sanitary conditions at the camp for the next few days were terrible. Doctors worried about the spread of contagious diseases.

Every so often the consulate general of Spain sent members of its staff to Japanese internee camps. Mr. A, consul general in San Francisco, visited us in person on July 12. The Japanese office presented our requests and demands. That evening he gave a speech in which he reported on a resolution passed by the Imperial Diet stating that it would continue to monitor the situation of its citizens interned in enemy countries. It expressed the hope that everyone would be optimistic, take care of his health, uphold Japanese pride, and wait patiently for the day when the peace bell would ring. The consul general spoke in Spanish, so Mr. Jo, a Mainlander, interpreted for us. Mr. Kano, our secretary and a doctor of agriculture, met with the consul general that day.

There was a broadcast that night in which Dr. Furugouchi reported on camp sanitation. He warned that the Japanese-style baths in the barracks should not be used until the water shortage was over. Also, because our supply of fresh milk was gathered from many different dairies and not inspected, he could not guarantee its purity.

Passengers for the Second Exchange Ship Announced

Since my arrival at Santa Fe, a few internees from the Mainland had been paroled. However, the FBI was continuing to send people from the relocation centers to Santa Fe for internment. Thus far no one from Hawaii had been moved or sent home. On June 30, 1943, a list of about fifty men to be released at the beginning of July was announced. It contained the names of only Mainland internees and included Mr. Yasushi Nakaarai, with whom I had been on friendly terms since our stay at Angel Island, and elderly Mr. Kishi, a member of my *noh* chanting group.

Eventually Hawaii internees began moving out. Of those who had applied for cohabitation with their families, six internees (Dr. Motokazu Mori, Messrs. Konosuke Iwakami, Masaru Suzuki, Hideji Kimura, Kentaro Hirashima, and Shigeichi Torisawa) left on September 10 for the family camp at Crystal City. Among parolees from the Mainland, Mr. Masayoshi Uehara of the former Kewalo Inn left Santa Fe for Salt Lake City on August 12. Eighty-five internees from Sharp Park, California, were sent there on August 15, including seventy-seven men from the eighth and ninth groups who had left Sand Island for the Mainland a little less than a year ago. Among them were Messrs. Yoshinobu Kato, Hyotaro Nakami, Yuichi Nakaichi, Kanji Tanaka, Ichiro Nakamura, Tsuneichi Yamamoto, Kiyoshi Yonemura, Shigeru Yano, Yaichiro Akada, Kikujiro Kondo, Isuke Horikawa, and Nizo Arita and Kuwasaburo Sakaguchi, two men who had been involved in a highly publicized fraud case just before the war started.

At this time the camp was buzzing with talk of returning to Japan, moving to be with families, and applying for review. There was also talk about the disagreements between orderlies and Dr. Masayoshi Tanaka at the hospital and about the complaints of workers at the barber shop. Both situations were said to be reaching a boiling point, but they were fortunately dealt with before they became big problems.

When a list of sixty-seven internees assigned to the second exchange ship, the SS *Gripsholm,* was announced on the afternoon of July 15, everyone became excited. These men were to be accompanied by families waiting at relocation centers. An additional thirty returnees were suddenly announced on the evening of August 21, bringing the total to ninety-seven. The news created an uproar. Some of the internees who had been left out appealed to the consul general of Spain or the State Department in Washington, D.C., by sending cables or through other means. Mr. Sutematsu Endo pleaded illness, and to his relief was later added to the list. On the other hand, Mr. Chin-ei Kinjo and Rev. Takashi Kamae were dropped. In the case of Rev. Kamae, however, a cable received on the day of departure allowed him to return to Japan.

Calm Returns

Five more internees were added to the list on August 26, and another three two days later. We all began speculating on the criteria for obtaining returnee status. No one could get any information from the authorities; we were in a sea of doubt, but it seemed that the authorities were also at a loss. Many of the internees who applied for returnee status could not make up their minds. One man flip-flopped in his decision three times in one day, canceling his application to return to Japan in the morning, rescinding his cancellation request at noon, then rushing to arrange to remain in the United States that evening. I am sure one of the reasons for the confusion at the consulate general of Spain and the State Department was the indecision of internees.

While the lists were being cabled from Washington, the camp authorities were busy preparing for the departure of the returnees. Inoculations against smallpox, typhoid, and cholera began on August 24. A farewell party for only Hawaii returnees was held on the evening of August 24 at the Lower Town mess hall. There were 426 of us at that time; 23 were returning to Japan. Mr. Kango Kawasaki gave a farewell speech, Mr. Hiseki Miyazaki led three *banzai* cheers, and Mr. Kyoichi Hamamura spoke on behalf of the returnees. The party was very simple. There was neither drink nor entertainment. Each man received a lei made from the red paper used for wrapping fruit.

A farewell party for all the returnees, sponsored by the Japanese office,

was held on the evening of August 25 in the open-air theater. Mr. Yasumasa Yoshizumi, assistant general manager, served as master of ceremonies; Mr. Ichikuro Kondo, administrator, gave a farewell speech; and Mr.
Shungo Abe gave a speech of appreciation on behalf of the returnees. Later
a meeting of barracks representatives and returnees was held at the Lower
Town mess hall. Many important matters were discussed and the meeting
proved very fruitful.

A seat and berth number were assigned to each returnee on August 27.
A strict inspection of their luggage began. All books in either Japanese or
English, letters, notes, as well as radios and similar mechanical apparatus
were prohibited. Returnees could carry no more than three hundred dollars in cash. It was a noisy and restless time for everyone. On August 29,
the day before their departure, our peace dormitories were in charge of
KP. My role was to control traffic in the mess hall. At five o'clock that evening, all the returnees shook hands with us before being taken to the classrooms in Upper Town. After that, all communication between returnees
and internees was forbidden. That day, August 29, marked the one-year
anniversary of my internment on the Mainland.

At around seven o'clock the next morning, the returnees boarded ten
buses, accompanied by several armed soldiers sent especially from Lordsburg. They left with our rousing cheers ringing in their ears. Then the
camp was suddenly quiet; it was like "the calm after the storm." Among
my good Hawaii friends who left that day were Eimu Miake, Takashi
Wada, Sutematsu Endo, Shin-ichi Hashibe, Shoten Suetomi, Takinosuke
Toyama, Jusui Isobe, Yoshiai Mikami, Shozo Hirama, Kyoichi Hamamura,
Shogo Miwa, Koshin Yamane, Koshiro Tofukuji, Ishichi Matsuda, Takeo
Akekarasu, Utanosuke Fujishiro, Hakusaburo Tani, Horyu Asaeda, Mine-
taro Hori, Isamu Kudo, Senpei Tominaga, Shishin Toda, Shun-ichi Neko-
moto, and Goichi Yamane. Friends from the Mainland included Shungo
Abe, Yasumasa Yoshizawa, Michiro Ito, Deiso Takayama, and Masahiro
Konomi.

Sent Back to Santa Fe

The returnees traveled eastward aboard a local train, where they were
treated well. They sailed out of New York on the SS *Gripsholm* on September 1, rounded Africa, and met up with the exchange ship from Japan, the
Teia Maru, at Goa (a Portuguese territory), on the west coast of India. Now
aboard the *Teia Maru,* they headed for Japan. Besides the returnees from
Santa Fe, Mr. Tokue Takahashi and his son, Mr. Konosuke Iwakami and

his two children, and all seven family members of Mr. Shoichi Asami of Hawaii, who had been interned at Crystal City, were aboard. Also among the passengers were Mr. Torataro Onoda of Sumitomo Hawaii and Mr. Kenji Kimura of Nippon Yusen Kaisha Hawaii, who had missed the first exchange ship. By journey's end, the returnees would have traveled more than ten thousand miles in two and a half months.

Something unexpected happened in New York almost immediately before the *Gripsholm*'s departure: Ninety-seven returnees were sent back to their camps because the passenger capacity of thirteen hundred had been exceeded. Sixteen men returned to Santa Fe on September 7, crushed and heartbroken. Among them were Mr. Tokuji Onodera and Mr. Wataru Takamoto from Hawaii, Mr. Dotatsu (Shonan) Kimura from the Mainland, and Mr. Tadashi Mitsui. Mr. Kimura had been chairman of the Return to Japan Committee. How ironic that he was left behind! The luggage for most of the internees had been loaded ahead of time, so nothing could be sent back until the ship docked in Goa, India. Unfortunately, those sent back were inconvenienced for quite some time. They had prepared everything, endured all the cumbersome procedures, gone through the immigration station on Ellis Island, seen the SS *Gripsholm* before them, had their luggage taken, and then they were turned back. They must have felt terribly frustrated.

We do not know how this kind of mistake happened. It seems there was a shortage of passengers on the first exchange ship, so for the second ship, the limit was purposely extended to avoid a similar problem. If this is true, those who were turned back at the last minute were truly unfortunate. Their only consolation was that they saw a part of the great city of New York.

The number of internees who returned to Japan totaled eighty-one, including the nine sent on the first exchange ship. At Santa Fe Camp, we received their letters sent from Rio de Janeiro and Goa. I received several from Mr. Asami, Mr. Miake, and others, who reported that the sailing was unexpectedly smooth, the services aboard ship were satisfactory, and everyone was in good spirits. They were expected to arrive in Yokohama on November 13. I received their letters on November 11. We had asked the returnees to give our regards to relatives and friends in Japan with whom we had not communicated for a long time. Because they were not allowed to carry letters or memos, they had to memorize our messages. Mr. Eimu Miake was asked to relay seventy messages to various people. According to the letter I received from him, he had memorized all of them, including the addresses, and recorded them in a notebook. I was amazed by his powerful memory.

Incidents Happen One after Another

Just before the departure of the returnees, the camp went through other changes. To our relief, a new mess hall was erected on the site of the old one, but not before an additional hall had been completed near the hospital. At the time, Mr. Ichikuro Kondo, a farmer from San Jose, served as administrator and dealt with many difficult situations. Mr. Hisanori Kano assisted him as chief secretary. People gossiped about them, but Mr. Kondo was a sincere man and Mr. Kano was devoted to his job. Both were especially fluent in English and made a good team. Ambitious barracks leaders coveting their positions proved troublesome. Eventually Mr. Kondo and Mr. Kano asked to resign, so we decided to put their request to a vote. On August 19, 1943, more than 60 percent of the nineteen hundred internees voted in favor of the current administration. Those who had led the opposition, barracks leaders Fukuda, Tachibana, and Motoyoshi, were defeated. The Reverend Fukuda was a bishop of Konko-kyo sect, Mr. Motoyoshi was a minister, and Mr. Zenshiro Tachibana, although well-meaning, habitually led the dissidents. Despite the results, the Kondo administration was determined to resign, so an election was held, and Mr. Kango Kawasaki of Hilo became our new administrator after the usual political wrangling and maneuvering.

In August, there were three funerals. Mr. Toyonosuke Hitosumi from Alaska died on August 18, and both Mr. Yasutaro Okamura and Mr. Fusakichi Takao died in the hospital on August 22. The first two men died of stomach cancer, the third of cancer of the esophagus. I felt especially sorry for Mr. Okamura because he was one of the returnees. It seemed to have been a month for misfortune. During a game of golf, a Maui internee's flying ball hit a Mainland internee in the eye. Although it was treated, the eye had to be removed.

Mr. Kawasaki, the new administrator, and his group made their first visit to Mr. Jensen, chief of the government supervisory bureau, and Mr. Schreiber, his assistant, on August 26. At the meeting they were told unexpectedly that broadcasts on certain topics would no longer be allowed. Apparently the authorities had been aware of the inflammatory comments made by two announcers, Mr. Fukuda and Mr. Tachibana, and were prepared to take legal action if necessary. It was decided that Mr. Toshio Sakaguchi and Mr. Muin Ozaki would replace the controversial pair. This was one of the problems Mr. Kawasaki faced as soon as he took over as general manager.

During this time picture taking in the camp was very popular. Internees wanted individual and group portraits taken, so a photographer from Santa Fe was called in. Many people had their pictures taken at memorial services, home prefectural gatherings, and other events. In the winter, Hawaii men were especially eager to have their pictures taken with snow scenes in the background. The photographer was an elderly Jewish man of about sixty. He charged a dollar a picture and refused to give a discount no matter how many reprints were ordered. We tried to negotiate better prices, but he never conceded. There were three photographers in Santa Fe, but for some reason only this man was allowed into the camp. We were so offended by his inflexibility that we called for a boycott and finally got a few discounts. He must have reaped quite a profit from us internees, because we heard later that he bought a luxury car. I realized that it is very difficult to get the better of a Jewish businessman unless you are very patient.

Profiles of Prominent Mainland Internees

There were nearly two thousand internees at Santa Fe, so of course I did not get to know all of them. I do not claim that other people would concur with me about those whom I mention below. I simply want to record here, briefly, my honest impressions of some of the people I met at the camp.

Mr. Miemon Minami, who supposedly was a millionaire, looked like an exemplary farmer as well as a millionaire. Mr. Sei Fujii, president of the *Kashu Mainichi* (California Mainichi), was a politician type who understood even the psychology of farmers. Mr. Shoroku Ono of Goshado combined sincerity with exceptional business acumen. Mr. Katsuma Mukaida was a shrewd man and what you would expect of someone who was said to be an adviser to the Tokyo Club. Mr. Gongoro Nakamura was of great character, a rare thing among lawyers like Mr. Fujii and Mr. Mukaida. Mr. Shonan Kimura, also in the law business, was amiable but timid. Mr. Toyosaku Komai, president of the *Rafu Shimpo* (Los Angeles News) was not a man of the pen but of business. Mr. Takeshi Ban became famous because he conducted funerals in the camps wearing a Ph.D. robe. Dr. Masayoshi Tanaka was a boor but skillful at his profession. Dr. Teiichi Furugouchi was a kind and intelligent physician. Mr. Kenji Kasai was a more agreeable businessman than his elder brother, Diet representative Juji

Kasai. Mr. Kamekichi Sasaki was a devoted scholar who rarely ventured out. Rev. Kiyoshi Ishikawa was a bookworm. Mr. Enryo Shigefuji of the Hongwanji Fresno Betsuin Mission was a scholar with no head for business. Mr. Gisho Maeda had many talents but was not very well informed. Rev. Dojin Ochi of the Soto Mission was a man of exceptional insight and the foremost authority on Buddhism in the United States. Mr. Michio Ito, the famous dancer, was a true gentleman. Mr. Hisanori Kano substantiated his beliefs with his conduct. Mr. Masaru Akahori (Hyoroku Oishi) was a gifted writer and speaker. My quick sketches may not be entirely accurate, but I hope they will provide some sense of the characters of these important men.

Mr. Hisanori Kano, the second son of Viscount Kano, prince of Ichi-no-Miya, managed a fairly large farm in the Nebraskan countryside and had been engaged in missionary work for many years. He and I became good friends as soon as I arrived at Santa Fe. Compared with his older brother, a former manager of the London branch of Yokohama Specie Bank, Mr. Hisanori Kano was smaller and lacked presence, but his steady gaze reflected his character. He had a degree in agriculture from Tokyo Imperial University and was a well-respected priest of the Episcopal Church. Although many Japanese were just visiting the United States at the time, Mr. Kano arrived with the intention of making this country his home and has never returned to Japan. His wife was a sister of Mr. Fumio Goto, a former minister of the interior. When the war between the United States and Japan began, the couple had already been here twenty-five years. He has two sons. In addition to farming and missionary work, he traveled widely in this country on behalf of Japan's Ministry of Agriculture, providing it with reports on American farming and other related matters. This was probably the primary reason for his internment.

Well versed in English, Mr. Kano worked hard and served cheerfully as our chief secretary. He also kept busy delivering sermons and lectures and was never idle. He dressed like a poor laborer and spared no effort to help others. There were some internees who spoke ill of him behind his back, but he did not care at all. I admired him for his sheer character. His "Lectures on the United States" and hands-on knowledge of natural history were invaluable.

Eccentrics

Among the nearly two thousand men in the camp, there were sure to be a few eccentrics. One of them was a man named Yamada, an amateur fortuneteller who loved cats. His father, Mr. Ittokusai Jirokichi Yamada, regarded as the last great Japanese sword master of modern times, was a teacher of *kendo* swordsmanship at Hitotsubashi Commercial College. This man was by far more experienced than Mr. Takano, who had participated in a famous *kendo* tournament before the emperor. Dr. Kenjiro Yamakawa was strongly influenced by the senior Mr. Yamada and asked his opinion before writing a history of Japanese swordsmanship. Although he was quite amiable, our Mr. Yamada was unworthy of so illustrious a father. He had wandered throughout the United States for many years. He liked to tell fortunes when his fancy struck him. He was said to be accurate 85 percent of the time. He loved and took very good care of homeless cats. (The camp was full of cats. We were forbidden to have animals of any kind, but this rule was overlooked if they were kept outdoors. Men like Mr. Yamada made pets of the stray cats, treating them like their own children. Whenever the cat population got out of control, the guards thinned it out.)

An elderly carpenter from Hawaii who had fought in the Russo-Japanese War was good at the "*kanaka* dialect" (Hawaiian pidgin) and used it even when talking in his sleep. He would shout "Charge!" and leap onto a nearby bed in the middle of the night. At first it shocked everyone, but soon no one paid much attention. Those who slept next to the man kept sticks handy; when he began his routine, they would give him a light spank. As soon as he realized he had only been dreaming he would return meekly to his bed. All of us sympathized with him, realizing that he was reliving his personal war experience.

There was an extremely fastidious man who would wipe the toilet bowl with paper two or three times before using it. He became angry if anyone sat on his bed. In the mess hall, while everyone else used one tray for his meal, this internee had his own bowl for rice. He would then eat only the center portion and discard the remainder. There was also a good Christian who endeavored to attend every class offered at the camp, regardless of the subject. His love of learning was praiseworthy, but in a particular German class, he always appeared near the end of the lesson, so the teacher finally refused to let him into the classroom. Then there was a man who painted in oils quite well, but he had an untidy, scraggly beard and wore a soiled government-issued outfit. I do not know if it was true or not, but he said he had been a secretary to Prince Konoye. He always kept two paper packets in the pockets of his worn-out shirt. We all wondered what could be in those packets because they looked heavy and unwieldy. Finally, there was a man who went out for walks stripped to the waist in the dead of winter, even when it was snowing. A doctor cautioned him, but he would not listen. Eventually he got sick and was hospitalized.

Signs and Broadcasting

No place had more "Do not" signs than Santa Fe Camp. "Do not pick flowers," scolded the sign in front of the Japanese office. They were especially numerous in the toilets. One admonished, "Do not wash your feet in the basin," which of course meant that someone must have already done so. I once saw a man washing a dog under the tap in the laundry room and felt that he and I would never be able to get along. At the entrance to the woodshop, a notice read, "Carpenter room not for use." Someone added a comma, changing it to "Carpenter, room not for use." One of the carpenters altered the sign further: "Except for carpenter, room not for use." In the camp, there were many good trees for hanging oneself. They should have put up a sign on each one saying "Do not hang yourself on this tree."

I was quite annoyed at the Japanese of the announcers. Small mistakes are inevitable, but here is a list of some things that I felt were extremely irritating:

> *muyo no nagamono* for *muyo no chobutsu* (useless things)
>
> *yosai* for *shosai* (details)
>
> *sonshu* for *junshu* (observance)
>
> *obo* for *oho* (visit)
>
> *shuppon* for *shuppan* (sailing out)
>
> *kakusho* for *oboegaki* (memo)
>
> *yuzetsu* for *yuzei* (canvassing)
>
> *kagawa* for *kasen* (river)
>
> *usuho* for *kyuho* (mortar)
>
> *kodai* for *kakudai* (expansion)
>
> *teryudan* for *shuryudan* (hand grenade)
>
> *hitokeri shite* for *isshuu shite* (giving a kick)
>
> *issetsu* for *issai* (all)
>
> *zenhabateki* for *zenpukuteki* (to the full)
>
> *yotaku* for *yokai* (meddling)
>
> *keiniku* for *geiniku* (whale meat)

One man's pronunciation of not only Japanese but also English was muddled. He claimed to have graduated from the University of Southern California. He repeatedly pronounced Pearl Harbor as "Pole Harbo," Eisenhower as "Aizen-no-hawah," and Iowa as "Aioh." All of the announcers were newspapermen, teachers, or interpreters from the Mainland. I noticed only one Hawaii man who pronounced *konrinzai* (by no means) as *kinrinzai*. I have no intention of faulting them for an occasional slip of the tongue, but what I have recorded here is what I heard on several occasions.

Whatever the pronunciation, the broadcasts on current affairs were very popular. Since the outbreak of the war, news was censored and there was too much propaganda. On top of this, people tended to lean toward wishful thinking, so that in the end it was difficult to determine what was true and what was not. Most of the internees were simpleminded. When Japanese victories were announced, they greeted the news with applause and instantly became cheerful. If they heard that the British or the Americans were making progress, they criticized the broadcast. Some announcers tried to flatter their audiences and were guilty of "selling out." Those who knew better thought this was foolish and stopped listening. The cooks in the mess hall were thoughtful. When good news about Japan was broadcast, they always placed a bun with the flag of the Rising Sun on each of our trays. Sometimes they served us *sekihan* (rice and red beans) to celebrate. I thought this was very amusing.

Double Field Poppies

In Hawaii we had been blessed with flowers all year round and had taken this for granted. Here in a world without flowers, we felt dreary beyond words. In Lordsburg I cannot recall seeing a single vase of flowers; there, even the smallest wildflowers were highly prized. So what pleased me most when I came to Santa Fe were the many small flower gardens. When I took my morning and evening walks, I made it a point to visit these gardens with their flourishing purple and white mallows and irises (similar to the rabbit-ear iris); marigolds; red, white, and purple nicotiana; garden zinnias; nasturtiums; small and lovely baby's breath; crocuses; larkspur; high-standing cosmos; big and colorful dahlias; violet bachelor's button. The California field poppy, a kind of opium poppy with a white and pink background, is graceful and reminded me of a beautiful Chinese woman. It is also known as the Flanders poppy, which became well known during World War I because of a popular song. There were many other flowers besides the ones that I have mentioned. Internees volunteered to tend these gardens. They were mostly from the Mainland, but there were some Hawaii internees who were good at gardening.

The Santa Fe highlands are alive with all sorts of flowers at the end of August. I was always busy memorizing their names when I went out for a walk. Experts on gardening taught me that, to obtain seeds, flowers should be thinned when they are in full bloom, and it is absolutely impossible to transplant field poppies, opium poppies, and sweet pea. One day Dr. U said to me: "You have not seen the double field poppy. You must take a look at it. The sight of one will be a souvenir of your time here when you go to paradise." I answered, "I don't want to go to paradise." "Then do you want to go to Hades?" "I would hate to go to Hades." "Then you want to stay in the middle?" "I am a middle-of-the-road kind of man, alive or dead." Talking such nonsense, we went out in search of double field poppies. Yes, they are voluptuous and beautiful, but the single field poppy appeals to me more. Even a single poppy at times seems a bit too thick for my tastes, a double field poppy doubly so. As with most things, the middle of the road is best. Flowers were always scarce in the town of Santa Fe and their prices were high. It was very expensive to offer flowers at funerals. Several flowers that grow in the camp turned black and withered miserably as soon as the weather turned cold.

A Sudden Change and Influenza

The temperature dropped suddenly in early September. On the twenty-ninth, the first snow covered the distant Rocky Mountains. On the evening of October 2, a blizzard raged on the mountainside. Outside the barracks, the early evening temperature was thirty-two degrees; on the morning of the twelfth, it was twenty-nine degrees and piercing cold. Then a series of three cold days followed by four warm days occurred. On the seventeenth, it got very warm, and on the nineteenth, it grew cold again. A strong wind blew and the nearby mountains turned white. After this cycle was repeated, it began to snow on November 26.

On September 24, eighty-seven internees who used the Upper Town mess hall began coming down with diarrhea from eating pork that had gone bad. The same thing happened on October 10 and November 5. I was one of the later victims. The food poisoning occurred only in internees who used the more popular Upper Town mess hall. Those who frequented the Lower Town mess hall were spared.

On November 2 the temperature stood at eighteen degrees at around

6:00 A.M. and at twenty-two degrees two hours later. I wore my army shoes for the first time. In just one day my feet developed painful blisters. I was so tired that day I drank coffee with the other internees despite knowing that later I would have to make three or four trips on the snow-covered road to the distant outhouse in the cold night air. This ordeal would give anyone a bitter taste of internee life.

With the sudden cold came an epidemic of influenza at the end of November. The number of victims increased by November 20, and the hospital soon was filled to capacity. On the twenty-second, the east classroom was turned into a temporary sickroom and housed several scores of patients. The room had neither running water nor toilets, so orderlies had to carry chamber pots to the ninth barracks. All lectures and meetings scheduled in the classroom were of course canceled. Later, the west classroom, the library, and the fourth barracks also became temporary sickrooms. Some influenza patients began to show signs of pneumonia. The Japanese office canceled all meetings and broadcasts for the time being.

It was very difficult to find space for the internees who were being evacuated from the fourth barracks. One stubborn patient who insisted on treating himself would not listen to the doctor nor allow him to take his temperature. He boasted that he would depend on no one. His behavior was irksome to those around him. The number of patients at that time was about 150, or about 10 percent of the population, and half of them were suffering from influenza. There was no oxygen, but fortunately many patients were not critically ill and the supply of the new medicine, sulfa, was abundant. Fortunately, I did not catch influenza this time. By the middle of December, the number of new cases was declining. We were all relieved.

Mr. Kohei Shimano, who had taught for many years in Southern California, passed away in the hospital on November 9. A Christian service was held in the square on the afternoon of the twelfth, with Rev. Ban presiding and Rev. Kano giving the sermon. Mr. Koichi Choshi, an outsider, was given permission to attend the service. Mrs. Shimano, who was in Boston, could not come because of illness.

On November 25, Thanksgiving Day, while we were in the midst of the epidemic, we were treated to a gorgeous chicken dinner.

Events Behind Barbed Wire

A memorial service for Mr. Masao Sogawa, who had passed away in Missoula Camp on September 5, 1943, was held at the Lower Town mess hall on the night of the ninth.[1] Mr. Tokuji Onodera led the service, Revs. Hiseki Miyazaki and Ryugen Matsuda gave sermons, and I said a few words of condolence. It was a quiet and solemn service. Mr. Sogawa was the first Hawaii internee to die on the Mainland. The next day, with the surrender of Italy, the news was full of reports favoring the Allied cause. This put all of us to shame.

An autumn exhibition of handicrafts was held on October 2 and 3. It was a spectacular event, with two hundred internees participating and several thousand items on display, including a *shakuhachi* (Japanese flute) made of hickory. At the request of Santa Fe citizens, the exhibition was extended another day for their benefit. The Santa Fe area produces stones of beautiful colors, quite different from Missoula stones. It is also famous for its tree, shell, and other fossils. A stone-polishing craze spread among rock hunters in the camp after the exhibition, and soon many internees were polishing stones from morning to night.

A memorial service for Mr. Masasuke Kobayashi was held in the west classroom on the night of October 10 under the direction of Mr. Tomoki Iwanaga of the Salvation Army. Mr. Kobayashi had passed away on October 4, 1940, and this was the fourth anniversary of his death. Mr. Iwanaga talked about the deceased in his sermon, "God's Carriage Horse," and it was very interesting. I was glad I attended the service; Mr. Kobayashi was a good friend of mine and I respected him.

One Sunday morning in late October I attended a church service, which was atypical of me. A passionately devout young priest from Honolulu was preaching that day. He was so overcome by his own sermon, he began to cry and was forced to stop. I find such behavior distasteful. To make up for the unpleasant encounter, I spent the afternoon chanting "Rashomon" and "Semimaru" with other *noh* friends.

It was comparatively warm on the morning of November 3, the birthday of Emperor Meiji. A celebration, sponsored by the Japanese office, was held in the open-air theater at 9:00 A.M. We bowed in the direction of the Meiji Shrine, sang the Japanese national anthem, and heard a speech by General Manager Kawasaki. After the ceremony a lucky-number drawing was held. That day there was a display of *tanzaku* (special paper strips used in formal gatherings of *waka* poem enthusiasts) that had been donated by the Japanese Women's Society of Boston. As a celebration committee

---

1. Masao Sogawa was among those who were interned on December 7, 1941, the same date as Mr. Soga. He was the editor of *Hawaii Shimpo*, a rival newspaper of the *Nippon Jiji*. Mr. Soga was once employed at *Hawaii Shimpo* when the newspaper was run by Mr. Sogawa's predecessor.

member, I was busy all day. An athletic meet was also held, so it was a very lively day.

Thanks to Mr. Goshado Ono, a sale of handicrafts and other goods was organized on November 7. The items were sold at 5 percent of their "price" to cover expenses. The event proved beneficial to all, so it was held regularly thereafter, one weekend a month. It was a flourishing business for the internees, with weekend gross sales averaging between five hundred and a thousand dollars.

Just after we celebrated Emperor Meiji's birthday, the United States and Japan engaged in two big sea battles off the Solomon Islands and the Bismarck Archipelago. News of Japan's amazing victories came trickling in. Around that time we also heard that in various places in Southern California some eighty fires had mysteriously occurred, which prompted some internees to spread the rumor that the United States was on the brink of collapse. On November 14, the military command in Hawaii announced the possibility of another bombing attack on the island within the next four months. Some scatterbrained internees began to tell others that Honolulu was already in ruins. I knew it was foolish talk, but my spirits sank somewhat. On December 1, Mr. Kango Kawasaki's term as general manager came to an end, and Mr. Ichikuro Kondo was elected to take his place. Mr. Shichitaro Fujii was now assistant general manager and Mr. Zenshiro Tachibana chief secretary.

Our Meeting with the Consul General of Spain

December 7, 1943, was the second anniversary of the attack on Pearl Harbor. A ceremony honoring the memory of fallen soldiers was held in the square in the morning. We bowed in the direction of the Imperial Palace, sang the national anthem twice, and observed a moment of silence. A speech was given by General Manager Kondo. After the ceremony, a packet of fragrant green tea, donated by the Japanese Red Cross, was distributed to each internee by the barracks chiefs. A large flag of the Rising Sun made with used paper was displayed in the Upper Town mess hall. This would have been a problem in the outside world, but here it did not seem to matter.

On December 9 it snowed heavily all day. The roads were slippery and dangerous. It was the forty-ninth day after the death in Italy of Mr. Akira Morihara, the third son of Mr. Usaku Morihara, a shopowner from Kona. A memorial service was held at the Lower Town mess hall in the afternoon, and many internees attended. This was the first service in the camp for a fallen Japanese American soldier. On the night of the tenth, the sight of the Rocky Mountains covered in snow and illuminated by the moon was bewitching and beautiful beyond description. On the night of the thirteenth, internees from Maui held a memorial service for eight Japanese American soldiers from Maui (including Mr. Yoshinobu Takei) who had been killed in Italy. The Reverends Ryugen Matsuda and Tamasaku Watanabe delivered sermons and Mr. Tokiji Takei said a few words on behalf of the families. It was later reported that, of Japanese American soldiers from Maui, 8 had been killed and 180 injured.

Led by the Reverend Ban, thirteen of us received permission to visit the Monument of Martyr Las Cass on the morning of the eleventh. This was my second trip to the monument; at the end of September, Rev. Kano had taken several of us to see it. Led by a guide, we took a shortcut up and down snow-covered slippery roads. After two hours, we arrived at the monument at the top of a hill, two miles from the camp. It had been built to commemorate the massacre of some Catholic priests by Indians in 1680. The view of distant snowy fields shining in the morning sun was really beautiful. We remained there for a half-hour before we made our way back, this time taking a less hilly route. On our way back to the camp, we saw a tidy military graveyard, a very old Catholic church, and some adobe houses. The scenes along the roads were unforgettable. We arrived back at the camp at around 10:30 A.M. I was quite tired, but it was a very memorable trip.

Mr. De Amato, consul general of Spain in San Francisco, and Mr. Benin Hoff of the State Department visited the camp on December 23. They met with the internees and Mr. Jensen, our camp manager, at the Lower Town mess hall on the afternoon of the twenty-fourth. Consul General De Amato made a few introductory remarks. Mr. Tachibana, chief secretary, served as interpreter. The consul general responded to each of the various questions or requests posed by the internees. The primary concern, family cohabitation, elicited some scathing criticism directed at the authorities for their vague answers and waffling behavior.

The consul general told us that he had received word that family cohabitation of all internees would be complete within the next six months. A Mainland internee replied on behalf of all of us: "If the American government does not follow through on this matter by January 31 of next year, we will cease cooperating with the camp authorities. If anything unfortunate should happen as a result of this, it will be on the heads of the Americans." Mr. Jensen announced that, as a first step, nineteen internees from Hawaii would be sent to the family camp in Jerome.

Mr. Fujii, the assistant general manager, translated our spokesman's remark "by January 31 of next year" as "within a week" and "cease cooperating with the camp authorities" as "strike." His translation, in my opinion, was reckless. Mr. Hoff, who was with the American embassy in Tokyo and had returned to the United States on the first exchange ship, was fluent in Japanese. Although he kept silent throughout the meeting, he later pointed out Mr. Fujii's faulty translation to Mr. Jensen. When the issue of food was discussed, a box of shriveled apples that had been delivered to the mess hall was brought into the meeting as evidence. Mr. Jensen gave a bitter smile.

First Month's Snow at the Foot of the Rocky Mountains

On December 24, the day of our meeting with the consul general, the thermometer showed six degrees and it snowed eight inches. Fog began thickening the night before, so visibility was poor. In the morning the fog changed to hoarfrost. I imagined the hoarfrost at Unzen that I had heard so much about. As the sun gradually rose, the snow began to glisten. The beauty of the scene was beyond words. I took a solitary walk in the snow. As you can see, even incarcerated men have a taste for aesthetics. Icicles hung like shining swords from the eaves of the barracks. The lengthy ones measured five to six feet, as long as Chinese broadswords. When they glistened in the sun, they looked magnificent.

On December 27, three trucks bearing "luxury goods" from the Japanese Red Cross arrived at the camp. These were being sent to Japanese living in enemy countries. We received 3,294 casks of *shoyu,* 158 casks of *miso,* 23 boxes of medicine, 6 boxes containing musical instruments, and 5 boxes of books. Everything was to be distributed through the Japanese office. The *shoyu* bore the Kikkoman label. Two casks were allotted to each internee. I was grateful to have them, as well as the green tea that had been sent to us earlier.

New Year's Day, 1944, arrived covered in snow. This was my third New Year's Day as an internee. I got up at seven o'clock and changed my clothes. I offered a silent prayer facing east. At nine o'clock, the internees assembled in the open-air theater to bow in the direction of Japan. After a speech by General Manager Kondo, we gave three *banzai* cheers and sang the Japanese national anthem. The donations from the Japanese Red Cross were distributed that morning. I did not check the temperature at the time, but it was terribly cold. The ground was covered by a thin layer of ice, and a cold wind blew down from the Rocky Mountains. While standing in the open-air theater, we felt almost dizzy with cold. New Year's breakfast consisted of rice cakes boiled with vegetables. Lunch that day was the most lavish meal any of us had ever had since our internment: eleven dishes of chicken, fish, soup, and so on. It was a thoroughly satisfying New Year's celebration.

It snowed almost every day that January. On the fifth, large snowflakes fell. The morning temperature was three degrees below freezing. On the seventh, we had the heaviest snowfall ever. The snow was so powdery it resembled smoke. On the morning of the eighth, the temperature dipped down to eight degrees below freezing. The slightly sloping road near the Upper Town mess hall caused many people to slip after a snowfall. Sometimes two or three people fell on top of each other. It was a very dangerous spot. Several men were hospitalized. I once sprained my wrist after taking a tumble, but luckily I did not suffer a fracture and my wrist soon healed.

On the morning of January 17, I gave a lecture entitled "My Thoughts on the Arms Reduction Talks in Washington" to Mr. Gongoro Nakamura's English class at his request. Mr. Nakamura had been a Washington correspondent for a Japanese magazine when the war broke out. After my lecture, we became friendly and went for a walk in the snow. Our conversation could have gone on and on, as he knew one of my relatives, Mr. Gunji Hosono, and Mr. Kilso Han, an anti-Japanese Korean. The night before there had been another mysterious announcement that the Japanese had attacked Pearl Harbor again and the upper side of Kaimuki had been completely destroyed. The source of this news apparently was a man from Hawaii. I was very annoyed.

On January 28 news spread that the Japanese army had massacred American POWs at Bataan and Corregidor two years earlier. The same news was simultaneously announced by Mr. A. Eden, the British foreign secretary. Many Americans became angry and there was talk that all Japanese should be shot on sight. The managers of relocation centers took measures to tighten security. That night the number of inspections more than doubled at our camp. It was a strange night.

Internees Moved Again

Some internees were screened and paroled or were permitted to go to family camps in October. Mainland internees were the first to go, then those from Alaska. Hawaii men were among the last. Mr. Hibutsu Murai (October 26), an Alaskan group including Mr. Kyosuke Yasui (December 3), Mr. Hisanori Kano (December 4), Mr. Ten-yo Yasaki (December 18), and Mr. Takeshi Ban (December 22) were all paroled on the dates indicated.

The tenth (and last) group of twenty-nine Hawaii internees, who had been waiting at Sharp Park for about a month, arrived at Santa Fe on January 9, 1944. Messrs. Kenju Otomo, Shinpuku Gima, Ichiro Deki, and Tomizo Tanigawa were among them. When this group left Hawaii, there were 150 Japanese Americans and more than 10 Issei at Honouliuli Camp. Twenty-one Japanese POWs (including four commissioned officers) had sailed with them to San Francisco.

Many Hawaii internees who had requested cohabitation with families already on the Mainland for more than a year visited the authorities on January 12 and demanded that their requests be expedited. A list was distributed on the eighteenth and received with much cheering. Although the dates were not fixed, some were to be sent to Tule Lake and others to Crystal City. As onlookers, we had sympathized with these men who had endured long delays and difficulties, so the good news lifted our spirits too, to some degree. More delays followed, however, until March 4 when the following people were temporarily paroled and left for Jerome (and eventually Tule Lake): Messrs. Keizo Miura, Sensho Hida, and Hiseki Miyazaki and five others; sixteen Hawaii men and one from the Mainland, including Messrs. Kyojyo Naito, Seikaku Takesono, Ryugen Matsuda, Tameshige Sueoka, Takahiko Chinen, Tsuruzo Hasegawa, and Yoshio Takahata (March 15); Messrs. Tokuji Adachi, Unji Hirayama, Minoru Nakano, Gijo Ozawa, Sei Odate, Tetsuou Tanaka, Muin Ozaki, Kouzan Nishizawa, Toraki Kimura, Gen-ei Miyagi, and about thirty others (March 23).

The parolee list of 162 internees from the Mainland was announced on January 13. Thirty people, including Messrs. Kenji Kasai, Hiroshi Suzuki, and Kenko Yamashita, left for the family camp in Crystal City on January 20, and twelve people, including Messrs. Gongoro Nakamura, Miryo Fukuda, and Toyoji Abe, also left for Crystal City on January 16. A list of forty-seven parolees from the Mainland was announced on January 27. More than fifty Mainlanders, including Mr. Shingetsu Akaboshi, left for Tule Lake on February 7. Mr. Shigehiko Nagaoka left for Jerome on February 10. Mr. Takuritsu Morita left for Hunt, Idaho, that same day. Mr. Tetsusho Matsumoto was scheduled to leave for Tule Lake, but due to an illness in his family, he was sent to Hunt temporarily, also on the tenth. Disturbing reports from Tule Lake were circulating at the time: Apparently tanks were patrolling the camp because of heated disputes between authorities and internees.

While we were at Lordsburg, we had heard that the parents of U.S. soldiers would be released. On February 17, a list was posted. Those from Hawaii could not return home, but they could travel anywhere in the free zone (anywhere in the United States other than the West Coast) or apply for entry to relocation centers. The authorities guaranteed their safety. They could also stay where they were if they wished. Twelve internees from New York arrived on February 20.

Third-Grade Kendo Expert versus Third-Grade Judo Expert

At the end of November, in the midst of all the moving and the influenza epidemic, Mr. Miryo Fukuda, a judo master, threw Mr. Seigo Takai to the ground. No one knew the reason for the altercation. It occurred just after a thaw, so Mr. Takai was covered in mud. Both men were barracks chiefs and from the Mainland. Fifty-year-old Mr. Fukuda, a large man and an ultranationalist, held the impressive title of Konko-kyo (Golden Light Religion) North America Mission Superintendent, and claimed to be a third-grade judo expert. He agitated the general public with his rousing argument that all Japanese in the United States should move to the Co-prosperity Sphere in the South Pacific after the war. Sixty-year-old Mr. Takai, a third-grade kendo (Japanese fencing) expert who was still full of fighting spirit, always competed against younger men in camp sumo matches. Surprisingly enough, he was also an officer in a Christian organization within the camp. When the Shintoist threw the Christian to the ground, elderly observer Mr. Imamura, who was driven to tears, bitterly chastised them, saying "How can religious leaders indulge in such behavior? It's abominable."

For the next two months, Mr. Takai nursed a grudge against Mr. Fukuda. Then, on the night of January 26, the evening before Mr. Fukuda's departure for Crystal City, Mr. Takai took his revenge. Carrying two kendo sticks, he charged into Mr. Fukuda's barracks, handed one to the judo master, and challenged him to fight. Once outside, the judo expert suddenly grabbed the arm of the kendo expert with one hand and began hitting his opponent over the head repeatedly with the other. Finally other people intervened and the fight ended. The kendo expert had gone in for wool but had come out shorn himself. He should have known better and acted his age. To be quite honest, Mr. Fukuda was something of a troublemaker at Santa Fe Camp. After he was moved to Crystal City, however, I heard that he behaved himself and became a different person. If elderly Mr. Iwamura had witnessed this second battle between the Christian and the Shintoist, he would no doubt have shed even more tears and lamented, "The end of the world is coming!"

It snowed heavily again on the night of February 25. On the twenty-ninth, forty-six men left for Crystal City in three trucks. They were accompanied by a smaller truck for the sick, with the chief nurse of the hospital in attendance. Messrs. Kumemaro Uno, Hyoroku Oishi, Kiyoshi Ishikawa, Kaichiro Yasutake, Shichitaro Fujii, Tsutomu Jo, Kumao Goketsu, and Yoshio Tagashira were among them and many of us saw them off. That night, Mr. Motomu Kanbara of Sacramento left for Heart Mountain.

Surprisingly the weather changed every two or three days. On March 1, it was too warm for an overcoat, but four days later it turned very cold and windy. We had a big sandstorm on March 14. The internee population as of March 10 was 1,061.

The Nisei Issue

Mrs. Yonako Abiko, president of the *Nichibei Shinbun* (Japan America News) in San Francisco, passed away in Philadelphia on March 4, 1944. A memorial service was held by her old friends in the east classroom on March 17. Rev. Shuntaro Ikezawa began the service. After a sermon by Rev. Tamasaku Watanabe, Mr. Shigeru Nagata served as master of ceremonies and memorial addresses were given by Messrs. Shoichi Nonaka, Toyosaku Komai, Ichikuro Kondo, and me. The service ended with a speech of appreciation by Mr. Akisuke Iseda. Born in 1880, Mrs. Abiko was the younger sister of Miss Umeko Tsuda. Her death at the age of sixty-three was due to breast cancer. She had been a great help to her husband, Mr. Kyutaro Abiko, a businessman. She was a wise and perceptive wife. We all missed her.

On March 18 in the east classroom I heard a lecture, "Nisei and the Geneva Convention," given by Mr. Sei Fujii, *Kashu Mainichi* (California Daily News) president. He referred to the pending court case of George Fujii, a young detainee at Poston Relocation Center who was charged with draft evasion and sabotage. The lecturer revealed the contents of the young man's letter justifying his conduct, which was sent to the Spanish consul at the request of the young man's father. The basic argument was that, unlike other second-generation Americans with blood ties to enemy countries, Japanese Americans suffered the same treatment as Issei Japanese, many of whom were not U.S. citizens. By subjecting its own people to unwarranted curfews and evacuation, the United States had violated its constitution and had no right to conscript Japanese Americans. Thus, if a Nisei refused to be drafted, he could not be charged with sabotage.

Because the topic was of interest to all of us, the classroom was full that day. Mr. Fujii's remarks elicited enthusiastic applause. Although he was an old acquaintance of mine, I was quite disappointed with his lecture. The government might be violating constitutional law, but this did not sanction similar conduct by Japanese Americans. The young man's letter could be used in considering extenuating circumstances, but his argument could not serve as a rule of thumb for Japanese Americans and their Issei parents. Worse, I believed it would be misleading and would only raise false hopes.

A request to return to Hawaii signed by 267 internees was presented to the authorities. I saw a copy of this document. The oldest internees to sign were Mr. Kinai Ikuma and Mr. Hanzo Shimoda, both seventy-two years of age, and the youngest was thirty-two-year-old Mr. Haruo Koike. Mr. Tachibana, his father-in-law Mr. Kobayashi, and several others were sent to Tule Lake Camp on March 27. Some Hawaii internees who had applied for cohabitation had their requests denied for unknown reasons and were ordered to remain at Santa Fe. By then most of the prominent men had left the camp. Just as we began to feel lonesome, 223 internees from Missoula arrived early on the morning of April 6. Among them were many old friends from Sand Island whom we had not seen in two and a half years, so it was an emotional reunion. Most were from Honolulu and Oahu: Messrs. Minoru Murakami, Kumaji Furuya, Daizo Sumida, Totaro Matsui, Torao Iseri, Itsuo Hamada, and Mankichi Goto, and the Reverends Masahiro Himeno, Kametaro Maeda, and Gendo Okawa. We spent some time exchanging stories, and the camp regained its liveliness. About three months later, seventeen internees (including Messrs. Joei Oi, Saichiro Kubota, Shoho Fujiie, and Iwaki Watanabe) who had stayed on at Missoula for business reasons arrived at Santa Fe. This group also included the men who had been sent to build roads in Kooskia.

Japanese and English Publications

The weather in the Santa Fe highlands changes as often as a chameleon changes the color of its skin. On the morning of April 9, clouds gathered. Suddenly strong winds followed by snow and hail spawned a sandstorm, and the day turned very cold. It forced us to cancel a festival in honor of Buddha's birthday, which was to have been held at the open-air theater that night. All the newcomers were surprised when the bad weather persisted. On April 12, Mr. Tetsuo Toyama, who had just arrived from Missoula, and several others (including Mr. Meijiro Hayashi) were paroled and left for Jerome. On the thirteenth, thirty-one internees, among them Messrs. Kamekichi Sasaki, Shinkichi Miyoshi, Motosuke Tsuita, and Shiro Koike, departed for Crystal City. The seven ringleaders of the "Tule Lake Incident" were brought to Santa Fe.[2] They were all from the Mainland; one of the two Nisei involved was the son of the Reverend Shisei Todoroki. The seven were separated and taken to the Upper Town barracks. Around that time, the only plum tree in the camp began to bloom, bringing back fond memories of home.

There were fifteen of our *Nippu Jiji* employees interned at Santa Fe, so our general manager, Mr. Kawamoto, invited all of them to a private gathering. Mr. Isomura, a cook, prepared chicken, sea bass *sashimi,* and tofu dishes. A small amount of liquor was somehow smuggled in and served. All of them spent an enjoyable evening. On the night of April 24, Mr. Keijiro Kawajiri and Mr. Taichi Tsuyuki, both ill, left the camp. On the morning of April 29, we held a solemn Shinto celebration in the square in honor of the emperor's birthday. During a broadcast we learned that Secretary of the Navy Knox had died of heart disease a day earlier, at the age of seventy.

At the end of the previous year, the Japanese Red Cross had sent us more than nine hundred books in Japanese, each of which had to be inspected by the authorities before we were allowed to see them. On May 15—half a year later—the books were finally displayed at the library, and from the eighteenth, they were available for borrowing. Within a day more than four hundred of them had been borrowed. All of the books were new, published from 1939 through 1943. Books on the war or current affairs were noticeably missing, but there were many good and recent titles on various subjects. We had been starving for books from Japan, so this collection was welcomed with indescribable nostalgia and appreciation. An extra

---

2. The Tule Lake camp became a "segregation center" in the fall of 1943, when the supposedly "disloyal" from the other War Relocation Authority administered camps were transferred there, while the "loyal" at Tule Lake were transferred to other camps. A great deal of turmoil took place at Tule Lake in the aftermath of these events. On November 4, 1943, a mass uprising took place (the "incident" referred to in the text) over a labor dispute, and the army was called in to restore order. Tule Lake remained under martial law from November 1943 to January 1944. See Michi Weglyn, *Years of Infamy: The Untold Story of America's Concentration Camps* (New York: Morrow, 1976), and Donald E. Collins, *Native American Aliens: Disloyalty and the Renunciation of Citizenship by Japanese Americans during World War II* (Westport, Conn.: Greenwood Press, 1985).

bonus was that we would be able to enjoy the latest publications not read-ily available outside Japan. The library was amply stocked with American books in response to our requests, but with the arrival of these books from Japan the librarians were suddenly very busy. In Japan there was a short-age of paper and other goods, so the printing and binding of the books we were sent were very poor. In contrast, I could see the extravagance in American publications despite strict rationing of materials. This clearly demonstrated the difference between the two economies during the war.

There was a fine farewell party on the night of June 3 for the Reverend Kametaro Maeda, who was scheduled to leave the camp soon. That day Mr. Watanabe, a fisherman from Terminal Island in southern California, fainted and died of a stroke while at a *go* club meeting. It seemed that home-brewed *sake,* which of course was prohibited in the camp, had played a big part in his misfortune. On the night of June 6, Rev. Maeda and Mr. Yazo Sato left the camp for the Amache Relocation Center and Denver, respectively. That was also the day the second European front opened.

It was time for our yearly physical examination. I was given a clean bill of health; my blood pressure was 154 over 92. On the afternoon of June 7, thunder and hail the size of big marbles fell, turning the ground white. Many horned toads that had been kept as pets in boxes outdoors were killed. A young man, Mr. Imahashi, caught a three-foot-long rattlesnake at the golf course. It had eight rattles and matched the color of its surround-ings so perfectly that we could not easily tell where it was when we placed it on the sand.

A Ray of Hope for Internees from Hawaii

It was the latter half of 1944 when Hawaii internees with sons in the U.S. military were paroled, on the condition that they would remain on the Mainland. Other internees had no hope of being paroled for the rest of the war, and no one could say how long that would be. This was the great-est cause of anxiety and frustration for internees. On June 13 Mr. Daizo Sumida received a letter from his wife revealing the possibility of parole for fathers whose sons were not in the military. It was based on a statement made by a Swedish Embassy representative, and it gave us a glimmer of hope for the first time.

On June 17, when the daytime temperature shot up to ninety degrees, Mr. William Hill, a Hawaii senator who was on his way home from the Republican Party Convention, met with internees from the Big Island. He took pictures along with them and paid them compliments, playing the shrewd politician as expected. On June 20, Miss Hoyler, an evangelist from Missoula, delivered a sermon in Japanese in the Upper Town mess hall in the afternoon. Having lived in Japan for many years, she was fluent in the language. She spoke like a true fundamentalist, but she had a warm personality. Mr. Thomas Taro Higa was our next visitor. He had been a student of Mr. Sasaki, a Windward Oahu school principal, and was returning home from the Italian front after being injured. He told us about various battles and the activities of Japanese American soldiers abroad. Although he spoke with a heavy Okinawan accent, his talk was very interesting.

This was an election year. At the Republican Party Convention in Chicago on June 27, presidential nominee General Douglas MacArthur received only one vote; the rest went to his rival, Thomas Dewey, the forty-three-year-old governor of New York. Mr. Bricker, governor of Ohio, was chosen as the vice-presidential candidate. The convention ended a day early, so Dewey gave his acceptance speech at eight o'clock on the evening of the twenty-eighth. I listened to his energetic thirty-five minute speech, delivered over the radio amid much cheering, at Mr. Kango Kawasaki's barracks. I listened to President Roosevelt's acceptance speech (his fourth) nearly a month later on the same radio. Looking at the pictures in the newspapers, I thought the president appeared haggard. But that night he delivered a powerful and dignified speech. Although it was short, it was far superior to Mr. Dewey's.

Seventeen more internees arrived from Tule Lake on July 1, again as a result of disturbances there. Mr. Tasaku Hitomi, a businessman from Sacramento whom I had met at Lordsburg, was seriously injured when he was mistaken for his brother and assaulted with a hammer. While these stories surprised me, I was truly shocked when a newspaper cable reported that someone had murdered Mr. Hitomi's brother four days after the attack. The perpetrator was never found. It was a messy and complicated affair, and both internees and the authorities were responsible for the tragic outcome.

A *Bon* Dance, a Picture Exhibition, and Sumo Tournament

The thermometer climbed up to ninety-two degrees on July 7, although morning and evening temperatures were comfortable. Mr. William Heen, a Hawaii senator in the territorial legislature who was on his way to the Democratic Party Convention, came to see Mr. Matsujiro Otani, president of Aala Market. According to Mr. Heen, Honolulu business enterprises of all types were doing unexpectedly well. Even Mr. P. Y. Chong's chop suey restaurant was crowded with customers.

According to the Japanese office, a review of every Hawaii internee's case would be conducted sometime in the near future. A Buddhist *bon* service was held on July 15 at the open-air theater. Unfortunately it rained, but the service went on as scheduled. As soon as the weather cleared, the *bon* dance began. It was like a scene in Honolulu before the war. Quite a few of the men dressed in women's costume, and the dance was a big success. Many beautiful *bon* lanterns were hung all around the theater. They had been made from the kegs of *shoyu* donated by the Japanese Red Cross. I was amazed at the ingenuity and dexterity of their makers. On July 20, I learned of the resignation of the Tojo cabinet during a broadcast.

An exhibition of internee artwork was held in the east classroom on July 22 and 23. About a hundred pastel drawings, watercolors, and oil paintings by students of Masao Ikeno were exhibited, along with about thirty Japanese-style paintings. It was a successful event. A meeting of exhibition committee members and exhibitors was held at the Lower Town mess hall the night of the twenty-third. Mr. Yoshinobu Sasaki, manager of the education department and committee chairman, addressed the meeting before the other attendees introduced themselves. Several dozen reactions placed in the comment box were read, and tea and cake were served. It was a fruitful meeting.

On the night of July 22, the Hawaii sumo team challenged the Mainland team in a tournament. Banners of popular sumo wrestlers and a standard sumo-wrestling ring were constructed. Rev. Kinai Ikuma, a Shinto priest, and Mr. Teizo Kimura, the referee, purified the ring. Mr. Hajime Nishimoto, who took pride in his strong voice, served as caller. The Hawaii team won more matches overall, but Mainland team members were awarded two of the three highest ranks: *sekiwake* (junior champion) and *ozeki* (champion). The tournament was a rousing success, but the festivities associated with the event were criticized by many internees as extravagant and out of place in light of their present situation.

On July 24 the liaison office informed us that our barracks, along with three shacks in the Lower Town, would be dismantled and sent to Crystal City to ease the housing shortage there. We were ordered to relocate the following day to a barracks of our choice, but we were not eager to leave; after all, we had just settled in, and most of the other barracks were overcrowded. After negotiations, we decided to borrow two rooms in the thirteenth barracks in Lower Town that had been reserved for a handicraft center. On the twenty-fifth, we cleaned the rooms, hung shelves, and moved luggage with help from friends. It took the entire day, and at the end we were completely exhausted. The thirteenth barracks was said to have once been a stable. It was a tasteless, dirty, and dilapidated barracks.

In the midst of the relocation commotion, we held a farewell party for General Manager Ichikuro Kondo on July 24 at the Lower Town mess hall. We presented him with a letter and gift of appreciation. Rev. Jodo Takahashi was the perfect master of ceremonies, and all were deeply touched by Mr. Kondo's thank-you speech. He left for Poston the next day. Mr. Matsujiro Otani was finally paroled and left for Amache on the night of July 25, but I was unable to see him off.

Two Hundred Internees Arrive from South America

Later that July, a Hawaii internee was caught shoplifting at the exchange store during a busy time. He had taken very little, but it created a problem because he was one of us. Our police department detained him for a while and checked his belongings. He became the talk of the town, and some of the Mainland internees were quick to condemn us in general. The fully repentant shoplifter mended his ways, and the matter was finally closed. In the past, Mainlanders had also been caught shoplifting, but their crimes were quickly covered up. Mr. Miyazaki, the longtime head of the police / fire department, was quite troubled by this incident and decided to bring in a few people to advise him. Mr. Yaemon Minami of California, Mr. Gikyo Kuchiba of Hawaii, and I were selected.

An election was held to appoint Mr. Kondo's successor as general manager. Mr. Totaro Matsui was elected but declined the position. On August 21, Mr. Katsuma Mukaida was elected and agreed to serve as our new general manager.

Sixteen internees from the Mainland, including Messrs. Yoshio Omae, Jodo Takahashi, Shisei Todoroki, and Sumio Arima, left for Crystal City on the morning of August 22. Two hundred and sixteen internees from Peru and Bolivia arrived at seven in the evening on August 23, 1944. They came from Kenedy Camp in Texas, where they had been held temporarily. Most of them were young Okinawans, and the camp grew lively again. They were all housed in the Lower Town barracks. The average number of internees per barracks now stood at forty-five. The newcomers reported that the temperature at Kenedy had been above a hundred degrees; they complained of not being able to sleep well here because of the cold.

The internees from South America brought many books from Kenedy and gave all of them to our library. In addition to a dozen books on music,

400 volumes were in Japanese, 171 in English, 150 in Spanish, 43 in German, and 2 in French. Many of these new additions pleased the book lovers among us. On the night of September 6, I saw the movie *Hawaii Calls,* starring Bobby Breen. The Hawaiian music was marvelous beyond words, and I was overcome by a wave of nostalgia.

Many internees needed dentures and spectacles. These were supplied by doctors in Santa Fe through the kind offices and at the expense of the authorities. Mr. Usaburo Katamoto served admirably as our liaison with the doctors. Because my reading glasses were no longer effective, I was taken on September 19 to an optician in the city along with several other internees also in need of glasses. The facility was well equipped and the optician very helpful. While in the city, I thought I would try to see as much as possible.

As I expected, Santa Fe was a small, quiet country town. There were many Mexicans, and their cultural influence could be seen everywhere. Santa Fe receives a large number of visitors from all over the United States, so the jewelry and dress shops offered a wide variety of goods, even more than the stores in Honolulu. The fashions and customs of the people on the street were quite different from what I was accustomed to seeing and they interested me greatly. I saw no Japanese except for one middle-aged lady, who kept looking at us with nostalgia.

The wife of the Reverend Masahiro Himeno of Honolulu came to Santa Fe with her cute baby on September 17 and stayed at a hotel in the city. She was scheduled to return to her parents in Amache on the twentieth. In the meantime, Mr. Himeno was paroled, but could not yet leave the camp. After suddenly receiving permission to do so by cable, he was packed up within half a day and left happily with his wife and baby. I suddenly felt lonely because I had lost a good friend in my barracks. Mr. Jensen had kindly arranged for Rev. Himeno's transfer. On the night of September 20, Messrs. Iwao Oyama, Taichi Takeoka, Shuichi Watanabe, and two others from the Mainland left to join their families at the Minidoka Relocation Center in Hunt, Idaho.

Paroles for Fathers of Nonmilitary Children

Toward the end of September, it got fairly cold and every barracks began to use their stoves. Our barracks began lighting them from the twenty-eighth. Although it looked easy, it was very difficult to do. The chore was not a problem for the Mainland internees, but we as a whole were not good at it. Apparently the trick was to get the coal to burn with consistency. That afternoon, the outcome of a sea battle near the Philippines was broadcast: Japan sank 1,008 American warships, including 18 key battleships, and shot down more than 2,000 airplanes. Its own losses amounted to 2 battleships and about 1,000 planes. Ecstatic over the news, we decided that night to present a show, which had already been postponed once before due to bad weather, to commemorate Japan's victory. Hastily arranged, the performance began at around eight and continued until eleven. It was favorably received. I cannot remember the first part of the show, but I do recall that "Kabuki Futaba Gunki" was not impressive except for the magnificent scenery and costumes. The finale was a comedy, "Erikin's Adopted Child," which was very light and witty.

The morning of September 29 was fairly warm but misty. The sky in the direction of old Santa Fe seemed covered in a black mist. On October 1, a rock exhibition was held in the east classroom under the sponsorship of the education department. With more than 120 exhibitors and more than 500 items, the show was a success. Generally speaking, Santa Fe rocks, especially fossils, are far superior to those in Missoula.

As of this day, Mr. Shoichi Furukawa of Lima was appointed chef of the Upper Town mess hall. (The chefs of the two mess halls rotated every two weeks.) When the war started, he was working for a rich family. After he was interned at Santa Fe, his former employer sent him a large sum of money as a token of sympathy and support. Before that he had been employed as a cook at the Japanese legation in Lima for many years. Talented and personable, Mr. Furukawa could prepare unusual dishes using whatever was at hand. It was a pity that his skills were not appreciated among certain envious cooks and many country folk with simple tastes.

On October 2, 1944, the distant Rocky Mountains were covered in snow.

At the end of September, we received the sad news that Mr. Hachiro Kishi, one of my friends in Honolulu, had died of stomach cancer earlier that month. A memorial service was held on the night of October 3 in the east classroom with more than forty friends in attendance. Rev. Ikezawa led the service, Rev. Kondo read from the Bible, Rev. Okamoto offered a prayer, Mr. Daizo Sumida read a personal history of the deceased, I gave a eulogy, Rev. Sugimoto gave a sermon, Rev. Watanabe offered another prayer, and Mr. Hatsuichi Toishikawa spoke on behalf of Mr. Kishi's family. Afterward, we had a picture taken. It was a fine service.

About that time parole notices began arriving for Hawaii internees with sons in the military. On October 7, Drs. Jiro Yoshizawa and Yokichi Uehara became the first Hawaii internees to receive parole notices although their sons were not soldiers. Dr. Yoshizawa said he would not leave the camp unless he could return to Hawaii, and Dr. Uehara replied that he had to give the matter some thought. A memorial service for Mr. Mitsuru Toyama, a member of the Kokuryu-kai, was held in the Upper Town mess hall on the night of October 10. The Kokuryu-kai was very active in the United States, and many of its members were interned. The authorities were watchful that evening.

A Stone Expert and a Mountain of Fossils

I mentioned earlier that many beautiful stones were on display at a camp exhibition in October and that the show was a big success. Soon afterward many internees began picking up stones around the camp and grinding them patiently with sandpaper, whetstones, or files. One man, who had practiced law and was a scholar of English grammar, was an especially avid stone grinder, working silently at his hobby every day. There was a doctor who was equally enthusiastic; everyone referred to him as "the doctor true to his name." [The doctor's name (not mentioned) could have had "ishi" or "ishiya" contained within it, for example, Ishida, Ishiyama, or Oishi. "Ishi" is doctor, but if written as "ishiya," it can also mean stonecutter.]

Santa Fe Camp had its own stone expert. This man also claimed to know a lot about movies because he had lived in Hollywood for many years. I think he knew more about stones. When he opened his mouth, he sounded like a professor of geology. He talked about glacial epochs and a place in Colorado where, if you buried something for a while, it would turn into a fossil. It sounded like some kind of wizardry and was very interesting. Elderly Mr. Iso had a fossil that looked like a lumpy yam, but nobody could tell what it really was. He showed it to the stone expert, who identified it as an 800,000-year-old fossilized cow's liver, scientific name such-and-such, and definitely a museum item. The old man was so pleased that he put it up on a shelf with his family gods. News of the treasure spread, and soon many people began dropping by for a look. Eventually Mr. Iso wrapped it up carefully and placed it in a trunk. The fossilized liver must now be hidden somewhere in his house in Honolulu, a precious family heirloom.

The stone expert became quite a celebrity after that. The manager of the education department, Mr. Yoshio Koike, set up a special class with the expert as lecturer. Many collectors brought their stones to him for his appraisal. Someone brought him a beautiful piece of jasper on a ring. According to the man, he had found it on a nearby mountain and ground it himself. The expert looked at it for a while and replied that the jasper was splendid, was at least twenty thousand years old, and had the scientific name such-and-such. It turned out that this blue stone was part of the celluloid handle of a toothbrush. After this experience, the stone expert became very wary.

Eleven thousand feet above sea level, or four thousand feet higher than the camp, there was a two-mile-square piece of land owned by a man called Mr. Sweetland. Located about thirty miles from Santa Fe, it was home to a fossil museum and of course many fossils. One day several internees received permission to travel there and purchased twelve hundred pounds of fossils at ten cents a pound. Mr. Sweetland was very happy because he received more than a hundred dollars in the sale. Those who visited the place told me they saw a large petrified tree, said to be a "bamboo tree," 275 feet high with joints every 5 feet or so. The tree rings revealed its age: 850 million years old. The only two living bamboo trees known to exist are in China and South America.

Every Man a Golfer

Twelve miles from Santa Fe Camp was a municipal golf course. The land on which it was built (255 acres) had been donated by Mr. C. C. Catland, a wealthy landowner, lawyer, and former member of the U.S. House of Representatives who apparently was "King of the Castle" in New Mexico. Because of the shortage of manpower during the war, the links had fallen into disrepair. The club owner contacted the camp and made an agreement with several internee golfers: If they agreed to take care of the links, they could use the course for half a day. This arrangement was made chiefly through the kind offices of Mr. Hatsuichi Toishikawa. He was apparently a good *aikane* (Hawaiian for "friend") of Mr. Catland and got along well with the members of the club, so everything went smoothly.

On October 9, 1944, Messrs. Matsui, Isomura, Kawamoto, and I joined the regular team of groundskeepers/golfers. The twelve of us went in two cars and spent the entire day free of barbed wire and guards. For the non-golfers, who went through the motions of helping with the grounds maintenance, the outing was like a picnic. The lunch we brought with us was a feast, and for the first time in a long time we drank mugs brimming with Budweiser, which was sold at the clubhouse. I enjoyed myself tremendously.

In the wintertime, the links are sprayed with chemicals to keep the coyotes from eating up all the grass. Once this happens, the golfers must wait a long time for it to grow back. Speaking of coyotes, they are said to appear in packs at the beginning of November. As long as they have something else to eat, they will not attack people, but come midwinter when their prey is scarce, they become dangerous to humans. Once in a while, a wolf joins a pack of coyotes. If a hunter kills the wolf, the coyotes will eat it bone and all before the hunter can skin it. Coyotes are basically timid and shy away from humans. What is frightening is that if a man slips and falls, they will attack and eat him.

At Lordsburg there were quite a few beginning golfers, but at Santa Fe their numbers took a giant leap. This was all well and good, but the sudden popularity of the sport gave rise to blatant disregard for playing rules and proper etiquette, leading to many dangerous situations. The fact that we had relatively few accidents was a miracle. They may have been beginners, but many golfers owned top-quality clubs purchased as a military privilege from a golf club in Santa Fe. In time, a number of internees could be seen in fancy golf attire, toting expensive clubs.

Road Construction in Kooskia

Like Drs. Uehara and Yoshizawa, Mr. Shujiro Takakuwa was paroled without having any family members serving in the U.S. military. On October 13, my family informed me that they had applied to the provost marshal general for my parole. My case would be up for review again. Once paroled, Hawaii internees had to remain on the Mainland; they could not return to Hawaii until the war was over—and of course no one knew how long the war would last. The news from my family made me happy, and yet it seemed like a pipe dream. Mainland internees could join their families as soon as they were paroled. They did not have to worry as soon as they left the camp about the high cost of housing or making a living. This was the biggest obstacle for those of us from Hawaii facing parole.

It was announced on October 18 that Mr. Jensen would be leaving the camp to head the immigration office at Ellis Island, New York, and that Mr. William, the manager of Kenedy Camp, would succeed him. Twelve internees who had been in Kooskia, Idaho, for road construction work returned on October 19. Kooskia is located about four hundred miles from Missoula, a day's ride by truck. It is an exceptionally scenic spot, but it is lacking in amenities. About 150 Japanese internees helped to build roads for fifty-five dollars a month if they worked every day. But there was no work on Sundays or rainy days, so the most they could earn was about forty dollars. They contributed twenty dollars each to operate a canteen that sold luxury items, including beer. Gambling was fairly popular among the workers.

Some internees voiced strong opinions against working in Kooskia because they believed that the roads would be used by the military. This proved not to be the case. They were used primarily by hunters. Kooskia is a popular spot for deer hunting. According to an internee who returned from Kooskia, a fawn captured in the mountains by a Japanese can be domesticated, but in the case of a white hunter, try as he may, the fawn will simply run off. The internee surmised that centuries of hatred against brutal white hunters was ingrained in the minds of all young deer. What a frightening thought.

For several days prior to October 22, the broadcasts from Tokyo were full of reports stating that more than 80 percent of Japanese in America were helping the enemy and that these people would be dealt with accordingly after the war. Some announcers even hinted that internees were being paroled for their cooperation. Those who had just received their parole notices were seized with panic. Earlier, when short-handed fruit farmers in the area had appealed to camp authorities for workers to help with apple picking, some internees had expressed interest in the job. The broadcasts and the implication that they were collaborating with the enemy led to the sudden withdrawal of applications, and the uneasiness continued for a while. I was indifferent to such silly broadcasts.

On October 23, 1944, the newspapers reported that martial law had been lifted in Hawaii. For those of us from Hawaii, this was one of the most significant pieces of news we had heard since the war began.

Apple Picking

Apple picking was something of a novelty for Hawaii internees, so quite a few signed on out of curiosity. On October 24, several young men from my barracks applied. A number of apple farms were in the vicinity; these fellows were driven some fifty miles to a place called St. Petero, the farm farthest from the camp. They were greeted by scores of fruit trees, each one weighed down with perhaps two thousand apples. The view was magnificent. With no one to pick the apples, the fruit farmers had been resigned to the crop loss, so they welcomed the new laborers with open arms. For their part, the men found apple picking easy work; what's more, they could eat as many delicious apples as they liked, and they got paid three dollars a day. Thus the arrangement benefited both sides. In the morning the men, shivering with cold, sped out to the farm by truck at sixty miles an hour, and returned with freshly picked apples, which we all were able to enjoy. Golden Delicious apples were best. (Surprisingly, apple production in New Mexico rivals that of Oregon. Annual average production before the war was about 500,000 cases at $3.50 per case. Because of the wartime labor shortage, in 1944 production fell by 50 percent; in 1945 it was reduced to 150,000 cases.)

For some time internees had been soliciting donations for Japanese POWs. On October 25 we had about twelve hundred dollars. Considering the camp population at that time, I estimated that each internee on the average had donated one dollar. In November of last year (1943), we had collected $737 in cash in addition to gifts and books for Japanese POWs. General Manager Kawasaki had sent everything through the American Red Cross on November 24.

In October, Mr. Hikoichi Hara of Peru, originally from Hiroshima prefecture, had an appendectomy at the camp hospital. The operation was too late, however, and he died on October 27.

General Manager Katsuma Mukaida, Assistant General Manager Taka-ichi Saiki, Sports Department Manager Hatsuichi Toishikawa, and Baseball Department Manager Sawajiro Ozaki invited about 160 baseball team members and their supporters to a party in the Lower Town mess hall featuring the house specialty, *udon* noodles. This was probably the first big "banquet" held at the camp. The food was good, but there were no speeches from the organizers. It was a strange and boring party.

November 3, 1944, was a clear, cloudless, and unusually warm day. At nine in the morning, we celebrated the birth of Emperor Meiji at the open-air theater. Mr. Yoshio Koike served as master of ceremonies and General Manager Mukaida gave a speech. Every internee received an orange, and the total expense was said to be sixty-three dollars. In the afternoon, a baseball match between Lower Town and Upper Town was held, with strong cheering sections on both sides and good players among the young men from South America, which made for an enjoyable game. The dinner at the Upper Town mess hall that night featured an outstanding menu. Prepared by Chef Furukawa, it included clear soup, sashimi, a side dish, a vinegared dish, grated radish, tofu, festive red rice, and a cake decorated with the Rising Sun and the word "celebration." My understanding was that Mr. Furukawa had gone without sleep the night before, and I was truly humbled by his efforts and his determination to do his best in carrying out his responsibility.

Beer Is Sold behind Barbed Wire

The U.S. presidential election held on November 7, 1944, attracted world-wide attention. On the eighth, it was confirmed that President Roosevelt had been reelected. It would be his fourth term, an unprecedented feat in American history. We now felt that the United States would take it upon itself to end the war. On the afternoon of November 7, the Buddhist and Shinto federations sponsored a memorial service for soldiers of the Japanese Imperial Army and for internees who had died in this camp. It was held at the open-air theater, with the Reverend Kogan Yoshizumi officiating. Rev. Enryo Shigefuji of the Fresno Hongwanji Betsuin Mission suggested in his sermon that internees who had pledged loyalty to the United States and had been paroled were disloyal Japanese. Later he found himself in the same difficult position of being condemned when, ironically, he and his wife secretly applied for parole. Christians wanted to join the service, where they intended to pray for all of the war dead, but Buddhists and Shintoists insisted that only Japanese casualties be recognized, so there was no joint service. Even within our little barbed-wire world there were rigid divisions, strong divisive elements, and opposing views.

On the morning of November 9, the outdoor temperature was twenty-eight degrees. It had been very cold the previous night. The ground was covered with frost, but I went for a walk with friends as usual. We had our first snow at night on the eleventh but it did not pile up much. It got very cold on the fourteenth and fifteenth and snowed continually.

On November 12, I was at a calligraphy exhibition sponsored by the education department in the west classroom when a scatterbrained internee from Hawaii came running in, saying he had just heard on the radio that the Japanese air force had bombed Honolulu that morning. I thought this was more propaganda, but it made me uneasy. Of course there was no truth to the rumor. Messrs. Ryuten Kashiwa, Aisuke Kuniyuki, Hajime Nishimoto, and a few others were paroled and left for Amache on the fourteenth.

The sale of beer at the camp, which had been pending for some time, was finally approved by the authorities. At first the canteen sold small bottles for fifteen cents each, but later added bigger ones for twenty-plus cents. There were so many men loitering around the canteen that the authorities decided to turn Room A in the thirteenth barracks into a bar and stockroom and appointed a chief. This room was next to mine, so I was often annoyed by the noise, but I soon gave up trying to do anything about it. Roughly a quarter of the camp went there for drinks. Before the beer became available, rules were established: Internees could purchase one bottle of beer a day with a special ticket (distributed by the authorities) and only during specified business hours; the beer had to be consumed on the premises; drinking outside the bar was strictly prohibited. Of course these rules were difficult to enforce in this kind of place. There were frequent violations, and the bar was ordered to close for one or two days as a result. This happened again and again.

A radio broadcast reported that Mr. Polk Carter, my favorite news commentator, had died of a sudden illness in Hollywood, California, on the night of November 16 at the age of forty-six. This was very regrettable. Many people trusted and admired this British announcer, and his death was a sad loss to journalism.

Excludees and Going to Crystal City

Unexpectedly, dozens of Nisei internees from Hawaii were suddenly sent to Tule Lake, where they arrived around November 22. Among them were Mr. Shinsaburo Sumida and Mr. Takuzo Kawamoto, who sent word to their fathers here at Santa Fe. The new group at Tule Lake consisted of sixty-seven men, mainly Hawaii *Kibei* (Nisei who lived in Japan prior to returning to the United States). Among them were Mr. Sumida and Mr. Sakamoto of the Nisei Club, who were sent to the Mainland as internees and later returned to Hawaii; Mr. Shigeru Matsuzaka, a naturalized American; and other young men like Messrs. Shinagawa, Urata, Nishioka, and Uehara (eldest son of Masayoshi) who had been at Honouliuli Camp. All had been forced to go to the Mainland as "excludees." They boarded a ship in Honolulu on November 8 and arrived in Seattle on the nineteenth. They were immediately sent to Tule Lake Camp. Some of the younger wives, upon hearing of their husbands' being sent to the Mainland, asked to accompany them, but permission was never granted. A second group of sixty-seven excludees was sent to Tule Lake around April or May 1945, among whom was the younger brother of Mr. Uehara. At first the Hawaii excludees were kept apart from the other internees.

Around that time, the government began closing down the relocation centers. Only the Amache Camp in Colorado was still receiving internees, but that eventually stopped. Ten internees at Santa Fe, the fathers of soldiers, received parole notices on the condition that they remain on the Mainland, about which they all expressed dissatisfaction. The wives and children of Hawaii internees who had applied for cohabitation at Crystal City had already left for the Mainland. On November 22, Messrs. Totaro Matsui, Tokiji Takei, Shodo Kawamura, and others were notified that they would be joining their families at Crystal City within a month.

It snowed again on November 24. In the morning, I took a walk in the snow with Dr. U as usual. The roads were annoyingly slippery, but this was the best form of exercise for me. Later I spotted snow on the Rocky Mountains, shining in the evening sun and looking majestically sacred. Such grand scenery cannot be seen anywhere else.

The parolees going to Crystal City were to leave in early December. The Santa Fe Tanka Society had a farewell party for two departing members, Mr. Sojin Takei and Mr. Uemon Matsui, at our old office on the night of November 26. We had only noodles, rice crackers, and tea, but it was a pleasant party. On November 29, former Missoula internees and friends held a farewell party for Mr. Totaro Matsui at the Lower Town mess hall. It was a well-attended gathering of more than two hundred internees from Hawaii, the Mainland, and South America. Everyone was charged twenty-five cents; a small bottle of beer was served to each attendee. Mr. Minoru Murakami, one of the organizers, gave a farewell speech, and a fossil stone gift was presented to Mr. Matsui, who expressed his thanks. After an exchange of *banzai* cheers, the party ended.

On the night of December 2, former members of the Japanese Chamber of Commerce of Honolulu organized a farewell dinner for Mr. Totaro Matsui, Dr. Akio Kimura, Mr. Masaichi Kobayashi, and Mr. Shu Kato. Elderly Mr. "Chicken" Isomura prepared *kaiseki* dishes (a set menu served to guests on individual trays) using mess-hall trays. Of course beer was served. Mr. Kumaji Furuya[3] gave a farewell speech and Mr. Matsui expressed his appreciation. This was the most elegant farewell party held that week. On the evening of December 3, in the midst of steadily falling snow, I saw fourteen people (thirteen Hawaii men and one from the Mainland, Mr. Tsunematsu Kuwahara) leave for Crystal City. In addition to those mentioned above, Mr. Shinpuku Gima and Mr. Ichiro Deki were among those from Hawaii.

---

3. Kumaji Furuya, a furniture-store owner, was also one of those detained by the FBI on December 7, 1941, and spent his first night at the Immigration Station on Ala Moana Boulevard in Honolulu. He was among the first group of internees sent to a Mainland internment camp. Mr. Soga left on the fifth ship, so Mr. Furuya's experiences differed from those of Mr. Soga, until the two met in the Santa Fe camp. Mr. Furuya has also written of his camp experiences, and his book is in the process of being translated into English. He goes under the pen name of "Suikei."

The Third Anniversary of the Pearl Harbor Attack

Dr. Akio Kimura had been transferred to Crystal City, not because he had family waiting there, but because the camp had only a few doctors and Dr. and Mrs. Motokazu Mori were overwhelmed with patients. He had been practically forced to leave, so I felt sorry for him. We received news that Mr. Keijiro Kawajiri, a veteran correspondent in North America who had left for Hunt Relocation Camp because of illness, had passed away on November 26. He was seventy-seven years old. A memorial service was held on the night of December 2, but I could not attend it because of a previous engagement.

Sixty-six Hawaii internees who had come to the Mainland on the first ship and the thirty-plus "Internees of the Seventh" (those interned on December 7, 1941) got together to commemorate the third anniversary of the attack on Pearl Harbor at the Lower Town mess hall on the night of December 6. The attendance fee was thirty cents. We had handmade *soba* and beer. Other than Rev. Ninryo Nago's short speech, most of the time was spent reminiscing. We had a group photograph taken the next morning.

On the very cold night of December 9, Hongwanji priests in the camp held a memorial service for the Reverend Etatsu Takeda at the Lower Town mess hall. Led by Bishop Gikyo Kuchiba, it was attended by about twenty of his friends. On the same day three years earlier Rev. Takeda, a Nisei Hongwanji priest, had died while hospitalized for a serious illness. His death had been hastened by the shocking news of the Pearl Harbor attack. Because of the confusing times, his funeral had been a very simple one.

Real winter finally arrived—always a difficult time for those of us from Hawaii. At six o'clock on the morning of December 11, the temperature in the barracks was fifty-one degrees; outdoors it was ten degrees. That night at a certain Lower Town barracks, a well-known "boss" from Hilo and several of his henchmen somehow got their hands on four cases of beer, got drunk, and went on a rampage, attacking a minister and the chief of their barracks. Everyone in the barracks then turned on the boss and began beating him. The boss took out a knife and ran about wildly. Finally he was overpowered by several guards. The troublemakers were locked up in the temporary detention room next to the supervisor's office for several days. When they were allowed to return to their barracks, the residents barred their entry and refused to let them in. The authorities finally decided to put them in the only vacant shack, a space where "special" people were kept.

A right-wing youth group called Shichisho-kai (literally "Club of Seven Lives") held its first meeting in the east classroom on the night of December 12. I decided to attend. At the meeting, young people seated themselves in groups and roll was taken. Then they all stood up and chanted in unison: "We are the loyal subjects of the Emperor. We are determined to be reborn seven times and serve our country." After that Rev. Dojun Ochi talked about the great history of Japan, beginning with the Meiji era and going back in time. It was very interesting. The leader of Shichisho-kai was apparently a man from Tule Lake.

Mr. Kan-ichi Niitomi, a blind evangelist who had once visited Hawaii, came to visit acquaintances on December 16. On the morning and afternoon of the seventeenth, a Sunday, he delivered a fervent speech entitled "Christianity and My Experience," which greatly impressed us. Although he was almost blind and deaf, he was surprisingly full of life. I later learned that he had sent postcards to the families of those internees he had visited at Santa Fe.

On the night of December 18, I observed an extraordinary phenomenon in the sky: Venus appeared very near the crescent moon.

Shaven Youths Arrive

Mr. Ryuten Kashiwa, who had just moved to the Amache Relocation Center, received word that his wife had suddenly died of heart failure on the afternoon of December 13. Upon hearing this sad news, Hongwanji ministers arranged a memorial service for her a few days later. The Reverend Deme was master of ceremonies and Bishop Kuchiba and the Reverend Fujitani delivered sermons. Many of Mr. Kashiwa's friends attended. Bishop Kuchiba spoke with tears in his eyes. Only one other Hawaii man lost his spouse while he was interned: Mr. Koichi Iida's wife passed away while her husband was at Missoula Camp.

October 22, 1944, was the eleventh birthday of the crown prince of Japan. According to radio news from Japan, Her Imperial Majesty, the Empress, had arranged for candy to be sent to pupils and teachers all over Japan and made a ¥240,000 contribution through the International Red Cross to Japanese students living in enemy countries (including Australia). The crown prince was a fifth-grader at Gakushuin and was especially interested in airplanes.

Christmas mass at Santa Fe was held in the east classroom on December 24 and the Reverend Ikezawa's sermon was very good. On Christmas Day, snow from the previous night was piled six inches high. A dense fog made visibility poor. Hoarfrost on trees shimmered like jewelry and was beautiful to behold. In the morning, I took a walk with friends on the snowy road. Jacky, our mascot, came with us. He was a big German shepherd and quite partial to Japanese. He would bark with intensity at any Caucasian who entered the camp, which I thought was interesting (it seemed as if Jacky was protecting the Japanese from the Americans on American soil), but whether it was a guard or an official I felt sorry for that person.

That day on my usual walk I wore a brand-new pair of snowshoes I had ordered through the canteen. They worked well, in that I did not slip and they kept my feet warm. A year-end party organized by Masao Ikeno's painting class was attended by about fifty people, including myself, a former student. In the evening, the distant dome of a government building in Santa Fe was illuminated. My fourth Christmas as an internee passed quietly. On the twenty-sixth, it snowed again. The road was very dangerous. In the evening, I took a stroll alone in Upper Town.

A new theater with a seating capacity of six hundred was almost complete at the entrance to Lower Town. The authorities decided to move the stage from the open-air theater to the new one. Mr. Yamagata, a ship's carpenter from San Pedro, volunteered to head the effort. He devised a machine capable of moving a house and enlisted the support of the young people of Shichisho-kai. Together they worked all day on December 28 and succeeded in pulling the five-ton stage over a ditch with a steep slope, thanks to Chief Yamagata's untiring efforts. The newly arrived camp manager, Mr. William, watched the moving operations with admiration.

On December 30, all of us carried out a general cleaning of our barracks. In the afternoon, seventy internees arrived from Tule Lake, most of them young and all with their heads shaven. They were carefully checked at the Upper Town mess hall under the supervision of many guards and soldiers and were separated into different barracks in Upper Town. It was an elaborate operation. We later learned that they were all members of Seinendan Hoko-kai (Youth Group Service Association) and were regarded as extremists. Many were *Kibei* who had been taken from their families and sent to camps.

Two Seinendan Hoko-kai members were from Hawaii: a son of Rev. Kyushichi Hayashi and an Okinawan minister, Rev. Kenjitsu Tsuha of Ewa. The newly married Rev. Tsuha had been dragged out of bed at midnight on the twenty-seventh and taken to a waiting train. Mr. Zenshiro Tachibana, a former general manager at our camp, was now back among us, this time with a shaven head and an imposing mustache. (This would be his third time at Santa Fe Camp.) These men seemed to be the leaders. On the very cold early morning of December 31, one day after their arrival, these association members were outside doing calisthenics in vocal unison. Later they used an old office without permission for a secret meeting. Their behavior was certainly disquieting.

Tule Lake

A rumor spread that more of these "shaven heads" would be arriving from Tule Lake. The reason for their transfer will become apparent once I explain the situation at the camp. There was constant trouble between authorities and internees and among the internees themselves at Tule Lake Camp. A young man, Mr. Okamoto, had been killed. The murder investigation was still in progress when a Nisei from Oregon beat up a guard in early June 1944. I think it was about this time that Mr. Jensen, the Santa Fe camp manager, had taken a five-day trip to Tule Lake regarding the transporting of a number of internees to Santa Fe. Upon his return he had commented that the trouble at Tule Lake would probably continue. When the time came for the actual transfer, the selected internees were given only an hour's notice, then hustled off nearly half-dressed. Mr. Jensen thought the action taken was shameful, but nothing could be done about it.

Among the internees at Tule Lake, two groups that were constantly at odds with one another were the pro-Japan or "disloyal" faction and the pro-American or "loyal" faction. Such a division in thinking could be found at any relocation center or camp, but it was especially serious at Tule Lake. The pro-Japan group set up a spy ring to gather information on those who were sympathetic to the United States. They infiltrated various groups, placing certain individuals under surveillance and using gatherings to collect information about their enemies. They selected faction members who were to take direct action against the enemy through extraordinary measures. If this proved unsuccessful, they planned to report the enemy to the Japanese government after the war. Once a person was identified as pro-American, they intimidated him by throwing human feces at his house or even boiled feces at the windows. Families were afraid of what others might think and quickly and quietly cleaned up the mess. In July 1944, after a certain Mr. Hitomi had been murdered, fear among the pro-American internees reached a panic stage. Thirteen families fled to a separate enclosed barracks, leaving everything behind. Some of the soldiers who were asked to retrieve their possessions were said to be in sympathy with the pro-Japan group, because when they went to collect one person's belongings, they asked, "Where's the dog's luggage?" [4]

The internee population of Tule Lake Camp was eighteen thousand in October 1944. There were many families, so the camp resembled a town in Japan. Because there were many young girls at the camp, romances blossomed. This, fanned by an uncertain future, led to rash and impulsive behavior. Forty to fifty babies were born every month. Japanese-language schools were not allowed at relocation centers, but there were seven at Tule Lake, two of which were specifically named First National School and Second National School. Mr. Tokuji Adachi was a principal at one of the schools.

The Agony of Japanese American Soldiers and *Kibei*

Tule Lake Camp measured about a mile and a half on its northwest side and a mile on its northeast side. Seventy-four barracks housed two to four hundred people each. There was an administration office, hospital, schools, police station, fire station, post office, immigration office, baseball field, shops, warehouse, and graveyard. In one corner of the camp was a military barracks. There were two reservoirs nearby with a railway running parallel to them. Tule Lake is in northern California, near Oregon, so the climate is pleasant, even in winter. The hospital facilities were good, like those of a university hospital. There were five doctors, white and Japanese, including Dr. Hashiba (a brain surgeon from the Mainland) and Dr. Kazuo Miyamoto from Hawaii. They were always shorthanded. Doctors and technicians were paid $19.00 per month, all others $16.00. Workers were given a stipend of $3.50 per month for clothing.

As I mentioned earlier, the conscription of Japanese Americans was a hotly debated and sensitive topic for Issei and Nisei. The following incidents took place at Tule Lake: The mother of a soldier tearfully begged her son to kill himself on the way to the front because it would be a disgrace

---

4. On May 24, 1944, Shoichi James Okamoto was shot to death by a guard at Tule Lake. Later, on July 2, 1944, Yaozo Hitomi, the manager of the Tule Lake co-op, was killed when his throat was slit with a knife. These events were symptomatic of the continued tensions at the camp between the various factions of the internee population and the camp administration. In order to defuse tensions, various "troublemakers" were transferred to Santa Fe over the next few months, as described by Soga. See Richard Drinnon, *Keeper of Concentration Camps: Dillon S. Myer and American Racism* (Berkeley: University of California Press, 1987), and the works by Weglyn and Collins cited in n. 2.

to their ancestors if he shot at the flag of the Rising Sun. The son answered that he would not kill himself but that he was among the three hundred Nisei soldiers who had pledged not to do battle in Japan. His mother was satisfied and let him go. In another instance, a commander wanted to send a Japanese American soldier fluent in both Japanese and English to Japan. He promised to pay him three times the usual salary. The young soldier asked the officer to consider his feelings and to send him anywhere but Japan. The commander was impressed by the young man's sincerity and agreed. These are just two instances in which the U.S. military considered and respected the feelings of Japanese American soldiers.

Internees at Tule Lake included four categories of Issei and Nisei—those who wanted to return to Japan, those who had refused to pledge their loyalty to the United States, those who were known to be disloyal at the time, and families of these men who requested cohabitation. There were about five to six thousand internees in each group. Not everyone at Tule Lake was disloyal or hostile to the United States, however. There were many whose classification had been determined by their responses to the formal questionnaire (Application for Leave Clearance). For example, when Issei were asked, "Will you pledge your loyalty to America or not?" they were often at a loss. It was an almost meaningless question for them, because they could not become U.S. citizens anyway. About 80 percent of Japanese at Tule Lake had sent their children to school in Japan or wanted to return to Japan themselves for family reasons—but they did not want to sever all ties with their second home, America. Most of the Nisei at Tule Lake had returned to the United States after being raised and educated in Japan. Not surprisingly, these *Kibei* could not get along in wartime America given their upbringing and education.

Given their situation, some of the Tule Lake internees openly expressed their discontent by shaving their heads and organizing the Sokuji Kikoku Hoshidan (Immediate Return to Japan Services) and the Hokokudan (Patriots Association). The first attracted mostly Issei, the second Nisei, and trouble erupted between the organizations on one side and the authorities and other internees on the other.

My Follow-up Interview Session

With the arrival of the "shaven heads" from Tule Lake, the atmosphere at Santa Fe Camp changed, becoming even more depressing than before.

January 1, 1945, was a fine and pleasant day. The thermometer held steady at nine degrees in the morning. It was my fourth New Year's Day as an internee. About nine hundred of us gathered at nine at the newly completed theater to bow solemnly in the direction of Japan. Mr. Shu Nakayama, manager of the education department, served as master of ceremonies and General Manager Mukaida gave a speech. Then, suddenly, the new group from Tule Lake pushed their way into the building and into the seats at the front of the theater. I thought their behavior was somewhat unruly. Mr. Langston, head of the liaison office, later prohibited the "shaven heads" from gathering as a group—even for calisthenics—and wearing insignia with words or messages like "patriotism" on their clothes. There were some fine young men among the new arrivals, but there were also some extremely impertinent ones. The Issei leaders in general were apparently at fault, judging by their lack of understanding as evidenced in their criticism of the Hawaii excludees sent to Tule Lake. No sooner had they arrived here, than these leaders began making disparaging comments about the Santa Fe internees in general.

On January 3, Santa Fe Camp, which had been called a "detention station," was redesignated an "alien internment camp." About a week later, by order of Mr. Ennis and Mr. Kelly in Washington, D.C., my parole application was reviewed by Mr. Morris, a camp immigration officer. He asked me about my life in Japan and Hawaii and my opinion of the war. I answered him as candidly as possible. I added that while I hoped to be paroled to Hawaii, I would consider parole on the Mainland. I was questioned as follows:

Q: Do you hope Japan will be defeated?
A: No. I am a Japanese citizen. I do not hope that Japan will be defeated. At the same time, as a permanent resident of the United States, I do not wish to see the United States defeated. Instead, I pray for peace between the two countries.
Q: Do you have any relations with Japan as a Japanese citizen?
A: I think I have certain legal obligations because I am a Japanese citizen.
Q: I retract the previous question and will ask you this instead: Do you have any reason to engage in hostile activities against the United States?
A: No.
Q: What do you think of Japan's policies?
A: I am fundamentally a liberal. I have often disagreed with Japan's policies, especially military ones, and have angered Japanese authorities several times. All of this was recorded in the newspaper I managed.
Q: Who do you think will win the war, Japan or the Allied Powers?
A: I do not know.

Q: Do you believe the information of the U.S. Wartime Intelligence Bureau?

A: I believe most but not all of it.

Q: Do you follow the progress of the war?

A: I think I follow it fairly closely.

Q: Do you wish to be paroled?

A: Yes.

Q: Have you applied for return to Japan?

A: No.

Q: Do you have any relatives among U.S. military personnel?

A: No.

Q: Do you have any assets in Japan?

A: No.

Q: Do you have any relatives in Japan?

A: Very few, but my wife has more.

Q: Did you correspond with these relatives?

A: Yes.

Q: Do you intend to go back to Hawaii?

A: Even if the war continues, I would like to go back.

Q: Do you intend to return to Japan for good?

A: No. Hawaii is my home.

At this point, the immigration officer asked sarcastically, "A Hawaii occupied by Japan?" He looked quite serious. I was somewhat offended and answered, "I have never thought of Hawaii being occupied by Japan." Sitting beside him, the young Spanish stenographer, Mary, giggled.

Snow, Snow, and More Snow

The Santa Fe authorities kept close watch on the Tule Lake group, who continued to do their calisthenics every morning without regard for the rest of us who were still asleep. The members of Shichisho-kai routinely held daybreak meetings on the seventh day of each month. Ostensibly they were meeting under the auspices of the Buddhist and Shinto federations, but that was just a subterfuge, and the authorities never suspected otherwise.

On the night of January 7, our Japanese culture class invited Mr. Ochi to tea. He gave us a special lecture on his experience of the 2–26 Incident, a military rebellion that took place in Tokyo on February 26–29, 1936, in which several government leaders were killed. From January 11 on, forty acres of hillside beyond the barbed wire-fence were made available to us.

The new theater was still without flooring, so four heaters were brought in—to no effect. Every week a very old movie was shown, but I always left in the middle because it was too cold. The no-smoking rules were never enforced, so the billowing cloud irritated my throat and also made viewing difficult. Worse yet, some men urinated in the theater. Throughout the United States, cigarettes were in short supply. From January 19, internees were no longer able to buy them by the carton; only two packs per person per day were allowed. Internees began hoarding cigarettes, so barracks chiefs were ordered to distribute them instead. We were all greatly upset when we heard about the murder in Hilo of the wife and daughter of Mr. Mitsuji Kasamoto, who had been sent to the East Coast. Airmail postage between the Mainland and Hawaii was lowered from twenty cents to fifteen cents.

Winter finally arrived. It began snowing from around January 17 or 18 and piling up on the twenty-first. At seven that morning the temperature stood at zero degrees; an hour later it was three degrees. There was an unusually heavy snowfall on the twenty-fourth. The next day Dr. U slipped and fell near the hospital while we were taking our evening stroll. The sight of the tall man falling on his rear was quite comical. It snowed and snowed all through the following morning and afternoon. Going for a walk was out of the question.

It snowed heavily again on the twenty-seventh. A dense fog obscured everything, but by evening the moon appeared especially clear. On the morning of the twenty-ninth, the temperature stood at ten degrees. Summoning up my courage, I took a walk, but it was piercing cold. It was very cold on the thirtieth. We stoked the stoves quite a bit the evening before, but the room would not warm up. The temperature in our barracks was zero degrees at 7:00 A.M., five degrees at 8:00 A.M., and nine degrees at 8:30 A.M. A half-hour later, the temperature suddenly shot up to thirty degrees. The morning of the thirty-first was also cold. The snow on the roads had frozen, and I could not go out for a walk. I felt I had had enough of Santa Fe snow.

On January 22, we received the sad news of the death of Mr. En ichi Saiki of Kauai, a former chemist at the camp hospital who had been ill. A memorial service for Mr. Itsuji Hamada, father of Mr. Itsuo Hamada, the Maui branch manager of my newspaper, was held on the afternoon of January 28.

One hundred and seventy additional internees arrived from Tule Lake on January 29. Most were young people, but among them were a few older men returning to Santa Fe: Rev. Unji Hirayama, Messrs. Shingetsu Akaboshi, Tetsu Tanaka, Seikaku Takezono, and Gikou Abiko. Young Mr. Ige, whom I had last seen at Sand Island, was also in the group. Around February 1 some public-spirited fellows began adding manure to the flower gardens that had been abandoned when the frost and snow arrived. The cooks were now making tofu, so the leftover soybean meal was also added to enrich the soil.

"Permission" to Return to Hawaii

An elderly man, Mr. Hanzo Shimoda, had applied for parole through his son in Honolulu. On January 24, 1945, he received from Lieutenant General Richardson an official letter dated eleven days earlier that said: "You have been paroled. You may return to Hawaii with the first group on the next available ship." This was the first letter of its kind to be sent to a Hawaii internee. We were all ecstatic, and for the next few days it was the main topic of our conversations.

On February 10, a cable arrived from the Justice Department in Washington, D.C., addressed to Messrs. Hanzo Shimoda, Teiichiro Maehara, Ryozo Izutsu, and Kichitaro Kouchi, fathers of U.S. soldiers. It said, "You may return to Hawaii on the next available ship together with family members interned on the Mainland." On February 11, a similar cable arrived for twenty-one internees, including Messrs. Tatsuo Ito, Hikohachi Onoye, Hikoju Otsuka, Tajiro Suzuki, Yonematsu Sugiura, Saichiro Kubota, Kumaji Furuya, Touichi Takada, Futoshi Ohama, Toraichi Kurakake, Mankichi Miura, Shinjiro Matayoshi, Chuji Torii, Hatsutaro Toyofuku, Gihei Tanada, Wasaburo Uranaka, Shinjiro Yoshimasu, Ushitaro Yonezaki, Makitaro Tamura, Katsuichi Tanaka, and Shigeji Terada. On February 13, the notification came for thirty men, including Messrs. Zeichi Fukunaga, Jinshichi Tokairin, Kodo Fujitani, Hozui Nakayama, and Kakichi Okamoto. All were fathers of U.S. soldiers except Mr. Kumaji Furuya, whose son had not yet joined the military. Mr. Hikohachi Onoye did not wish to return to Hawaii but asked instead to be sent to Japan.

The fifty or so internees who had received cables informing them of their return to Hawaii were walking on air for a while, thinking they would be leaving soon. However, even the camp authorities could not say when the next available ship would sail. The internees all began to grow impatient. It should be mentioned that not everyone who had a son in the military service had received a similar cable. As for the rest of us, we wondered if we would end up like the twelfth-century Buddhist priest, Rev. Shunkan—alone in a deserted penal colony on an island. Dr. Ryuichi Ipponsugi and I were granted parole on the Mainland on February 3.

Since the arrival of internees from Tule Lake, the population at Santa Fe had grown to 1,409. The Upper Town mess hall now served more than six hundred men. KP duty, which came around about once every two weeks, was a bit more demanding. Since coming to the Mainland, I had been excused from work because of my age, but at Santa Fe I volunteered to help in the kitchen, although I was more like a fly in the ointment.

I worked diligently at the task of handing out the silverware. Things could get quite hectic, but I somehow managed to do an adequate job. Everyone teased me, saying I could make a living at it on the outside. Sometimes I was given the task of cutting vegetables, but my fingers became stiff from the cold, and my fingertips hurt because of my lack of experience in using the knife. Scum from the potatoes and carrots also stained my fingers black. Although the job of cutting vegetables was for only three to four hours a day, I preferred my usual task of handing out knives, forks, and spoons three times a day.

Relations between Authorities and Tule Lake Group Worsen

Mr. Kelsey, an immigration supervisor, arrived at Santa Fe on February 13 and stayed for a few days. He came to discuss the construction of additional barracks. It seemed that more internees were going to be transferred from Tule Lake. It was also rumored that some of the fathers of U.S. soldiers would not be allowed to return to Hawaii.

At this time a play was performed for two nights under the sponsorship of the entertainment department. A table, cashbox, and even envelopes were set up at the entrance of the new theater to encourage donations. This kind of thing would not have been welcomed on the outside—and it was certainly resented by those of us behind barbed wire. Although the audience liked the play, they did not like being made to feel guilty. We all knew that the entertainment department was in need of money. It was later suggested that donations be solicited from each barracks to make up any difference not covered by the welfare fund subsidy.

A few internees had been canvassing to return to Hawaii as a group. They met on February 16, and Mr. Shigeo Shigenaga, an intermediary, made a lengthy progress report. According to him, Mr. Williams, the camp manager, told Mr. Kazuto Takeda, the assistant general manager, that those who had not yet applied for parole, whether they were fathers of U.S. soldiers or not, should apply directly to Mr. Kelly, the chief in Philadelphia. On the same day, a broadcast reported that fifteen hundred U.S. planes had initiated bombing raids on Tokyo, taking off from aircraft carriers three hundred miles away. On February 17, at the barracks managers' meeting it was reported that 22 internees had died in the camp since September 1944. Out of a population of 1,409, close to 900 internees [ca. 64 percent] had applied for repatriation to Japan.

A cold had left my voice completely hoarse. After visiting Dr. Kohatsu, I went to the canteen to buy some honey. I was told that the sale of rice and honey had been stopped because they had been used to brew sake. (I noticed that the sign "malted rice sold here" was no longer posted.) Of course brewing was banned, but people managed to make sake. Once in a while there was an informant and guards would suddenly appear, confiscating all the tools used for brewing and pouring whatever had been made down the drain.

A fellowship gathering of Big Island internees was held in a mess hall on the night of February 20, in the midst of a heavy snowfall. Of the 151 internees from the Big Island, 98 were at Santa Fe, and at the time 3 had passed away. I was told that for an attendance fee of one dollar, guests were treated to a sumptuous meal with two bottles of beer each.

Since the arrival of the Tule Lake internees, the volume of mail between our two camps had increased dramatically—as did the number of letters with contents that violated mail regulations. The mail inspectors were kept busy: Many letters had portions cut out, and some were returned. The resentful Tule Lake group sent the inspectors a threatening letter, allegedly written by the Kesshi-dan (Blood and Death Group.) One of the leaders of the Tule Lake gang, Mr. Wakayama, was summoned to Mr. Williams' office, causing the situation to deteriorate even further.

War and a Tragedy of Interracial Marriage

On February 22, we heard that twenty-one Japanese POWs detained at McCoy Military Barracks had committed suicide, but we could not tell whether this was true or not. On February 24, Mr. Takaichi Saiki and Mr. Sawajiro Ozawa were elected general manager and assistant general manager, respectively. On February 27, a newspaper reported that Mr. Hoshiro Mitsunaga, former president of Dentsu, Ltd., and a member of the House of Peers, had passed away at the age of seventy-eight. According to a broadcast that morning, the Japanese army was nearly defeated in a battle on Iwo Jima. Reports from Tokyo, however, reported a glorious Japanese victory, which caused an uproar in the camp. I could not tell which broadcasts to believe.

At the beginning of March, alopecia, a disease that causes baldness, began spreading in the camp. More than 120 internees, mostly from Tule Lake, were suddenly infected. There were no adequate provisions for disease control, so the doctors were thrown into confusion. The outbreak lasted for a while, so a temporary barbershop for patients was set up. Everyone was nervous, but the disease did not spread much further.

On March 5, a snowstorm developed in the afternoon. I was on KP duty when I heard that some six hundred internees had consumed seventy-five gallons of coffee earlier in the day. This coffee-in-name-only would be shunned in the outside world, but the cold weather made it especially popular in the morning. At the time, 293 internees were engaged in some kind of work at a daily wage of eighty cents; 102 internees were looking for work.

I was shocked to hear during an evening broadcast on March 5 that the only son of former Ambassador Kurusu and his American wife had died gallantly in a battle against American B-29s. According to an article in the *New York Times,* the young pilot had survived the crash landing, but farmers outside Tokyo mistook him for an American and clubbed him to death. The story moved me to tears and brought home to me the tragic impact of war on interracial marriages. The ambassador and I were old friends. Before the war, I had become acquainted with Mr. Kurusu at the residence of the consul general of Japan in Honolulu. One evening a memorable dinner was held there in honor of the ambassador, who was stopping over on his way to Washington. I thought of the grief-stricken ambassador's wife, whom I had seen many times, and deeply sympathized with her for her loss.

On March 5, before the arrival of more than a hundred more internees from Tule Lake, the authorities began assigning them to already over-crowded barracks. There were bitter complaints, but we could do nothing. Two days later, 125 men arrived. They went through a strict check under the heavy supervision of mounted guards and were placed in the preassigned barracks. In our barracks, ten were housed in Room E, which had been used as a recreation room, six were taken to Room C, and four to Room B. The barracks had never been so crowded. All the new arrivals had shaven heads. Many of them wore a "patriotism" emblem on their shirts. One of them wore a shirt with the following message in big, conspicuous letters: "Not words but action. Trust the mother country, Japan. Crush 'em to bits." Soon a notice from Mr. Williams appeared: "To Internees from Tule Lake: If you have shirts with "patriotism" written on them, you must bring them to the office by 4:00 P.M. on March 10. Violators will be prosecuted."

A Bloody Incident

March 10 was a warm spring day. The daytime temperature was sixty-five degrees, but this was sure to change. Suspecting that internees from Tule Lake were concealing swords and other dangerous weapons as well as shirts with "patriotism" emblems, Mr. Williams ordered dozens of guards to go through their belongings again. A few items were confiscated. This was the lull before the storm.

On March 12, I heard that Mr. Langston, chief of the liaison office, had been checking the theater, the east and west classrooms, and buildings other than the barracks from early that morning. At the Lower Town on our way back from breakfast, we saw Rev. Kenjitsu Tsuha and Mr. Zenshiro Tachibana being led away with their belongings toward Upper Town. Many Tule Lake internees were following them. Their behavior did not seem especially violent, but when they approached the Upper Town mess hall, waiting guards suddenly threw tear-gas grenades at them. Unfortunately the guards were downwind, so the thick smoke drifted toward them, which created an uproar among the Tule Lake internees.

That was the beginning of the conflict. The "shaven heads" were chased down with clubs and attacked from both sides by the guards patrolling the entrance to Lower Town. Tear-gas grenades were thrown again. Defenseless internees began falling one after another under blows from the clubs. Messrs. Gontaro Ono, Akira Osugi, Isamu Uchida, and Moto Hirashima fainted from bloody head injuries. They were thrown into a truck and taken to the hospital. A terrible incident had taken place in what felt like a matter of seconds.

The authorities must have anticipated a confrontation that afternoon. Mrs. Carter, the head accountant, and Miss Merry, the stenographer, did not report to the liaison office as usual, and guards from El Paso had been brought in. All internee meetings were now prohibited and all work stopped except in the mess hall, hospital, and canteen. In the afternoon, only the barracks chiefs were allowed to hold an emergency meeting to select seven members to serve on a counterplan committee.

The authorities were planning to segregate some three hundred Tule Lake internees. The Japanese office wanted to find another solution. That night mounted guards patrolled in and around the camp; everyone was uneasy. All internees were advised to remain in their barracks. We were surprised the next morning to find that overnight a fence had been built around the sixty-third to sixty-ninth barracks, near the baseball field in Lower Town, by Mexican laborers. The authorities flatly refused to listen to any suggestions from the barracks chiefs. On the fourteenth, the Tule Lake internees were taken to the barracks in the newly fenced-in area and internees who were currently occupying those barracks were moved out. The mess halls remained under guard. We felt as if we were living under martial law.

More Aftereffects

We were afraid for the lives of the four internees who had been beaten, but it soon became apparent that their injuries were fairly light, with the exception of Mr. Osugi's. His wound was deep enough to reach the periosteum and required four stitches. If anyone had died, there could have been more incidents.

On March 14, the reshuffling of internees between Upper and Lower Town barracks was like the confusing aftermath of a fire or similar disaster. Guards were shooting movies of the chaos. Two Tule Lake men left our barracks and four other internees moved in, so we suspended our belongings from the ceilings, but there was still barely enough space to walk. Every barracks faced a similar situation. The moving was somehow completed by that evening, but the segregated area was rechecked again, and books and other items were temporarily confiscated and some belongings lost in the confusion. Our contact with the segregated internees was cut off completely. They could not go out for walks or exercise. Meals were brought to them from the mess halls. It was a dismal and heart-wrenching situation.

After dinner Mr. Orimo, chief of the fourth barracks, was taken to the fenced-in area by the authorities. He was not from Tule Lake, but the reason given was "camp security." This caused another problem. The *Santa Fe Times* temporarily suspended publication.

On March 15, four days after the disturbance, there was still some confusion because people's belongings were not yet sorted out, but it felt like the day after a big storm. The emergency meeting of barracks chiefs lasted from morning to evening, in part because the Japanese office leaders in attendance were not familiar with procedural rules. A few stubborn individuals added to the problem. It was made clear at the meeting that both Rev. Tsuha and Mr. Tachibana, leaders of the Tule Lake group, had been partly responsible for the disturbance. Mr. Williams issued a statement saying that all internees except those in the segregated area could expect camp life to return to normal.

After dinner on the fifteenth, several guards wearing gas masks entered the segregated area and approached Mr. Wakayama, chief of the sixty-ninth barracks and leader of the first group to arrive from Tule Lake. Within a half-hour, they gathered his belongings and took him away. Early on, Mr. Wakayama had cooperated with the authorities; his barracks had been passed over when guards were conducting searches for "patriotism" emblems. It was rumored that Mr. Wakayama was taken away for his own protection. That day Mr. Kelly arrived at the camp to investigate the disturbance of March 12 and to review the parole applications of fathers of U.S. soldiers. During this period two of the camp's mail inspectors were kept busy acting as interpreters for Mr. Kelly's investigation, so mail came to a standstill. Nothing was delivered or sent out, which was quite annoying.

Mr. Kelly and Mr. Williams were still investigating the Tule Lake incident on March 21. That day the four internees who had been hospitalized were moved to the meeting hall outside the barbed-wire fence. Although barbed wire was strung around the hall, these four and fourteen other Tule Lake men were eventually moved elsewhere on the twenty-third.

My heart sank when I heard that Lieutenant General Tadamichi Kurihara, commander of the Iwo Jima Defense Force, had sent a cable to report that he and his men had run out of bullets and water and had decided to commit suicide.

More Gloomy War News

We received word that thirty family members of the eight Hawaii internees scheduled to go to Crystal City had finally arrived on the Mainland. Mr. Schreiber, deputy camp manager, announced on March 25 that the eight internees would leave within a week to join their families. Messrs. Takegoro Kusao, Yaichiro Akada, Junji Oda, Kazuaki Tanaka, Konin Matano, Shunjo Shiratori, Nizo Arita, and Taizen Imamura left on the evening of March 28. A young man, who had cut his wrist on the train from Tule Lake because he had been treated "like a dog" by the other internees, left with them. With the departure of Mr. Kusao for Crystal City, Mr. Toshio Sakaguchi took over as manager of the newspaper department.

An immigration officer arrived to review the parole application of Mr.

Kujuro Ishida, who was immobile and had been hospitalized for paralysis. At the time, we all wondered why Mr. Ishida, the father of a U.S. soldier, was being investigated further, but later we learned of similar cases. A reinvestigation was a general rule and no exceptions were allowed. In the camp at the time there were 119 Hawaii internees and 16 Mainland internees with sons in the military.

Mail from sons at the front did not come regularly. Someone from Kona received fifty-eight letters all at once at the end of March from his son in France. In our case, outgoing letters were often returned from the inspection office at about the time they should have been being delivered to the addressee. For example, an airmail letter sent to my family in Honolulu on March 13 was returned to me undelivered after the twentieth. (I had made the mistake of alluding to the Tule Lake incident.)

The barbed wire around the segregated area was finally taken down on March 31, two weeks after the incident, and everyone was allowed to communicate freely. The atmosphere of the camp brightened noticeably. The young internees from Tule Lake gathered at the library, on the hillside, at the canteen, and in the broadcast area in the evening like birds released from a cage. Cut off from the outside world for two weeks, they were especially hungry for news.

We received word that Mr. David Lloyd George, Britain's prime minister during World War I, had passed away peacefully in London on March 26. From the end of March to the beginning of April, there was nothing but bad news for Japan. On March 27, the U.S. Navy and Air Force attacked the main island of Okinawa and landed on the islands of Tokashiki, Zamami, and Aka. That day Argentina declared war on Japan and Germany. On April 1, a large U.S. force landed on the main island of Okinawa.

On April 4, Mr. Williams informed the Japanese office as follows: "The Spanish embassy is no longer responsible for protecting the rights of Japanese in the United States. Camp authorities will continue to treat internees in a fair manner. Please bring all requests and other matters to the authorities here. Matters that cannot be decided here will be promptly forwarded to the central authorities."

On April 5 the Koiso cabinet resigned. A few days earlier Shinsei-to (the New Political Party), headed by General Jiro Minami, had issued a statement hinting at the cabinet breakup. At the time I had been outraged, but I realized that it was a sign of worse things to come. The simpleminded men in the camp were convinced that the cabinet change proved that Japan was calm and composed. Later news revealed that General Kantaro Suzuki, president of the privy council, had received an imperial mandate to form a new cabinet. What really had a chilling effect on me was the news that the Soviet Union had abrogated its neutrality pact with Japan on April 4, the very day that the Koiso cabinet resigned.

The Death of the U.S. President and Our Reactions

On April 7, General Manager Saiki was ordered to compile a list of internees who were over seventy years old along with the addresses of their families. He submitted the names of those over sixty-five and of those in the hospital. One rumor was that the authorities might be preparing paroles, while another was that older internees were going to be transferred to other places. There were 115 men over sixty-five at the camp. Around that time it was learned that the broadcasting staff had stolen beer from the bar and held a small party. The bar was closed for three days, which annoyed drinkers considerably. The wartime food shortage was of course felt at the camp and became especially apparent that month, affecting the quality and quantity of the food. A man who seemed serious asked one of the doctors if he could develop night blindness as a result.

On the evening of April 10 we heard that Mr. Shigenori Togo had been appointed minister of foreign affairs and concurrently minister of Great East Asia. The camp population that day was 1,504. The mail situation had not improved, so we decided to voluntarily limit outgoing letters to just the essential ones.

In early April there was news that the tide of war was turning against Germany. On the twelfth a cable arrived informing us that President Roosevelt had died of apoplexy at 4:35 P.M., at Warm Springs, and that Vice President Truman had assumed the presidency. The Stars and Stripes flown in front of the supervisor's office was immediately lowered to half-mast. The president was sixty-three years old. The funeral, attended by about three hundred people, was held at the White House on the morning of April 14. The burial service took place at Hyde Park the next morning. On that day, snow from the previous night had piled up considerably. For the most part, internees received the news of President Roosevelt's death quietly and respectfully, which was heartening to see. All sporting events were postponed.

Mr. Shujiro Takakuwa received a letter from the military authorities in Hawaii at the beginning of April informing him that his request to return to Hawaii had been approved. He had permission to leave in a few months, as soon as a ship became available. He left for Denver on the night of April 12 with the intention of going to see his younger brother in California. Like Mr. Takakuwa, I received a copy of a similar letter from my family on April 13. On the nineteenth, I received the actual letter, dated April 4, from Major General Morrison of the Hawaii Security Office. It was finally clear that I would be allowed to return to Hawaii someday.

On the seventeenth we heard that, a few days earlier, two hundred B-29 bombers had flown over Tokyo, primarily targeting shrines, temples, and hospitals. The Meiji Shrine, the Asakusa Kannon (the Goddess of Mercy), and Junten-do Hospital were completely destroyed. April 20 was Hitler's fifty-sixth birthday. On April 29, we learned of the B-29 bombing of Japan in greater detail. A quarter of Tokyo was ruined. In Osaka 1,500,000 homes were destroyed and 500,000 people were killed; in Nagoya, 60,000 homes and 230,000 people; in Kobe, 100,000 homes and 260,000 people. The numbers for Shizuoka and Yokohama were not yet known. The pope visited Tokyo and surveyed the ruins of many famous buildings, including Senso Temple, Meiji Shrine, Junten-do Hospital, Tokyo Dental College, and Japan Dental College.

On April 25 we heard that the long-heralded San Francisco meeting (where the charter that would be the foundation for the United Nations was developed) had finally been held.

Germany and Italy Collapse

At the end of April more internees were scheduled to arrive from Kooskia and Tule Lake. I was afraid the overcrowding would soon become unbearable. To cope with the problem, the authorities restricted us to either two suitcases or one trunk and one bag per person. Everything else was to be taken away for storage in two warehouses. This readjustment caused as much confusion as a camp move, and I was quite annoyed. Around that time the camp population was 1,503. Preparations were under way for the emperor's birthday celebration, but Mr. Williams would not approve any additional expense for a special lunch menu. We decided to take six hundred dollars from the internees' welfare fund to pay for the meal. Our request for more money was probably denied because the country was still in mourning for the late president. We celebrated the emperor's forty-fourth birthday at the new theater on April 29. General Manager Saiki gave a speech and each attendee received an orange as a complimentary gift, which I thought was an interesting part of internment life. After lunch a baseball game and sumo tournament were held throughout the afternoon.

In early May, the terrible news of the collapse of the Axis powers was quickly followed by one tragedy after another. The *Denver Post* reported on May 1 that members of the Communist Party had shot and killed Mussolini, his lover, and several cabinet members on April 29 in Milan. Their bodies were then mutilated by the crowd and hung upside down with their pictures attached. On the evening of the second, we heard that President Truman was preparing to announce the fall of Berlin and the death of Hitler. That was the beginning of the end. Germany unconditionally surrendered to the Allied powers at 2:41 A.M. on May 7. The United States and Great Britain declared May 8 "V-E (Victory in Europe) Day." Detailed reports were given on the celebrations in both countries. Even in this old town of Santa Fe, all businesses were closed to commemorate the end of the war in Europe. Two of the three countries that had aimed at world conquest were easily broken in the end, and the future of Japan turned dark.

Lieutenant Saburo Maehara, a son of Mr. Teiichiro Maehara of Puunene, was killed at the Italian front. On April 25, a memorial service was held at the Lower Town mess hall with the Reverend Ikezawa officiating. On April 26 and 27, there was an exhibition of more than 120 paintings by students of Masao Ikeno in the east classroom. A watercolor by Mr. Tosuke Tanikaga was especially fine. There were also a few good paintings by young men from Tule Lake. A group photograph was taken of everyone connected with the exhibition. At that time the immigration office began interviewing internees over sixty-five years old (including me) and those who wished to return to Japan. Fort Lincoln Internment Camp in Bismarck, North Dakota, invited two of our ministers, Mr. Rien Takahashi and Mr. Hosho Kurohira, to visit on May 3.

On May 6, ninety-six internees who had been building roads in Kooskia returned to Santa Fe Camp as expected. They were put in the newly built fourteenth and forty-ninth barracks. Most of them were from the Mainland. Among the group were Rev. Hozen Seki of New York and Mr. Hisashi Imamura, both members of a *noh* group from Lordsburg, and seven internees from Hawaii, including Messrs. Rincho Onaga, Ittetsu Watanabe, Hitoshi Hanamoto, and Koichi Kurisu. The population at the camp on May 8 was 1,596: 748 were assigned to the Upper Town mess hall, 731 to the Lower Town, 111 to the hospital, and 6 to the officers' mess hall. The immigration office distributed picture ID cards to each internee on May 10. These cards were mainly used when we went out to the hill behind the camp.

Delayed Mail

In early May an American commentator cynically likened the San Francisco meeting, which was still going on, to "mice meeting under the auspices of cats." I thought the remark was very apt. On the morning of May 14, the Stars and Stripes was back at full mast. The thirty-day mourning period for President Roosevelt was over. Mr. Shin-ichi Hashibe, a former schoolmaster at the Kakaako-Alapai Japanese Language School, left for Japan on the second exchange ship. His ailing wife had died in Honolulu, leaving their young daughter and her old mother behind. The news reached him at Santa Fe on May 15. I was sorry for their loss.

As I mentioned before, animals were not allowed in the barracks, but some internees openly ignored this rule. Suddenly, on May 18, the authorities began enforcing the regulation. A man in our barracks finally put his little dog in a box outside. I advised a Mainland man who kept a bird to set the animal free because it disturbed others, but I was ignored. The barracks chief let the man have his way, but eventually he released the bird. His conscience may have been pricking him.

Mail, the internees' only link to the outside world, was either late or seemed to have stopped altogether, especially for those of us from Hawaii. Letters from Hawaii arrived here after a while, but our letters home never seemed to get there. Both were sent on clippers. On May 19, I received a letter from my family dated May 10, in which they reported receiving nothing from me since March 19. Internees had been using the prescribed stationery for letters to Hawaii when suddenly we were told not to continue to use it and all mail already posted but uninspected was returned to the sender. We received no advance notice of this, which was very annoying.

On June 2, I received a letter from Honolulu dated May 26. I learned that none of the letters I had sent since March 20 or thereabouts had reached my family. Because no one had heard from me, rumors were circulating and people were worried. Mail within the Mainland was also delayed: A letter from the city of Santa Fe took a month to reach the camp. This state of affairs continued for a while.

The climate changed every five or six days. On May 1, it felt as though summer had arrived. All the mountains and fields turned green and weeds began sprouting. Fleurs-de-lis were blooming. Then, on the evening of the twentieth, it began to blow and snow in the mountains, and we shivered with cold. On the twenty-first, just as I was tiring of the book I was reading, Doctor U arrived. We went for a walk on the hill behind the camp for the first time in a long time. It was a fine, beautiful day without wind. Flowers, whose names I did not know, were just starting to bloom—yellow, violet, and white. We heard the sound of a *shakuhachi,* which was becoming popular in the camp. The old town of Santa Fe appeared before us like an oil painting. Although our lives were filled with many gloomy days, we were occasionally refreshed and cheered by sights such as these.

On May 21 we received word that His Imperial Highness Kan-in, general of the army, had passed away on May 19 at his villa in Odawara. He was eighty years old and had been ill. A state funeral was held for him. I used to look up at His Highness riding gallantly on horseback in Tokyo when I was a boy, so his death affected me quite a bit.

Sorrowful Confession of Japanese Scientists

Miss Shimeji Ryuzaki, secretary at the Swedish consulate in Honolulu, accompanied Hawaii families traveling to Crystal City. She was scheduled to come to Santa Fe Camp, but in early May we received word that the authorities would not approve her visit. The cement flooring for the new theater was completed and five hundred new seats were put in on May 23.

On May 22 I was shocked to hear of the death of Mr. Retsu Kiyosawa. He had died of acute pneumonia in Tokyo the day before. I had known him for thirty years, from the time he was a nameless reporter for the *Shin Sekai* (New World) in San Francisco. Supposedly he wrote an article critical of the San Francisco Conference. He was only fifty-five years old. We first received word of the "balloon bombs" at the end of May. These were launched from Japan and were carried by the jetstream to the United States. Most of them exploded west of the Mississippi and caused many mountain fires.

According to a broadcast from Tokyo on May 25, about five hundred B-29s had bombed Tokyo. The Imperial Palace, Omiya Imperial Palace, and Ginza burned down, and the Imperial University of Tokyo and Keio University were ruined. We later found out that Mr. Kikuji Ishii and Dr. Man Oda were among the victims of the bombings. That day Domei Tsushin, a Japanese news agency, reported that Lieutenant General Reikichi Taba, chairman of Kagaku Shinko-kai (Science Promotion Council) and an authority on scientific weaponry, had announced that suicide bombers were the key to winning the war. His statement was a clear indication that in this regard Japan was no match for the United States.

Families in Hawaii applied for the parole of several internees at Santa Fe Camp. The security office in Hawaii replied to their applications on May 28, saying that they needed to collect further information and, upon receiving instructions from authorities on the Mainland, they would in turn inform the families. These conditional letters were something new and were the cause of some speculation.

On May 30, the American flag was raised in Shuri, Okinawa. In China, Generalissimo Chiang Kai-shek resigned and Mr. Sung Tzu-wen took over his position.

The young Mr. and Mrs. Kenneth Stevens and their baby visited us from Hawaii on May 31. They met with more than ten internees and relayed news from their families in Honolulu. Afterward the couple promised that they would write each family to tell them about the meetings. The internees really appreciated their kindness. The American Friends Services Committee provided many such humanitarian services to internees during the war. I should mention that this organization, together with Dr. Gilbert Bowles and his family in Honolulu, extended aid to Japanese during and after the war, regardless of their religious beliefs.

Mr. Minoru Uematsu and Mr. Shigeo Kiino, inspectors at the camp, were always kept very busy. Mr. Setsuzan Sasaki and Mr. Kazuaki Kuwata were brought in from other relocation centers on May 31. At last this office was adequately staffed, but the inspectors were often asked to work as interpreters as well. Mr. Uematsu was a Japanese American from Kauai. Not all inspectors were monsters. On June 1, Mr. Tsuneyoshi Koba and Mr. Bunho Kuwatsuki were elected general manager and assistant general manager. They were both from the Mainland. Mr. Koba was a medical student and was called "Doctor" by the internees. Mr. Kuwatsuki was a minister.

Disagreeable and Distasteful Things—Again

For the 109 men who had sailed on the third ship from Hawaii, June 1, 1945, marked the third year of their internment on the Mainland. On that day, the remaining seventy or so internees (including Mr. Kango Kawasaki and Mr. Ichini Adachi from the Big Island and Messrs. Sadato Morifuji, Ryoichi Tanaka, and Kogan Yoshizumi from Honolulu) took a group photograph.

Summer arrived in full force on June 13. It was a very hot day. It had been rainy and chilly only a few days earlier. What a big change in the weather! Around that time *buyo* (sand flies) began pestering us during our walks on the hill behind our barracks and many internees were bitten. The flies also started to appear around the barracks. (People from Kyoto and the Kansai area say *"buto."* I do not know whether this is the same insect or not.) According to a man from Fresno, California, a small insect called a "vine hopper" is responsible for destroying vineyards. A gas is sprayed on the vines to exterminate the insect, but the gas can kill people, too. I remembered leaf hoppers were a big problem in Hawaii's cane fields.

A small man (like someone from Lilliput) with a big nickname that I have forgotten often visited his *aikane* [friend] in our barracks. He told obscene stories without batting an eye and lectured on a betting game called "4-5-6," which was popular among internees from the Mainland. Some people were impressed with what he had to say and befriended him. But his visits were always ill-timed, so I disliked him more than the *buyo*. One day in the middle of June, he arrived at the usual time and began to boast in a loud voice about the amount of tobacco and the number of pipes he had. A Mainland minister with a fiery temper could not stand it any more and shouted, "QUIET!" The man scurried away like a rat escaping a drowning. That was extremely gratifying.

June 14 was the second anniversary of my arrival at Santa Fe Camp. Three years and seven months had passed since I was first interned—the day of the Pearl Harbor attack. How much longer would the war last? On the evening of June 15, Mr. Buntaro Nakahara, a fisherman from Waianae, swallowed lye and died at the sixty-second barracks while we were all out for dinner. A wake was held at the new theater after the day's broadcast. The Reverend Hakuai Oda delivered a sermon. On the afternoon of the nineteenth, the funeral, led by the Reverend Kuchiba, was held at the same place. I attended both. Mr. Nakahara was a good-natured man and liked playing card games. I do not know why he committed suicide. A few days later, on the morning of June 21, elderly Mr. Koei Mochizuki of Yamanashi prefecture died in the hospital. That evening, the men in his barracks gathered; the Reverend Gendo Okawa read a sermon and everyone burned incense. It was a good, quiet gathering. Young Mr. Toyoaki Okuyama from Peru worked hard to arrange the gathering, but a doctor, also from Peru, remained in bed during the service. Everybody was disgusted with him.

Let me add one more disagreeable thing. In the evenings in the middle of June, an old man insisted on killing cockroaches with a burning newspaper. This was very dangerous and could have easily started a fire. I advised him of this quietly, but he would not listen to me. I felt like slapping him in the face.

The First Group to Return to Hawaii

The first group to return to Hawaii, which included Messrs. Shimoda, Maehara, Izutsu, and Kawachi, finally left at 7:00 P.M. on June 21, 1945. Many people saw them off. It was what all of us from Hawaii had been waiting for. Because their luggage tags were stamped "Seattle Airport," we thought they were traveling by air, but they took a train. The internees had received the order to leave about a month earlier, on May 22. We thought they would be going home the next day, so the entire process took quite a bit longer than we had expected.

Four hundred more internees were brought in from Tule Lake on July 27 and were housed in seven barracks in Lower Town. They were mostly old men, including Mr. Minoru Nakano and Mr. Kyuhachi Tanaka from Hawaii. The young men were mainly draft dodgers. About thirty men of other backgrounds were taken to barracks in Upper Town. As I mentioned earlier, the camp was already overcrowded. We had almost no elbowroom. Each man had a space about fifty inches wide and the length of the bed plus a foot to call his own. When we were lying down, we could reach out and touch the next bed. The cramped conditions were almost intolerable. Out of desperation, each man dug a foxhole under his bed where he could rest and get away from others. In some places, some dug so deep that the posts swayed. Mr. Langston of the liaison office circulated a "Do Not" notice prohibiting the digging of these holes, but in the face of necessity, many orders were ignored. In the end the authorities were forced to tolerate the holes.

On the morning of July 1, the mountainside was filled with smoke, which grew thicker by afternoon. People guessed it was a mountain fire. At night there were a thunderstorm and a hailstorm. The July 3 broadcast reported that Dr. Junjiro Takakusu had passed away at his home in Shizuoka. He was eighty years old. On the night of July 7, a memorial service was arranged by the camp's Buddhist association. Rev. Gikyo Kuchiba officiated and Rev. Kodo Fujitani served as master of ceremonies. Rev. Dojun Ochi gave a sermon. It was a very good service. Tributes to Dr. Takakusu were hastily written for the second page of *Hikari*, the newspaper of the Buddhist association. More than ten people, including myself, contributed eulogies of ten lines each.

July 4, Independence Day. Because of the war, it was not a holiday.

Mr. John Curtin, prime minister of Australia, passed away. It was a hot, sultry day. Since June 20 we had been receiving typhoid shots at the camp hospital; we finished the third and final round on July 5. Some of the internees turned blue or became ill, but fortunately I did not suffer any side effects.

For some time the mess halls had been serving broken grains of rice and unappetizing side dishes. All of us complained. We made up for the poor food with eggs from the canteen and sashimi, which was sold in convenient paper packages for fifteen cents. When it was available, there were long lines outside the canteen, which I often joined. I do not know why, but the sashimi gave many people a slight case of food poisoning. I fell ill several times. Speaking of food poisoning, people got sick from eating the mess hall food: When caused by bad jellyrolls or pork, the effects could be severe but not serious. Decent rice was finally served on July 6 and all of us shouted for joy. Japanese are nothing but bags of rice after all.

Informal Lecture on the Dishcloth Gourd

July 7, 1945, was the eighth anniversary of the start of the Sino-Japanese War. The conflict was now entering its ninth year.

We received a letter from the first group to return to Hawaii. They had arrived in Seattle on June 25, and six internees, including Rev. Kametaro Maeda and Mr. Kyoichi Miyata, from Amache and elsewhere joined them to form a group of ten. They boarded a ship bound for Honolulu on July 3. On July 17 we learned that they had arrived in Honolulu and were released on July 10. We were all relieved.

The east classroom, which had been being used for inspecting the luggage of Tule Lake internees, was at last available for lectures and other gatherings on July 11. The *Rocky Shinpo,* which had always been available to internees, was no longer delivered to the camp from the middle of July.[5] It seems the paper had printed something that had offended the camp authorities.

One of my close companions since my days at Lordsburg was the Reverend Gijo Maeda of the Fresno Hongwanji Betsuin Mission. A young man from Kishu, he had a long mustache like the old Chinese general

---

5. The *Rocky Shinpo* was a Denver-based Japanese American newspaper edited by James Omura. It was the only Japanese American newspaper to support the draft resistance movement by Nisei interned at the Heart Mountain "Relocation Center."

Kan-u, which earned him the nickname "Mustache Maeda." This reverend was an ardent student and read voraciously. His arguments were rational. He was an ultranationalist and used to tease me about my pro-American sympathies, but I liked him.

One evening in July, the two of us took a walk. We saw many dish-cloth gourds growing here and there in the camp. Rev. Maeda told me that the two vines of the dishcloth gourd grow together to form two-inch-long springs. When coiled around each other in opposite directions, these springs are able to bear the weight of the heaviest gourd. Nature really is amazing. The reverend talked about not only dishcloth gourds but also Buddhism in Japan and Islam. I appreciated hearing what he had to say because it was interesting and educational.

Lists of a second Hawaii group and an Alaska group arrived from Washington and were announced on July 17. There were twenty-nine names in the former, nine in the latter. One more was added to the Hawaii list the following day. They were to travel first by train, then ship. A sailing date had not yet been fixed. The authorities would begin inspecting luggage (limited to 170 pounds as before) at 1:00 P.M. on July 17. From this time on, government-issued items would not need to be returned. Among the thirty returning to Hawaii were Messrs. Shotaro Awaya, Makitaro Tamura, Sadasuke Hamamoto, Kyujiro Ishida, Mankichi Miura, Kakichi Okamoto, Tokikichi Sugimoto, Katsuzo Sato, Keiso Ban, Kan Ooka, Ryoichi Tanaka, Setsugo Togioka, Hatsukichi Yamamoto, Shutetsu Uyenoyama, Shinjiro Yoshimasu, and Kogan Yoshizumi. Fifteen had sons in the military, the rest did not. They came from various islands. I noticed that the list included internees who were hospitalized: Messrs. Ishida, Hamamoto, Tamura, and Ooka.

The daytime temperature in the barracks was ninety degrees on July 20. A few hot days followed. The *New York Times* strike continued for seventeen weeks. We finally received our July 1 paper on July 23. Britain held its general election on July 26. The incumbent prime minister, Winston Churchill, lost the election and resigned. The Labor Party won a big victory and Clement Attlee was elected prime minister. On July 27 the U.S. Senate passed the San Francisco Charter with eighty-nine ayes and two nays. Just after nine o'clock in the morning of the same day, a B-25 hit the Empire State Building in New York in a thick fog. Thirteen people died. Life continued in the outside world.

In camp, an elaborate play, a social drama, and a comedy were presented on the nights of July 27 and 28. They were fairly good, but the kabuki we had that night was not. It could not compare with what I had seen at Lordsburg. On the twenty-ninth an enjoyable and lively sumo tournament was held under the blazing sun and continued into the night. A sixteen-page sumo special issue was published. Twelve hundred copies of this mimeographed issue cost about sixty dollars. I contributed an article entitled "Unreasonably Difficult Problems." The camp population reached 1,986 on July 31.

The Atomic Bomb and the Betrayal of the Soviet Union

It was now August 1945. Soon Japan would be changed forever.

A friend of mine in camp received a letter from Mr. Kyoichi Miyata, who had gone back to Honolulu with the first group. He wrote to say that he had been invited to a party by some golfers. The meal was simple but cost $7.50 per person. Meat was scarce, but chicken was readily available. Other groups in Hawaii were beginning to take over fishing from Japanese, so more fish was anticipated in the markets. A simple two-bedroom house sold for $15,000. People sometimes bet $1,000 on a golf game. These facts sounded incredible, but they were all true.

Naughty old folks in the tenth barracks made fun of the office "beauties" passing by the windows of the Upper Town mess hall. Because of this, the mess-hall windows were nailed shut on the third. Three weeks passed. The mess hall was so hot we could hardly stand it. The authorities said we were all responsible, so we must all be punished.

On August 4 Dr. Yokichi Uehara received a letter from Major General Morrison permitting him to return to Hawaii on the next available ship. A few days later, Dr. Ryuichi Ipponsugi received the same letter. Elderly Mr. Daikichi Akimori received a cable adding him to their group, the second to return to Hawaii. The problem was that no one knew when the next ship would be available. It was probably not any time soon.

On Sunday, August 5, a baseball tournament opened with much fanfare. A band played and it was a merry event. The next day the authorities claimed that one of the songs performed by the band was "Miyo, tokai no sora akete" (Look at the dawn of the eastern sea), a military song and therefore inappropriate. Nothing came of it, however. The early-morning meetings sponsored by Buddhist and Shinto groups—held at dawn on the seventh of every month—were now banned. When Assistant General Manager Kuwatsuki was asked why the meetings always convened on the seventh, he had answered that it was in honor of Buddha's birthday. The authorities asked another minister, who answered that it was the day of the Pearl Harbor attack. From then on the authorities regarded Mr. Kuwatsuki as untrustworthy.

While we were troubled with these trivial matters, Japan and the rest of the world continued to experience the horrors of war. Atomic bombs were dropped on Hiroshima on August 6 and Nagasaki on the ninth. Both cities were nearly annihilated. The bombing caused a huge sensation worldwide. Bitter complaints were heard even in this country against the United States' use of atomic bombs. Detailed news reports from Hiroshima and Nagasaki came in one after another. We were further taken aback when President Truman announced that the Soviet Union had declared war on Japan on August 8. The next day the Soviets invaded Manchuria. This terrible betrayal by the Soviet Union could not have come at a worse time for Japan. Not surprisingly, we were all dumbfounded and utterly dejected by these reports. There was a big thunderstorm on the night of the ninth.

Most of the internees would not accept the reality of what was happening. They argued that the reports of the devastation caused by the atomic bombs were propaganda and that the Soviet Union's declaration of war against Japan was a ruse, concealing some hidden strategy. They indulged in this kind of wishful thinking to console themselves, which was understandable, but they were also speculating wildly and irresponsibly. Then came the surprising news of Japan's unconditional surrender.

On the Eve of Japan's Surrender

A group of young people issued a mimeographed magazine called *Sankure.* I was asked to contribute something to the second issue, which I did, but the piece was never printed. It appears below to give readers an idea of camp conditions on the eve of Japan's surrender.

A FEW THOUGHTS

People indulge in wishful thinking, construing whatever they hear or see to suit themselves. This was true during peacetime, but even more so since the war began.

It is necessary to be humble if we are to face reality and understand the truth of events or issues in the world

Whether news is bad or good, we should check its source carefully and think through what we have read or heard reasonably.

Yes, we should be wary of propaganda. At the same time, it would be foolish to dismiss all news simply on the basis of one's prejudices or biases.

There are many demagogues among us, as well as *nyo-nyo-to*s (camp lingo for "talkative people") who know nothing, yet like to hear themselves talk. If I listen to them, I develop a headache.

Everyone I meet asks me, "Is there is any good news?" This means news that one wishes to hear. Nonsense. We are at war. Good news is a luxury.

I have been troubled by the strange Japanese used in our broadcasts. Even more upsetting are the distortions and opinions. I had hoped that our broadcasters knew the difference between news and commentary.

To speak on current affairs one must be knowledgeable. To speak intelligently on military matters requires some expertise. It is a mistake to talk about something one does not understand. I become disgusted when I see people here so easily swayed by the words of those who pretend to know what they are talking about.

We have many old yet young men in camp. Age does not determine whether one is old or not. If a man is slow-witted and has lost his inquisitiveness, he is already an old man even if he is only thirty or forty years old.

Many of the religious men and educators here—regarded as leaders by themselves and others—have nothing to recommend them. I am not the only one of this opinion. Of course there are exceptions, but in most cases I have been disappointed in these men. Wearing a scarlet robe or claiming to have a doctoral degree does not make a man exceptional. Some sanctimonious church leaders are a greater disgrace than the common individual. Some schoolteachers try to teach despite their ignorance in the subject. An honest man is better even if he has no education or religion.

Even a trivial thing will give away a man's birth and education. Exaggerated manners in the mess hall are offensive, but no manners are worse. There should be courtesy, even among friends. If everyone put this proverb into practice, most of the problems of communal living would be solved.

I do not like melancholy old men or swaggering youths.

Generally speaking, I prefer the company of young people. This may be a common sentiment. Lest I be misunderstood, I must add that I like young people for their forthrightness and honesty.

Only the gourds hanging from the trellises seem alive. Everyone here is depressed. Where is our Japanese spirit?

I could speak frankly on other matters, but I will stop because I could face censure or worse.

—August 9, 1945

Japan Surrenders

August 10, 1945. I got up at 6:30 A.M. While I was changing and others were still asleep, Mr. Shonan Kimura from next door came in and said, "The broadcaster announced that Japan has finally surrendered." Whenever I received a piece of news I would usually ask a few questions, but this time I kept silent. I had been expecting this. I felt my head begin to ache. I ran out and walked around the flower gardens.

In every barracks, the *nyo-nyo-to*s chattered noisily. That morning the barracks chiefs held a meeting with Mr. Williams and his assistant, Mr. Schreiber. Mr. Williams asked that all internees remain calm. The number of guards was increased and light machine guns were secretly placed in the watchtowers. That evening several guards were stationed in front of the liaison office and two mounted guards patrolled the camp throughout the night. Beginning that day, every kind of rumor spread. We were all under considerable strain. I could not speak my mind. Even the most unlikely people were caught up in the rumors.

From the night of August 13 through the next morning, I could hear the people of Santa Fe celebrating Japan's surrender. Most of the internees would not accept it, of course. On the morning of the fourteenth, I heard President Truman on the radio at the newspaper office. Japan had accepted all of the conditions of the surrender outlined by the Allies in the Potsdam Declaration. The commander of the occupation forces was General Douglas MacArthur. "V-J Day" would be declared once Japan signed the surrender treaty. The war was over. I listened to all of this with Mr. Sakaguchi. There was no camp broadcast or newspaper that day, and the beer hall was closed. I did not sleep well. That night there were fireworks in Santa Fe, and a big mob appeared at the camp fence but was dispersed by the guards. I did not hear or see any of these things. I dozed off for a while early the next morning.

As soon as I heard of Japan's surrender, I expected disturbances in the camp and even a few suicides. Fortunately nothing like this occurred. Minister of War General Anami and several military officers committed suicide, as did General Sugiyama and his wife in mid-September. According to a few reports, several Japanese civilians had also committed "hara-kiri."

Mr. Williams issued another circular asking for calm while Rev. Ikugoro Nagamatsu of our barracks was angrily asking, "Why did Japan surrender?" An agriculturalist from Nevada, Rev. Nagamatsu was originally from Kumamoto prefecture. He was an honest and good-natured man but was as stubborn as a mule. He taught English in the camp, but his understanding of the language was doubtful: He only talked about Jesus Christ. He could not understand current events.

According to an August 16 broadcast, the Suzuki cabinet had resigned. His Imperial Highness Prince Higashikuni received an imperial mandate to form a new cabinet. That day the *Denver Post* reported that the emperor had issued a rescript concerning the surrender of Japan over radio. I read an English translation of it with tears streaming down my cheeks. On the fifteenth and sixteenth, people celebrated the end of the war throughout the United States. In San Francisco, soldiers and civilians, men and women, became intoxicated and disorderly, and eleven people died. None of the violence was racially motivated.

More False Rumors

Through all the false rumors and uncertainty in the camp I was able to keep abreast of what was happening in Japan thanks to a friend who listened to shortwave broadcasts from Japan. I escaped my noisy barracks whenever I could by taking walks in the morning and evening with other "traitors"— as the rabble-rousers called those of us who believed that Japan had been defeated. I also spent my time hunting for pretty stones on the hillside, visiting Dr. U in his underground "room," or reading in the library. The office of the *Santa Fe Times,* which adjoined my barracks, offered the best refuge, however. There I was able to relax and discuss current events or talk nonsense with the young people from South America or the Mainland.

On August 14, Messrs. Kanemori, Tanabe, Hotta, and Takemoto were added to the list of those returning to Hawaii on the second ship, bringing the total to thirty-five. Later Mr. Sakaguchi, manager of the newspaper department, also received permission to return to Hawaii. At that time, rumors in the camp began to intensify. Pearl Harbor and Honolulu had been devastated by a "double" atomic bomb. The United States had been demilitarized. The Panama Canal had been blown up, and so on. Quite a few people believed these stories. In the camp there was no shortage of rumormongers.

From August 23 the newspaper stopped publishing for a few days because of the commotion generated among readers, some of whom criticized even the minor points in an article. Mr. Murakami, a news staffer, and I went for a walk and shared our outrage over the fact that some of our good friends were among the rumormongers. That day the temperature was ninety-four degrees even in the shade, but for the next few days the weather turned chilly. From August 21 on, our mail was sent to Honolulu directly without passing through the New York inspection office. We were also allowed to use ordinary paper and envelopes for our correspondence. However, because they continued to inspect all incoming and outgoing mail here, there were still delays—in fact, they seemed longer.

We received a cable from Hawaii Times, Ltd., informing us that old Mr. Miyozuchi Komeya had died in Honolulu at 10:40 A.M. on August 18. His friends at the camp arranged a memorial service at the new theater on the afternoon of the twenty-third. The Reverend Kuchiba officiated and about twenty ministers from the Hongwanji Mission chanted a sutra. About two hundred internees attended the service, and photographs were taken to commemorate the event. It was a grand service, but someone commented that Mr. Komeya had died in peace because he had heard that Japan had won a military victory that day. It was his only consolation. I was quite surprised when I heard this remark.

A few days earlier, on the night of August 21, a quarrel started in the fourth barracks over whether Japan had won the war or not. Two men emerged from the fight, both bloody. The mustached Mr. Matsumoto had been hit on the head with a wooden clog and was given four stitches. His assailant was put in a temporary holding cell and the beer hall was closed again.

Following a barracks chiefs meeting, the *Santa Fe Times* began publishing again, but the articles were lukewarm because the writers were afraid of offending anyone. Nevertheless, a few days later, someone came to the office to complain about a certain article on the surrender of Japan. The newspaper stopped publishing for a day to avoid further trouble. This scenario was repeated over and over.

On the evening of August 27, a minister from our barracks burst in, looking serious. "Listen, everyone," he said. "Oshima has been appointed ambassador to the United States and will be coming here soon." When someone asked him where he got this information, the man answered, "Well, I don't know." The next day, this same man was explaining a *Life* magazine editorial, "The Meaning of the Victory," to internees in the barracks. According to him, the article clearly stated that the United States did not believe it had won the war yet. Here he was, making another wrong guess. I was amazed at the gall of this man who supposedly knew enough English to teach it to internees. Although it had been a wonderful day, I felt a pain in my heart when I thought of conditions in Japan.

Sorrowful Death Knell

A broadcast on August 29, 1945, reported that the first contingent of occupation forces had landed at Atsugi the day before. The 150 soldiers had been surprised that the Japanese citizens were cooperative and that the outlying coastal area had already been secured. Thirty-six people committed suicide by hara-kiri in front of the Imperial Palace. The youth group organized mainly by Tule Lake internees held a dissolution ceremony that night. I heard that their officers made speeches and burned all of the group's documents, including oaths taken. We did not know what prompted this.

Forty-five internees from Kooskia (including two Hawaii men, Mr. Onaga and Mr. Hanamoto) were ordered to Fort Stanton, New Mexico, and left on the morning of August 29. We heard they would be paid eighty-five cents a day. It should be noted that they were forced to move. That evening, Mr. Masajiro Kai, the ninth barracks chief and leader of the Japan Victory Party, was taken to a temporary holding cell for spreading false rumors. The camp megalomaniacs quieted down a bit but continued to gather here and there, whispering among themselves. Returning from my walk, I was stopped by the mustached reverend, who wanted to talk about Mr. Kai. I was surprised at his ignorance of current events. If he had been anyone else, I would have kept silent, but I decided to "cure" this man and explained the situation to him in detail. In the end my medicine proved to be too much: The reverend kept away from me for some time after that.

Mr. Eishu Asato, the former owner of the Honolulu Hotel, fell ill and died after returning to Okinawa on the second exchange ship. A memorial service was held on the evening of August 30 at the Lower Town mess hall with the Reverend Ikezawa officiating. The next morning someone spread the rumor that talks between Japan and the United States had broken off and that we were at war again. Shouts of joy could be heard throughout the camp.

Mr. Hiroshi Tahara, a schoolmaster from Papaikou who had been in the hospital for some time, passed away on September 1. His funeral followed three days later. In his eulogy, another schoolmaster remarked, "Mr. Tahara passed away knowing peace had finally come and Japan had achieved her purpose in this sacred war." I was amazed at this and recalled something similar that had been said at the memorial service for old Mr. Komeya the month before.

Japan formally surrendered on September 1 on the USS *Missouri* in Tokyo Bay. The city of Santa Fe broadcast news of the event on loudspeakers throughout the day. Church bells rang and fireworks went off continuously. To our ears, the bells sounded as solemn as a death knell. September 2 was designated V-J Day. The authorities ordered doctors to postpone surgeries on patients requiring hospitalization for more than twenty days unless it was absolutely necessary.

The rumors continued. On September 4 one internee announced that Japanese schools would be reopening in Hawaii with teachers from Japan. Men in my barracks were exultant, saying that here was proof that Japan had won the war. This was nothing short of insanity.

At that time we were all visiting the hospital for our annual checkup. On the fourth, I was told that my blood pressure was fine and that I was in good health. Fully clothed I weighed 110 pounds, which was about 20 pounds less than four years earlier. On the night of September 7, eight of the twenty-six Alaska internees were paroled and left for home through Seattle. On the morning of September 10, the weather turned cold; it felt like late autumn. That day 121 internees from Poston and other camps arrived. Most of them were young people who had renounced their American citizenship. The barracks became even more crowded; most were packed with nearly seventy internees each.

Here are some comments courtesy of "the man on the street." An elderly gentleman from Maui: "They say the Japanese army has landed in Hawaii." Mr. Fukunaga, chief of the Lahaina branch of my newspaper, to an acquaintance of mine: "People in my barracks say they cannot understand your boss." (He was referring to me.) Mr. Takeda, a former general manager: "I was asked by a minister whether the Japanese flag had finally been raised in Hawaii or not. I was at a loss . . ."

The Reverend Shigefuji's Sermon

Something big was on the horizon. On September 11, 1945, the Provost Marshal General in Washington, D.C., wanted to verify the number of internees returning to Hawaii, remaining on the Mainland, and traveling to Japan. That morning we heard that General Hideki Tojo, the former prime minister, had failed to kill himself with his pistol. What a disgrace! Five hundred senior military officers had supposedly committed suicide as a group by hara-kiri in Singapore, but this could not be confirmed.

Winter arrived suddenly. On the morning of September 12, the outside temperature was thirty-eight degrees; indoors it was fifty degrees. A cold wind blew. The internee population now stood at 2,035, including 426 from Hawaii. In this latter group were 50 men who wished to return to Japan and 366 to Hawaii, 130 of them having sons in the military. From September 14 the authorities began taking our fingerprints and photographs. They also announced that luggage checks would begin the following week for those returning to Hawaii.

A memorial service for the war dead was sponsored by the Buddhist federation and held at the theater on the night of September 14. Rev. Joei Oi began the evening by saying that the service would honor the war dead of both sides, which was commendable. However, in his sermon, Rev. Enryo Shigefuji of Fresno expressed opinions that clearly showed he did not understand the current situation. I was surprised at his ignorance. First he attacked the United States for its unlawful and unjust use of atomic weapons. This was admirable. Then he reported, "Japan was so incensed at the inhumanity of this act that it wiped out the entire American expeditionary force in the Far East in three days and forced the United States to surrender." Rev. Shigefuji was said to be a highly learned priest, so I wondered what had happened. Outside after the meeting, Mr. Komai, *Rafu Shimpo* president, and I were so dumbfounded that all we could do was exchange stunned looks. We were so amazed by his remarks that we were practically speechless.

Two days later, I heard a sermon by Rev. Shuntaro Ikezawa of the Christian church in the east classroom. The weather was very bad—rain, hail, even thunder. There were only a few priests and about a dozen people present. As I expected, Rev. Ikezawa had grasped what was happening. In his sermon, "Truth and Love," he talked about the atomic bomb: "What was wrong was not the invention of atomic energy, but the thinking that led to its use in war. If we use our inventions for good, all human beings benefit. His Highness the Prime Minister said to General MacArthur, 'You must forget Pearl Harbor and we must forget the atomic bomb.' These were wise words." The Reverend then prayed for the birth of a new Japan. I felt what he had to say was well worth listening to. Over the next few days the internees could not stop talking about Rev. Shigefuji's sermon while Rev. Ikezawa's was never mentioned. Rev. Shigefuji was praised for expressing his opinions without fear and was regarded as a hero.

Hummingbirds, or what we call "bee sparrows," often visited our flower gardens. They are small, beautiful birds that suck honey from flowers like bees. They fly as skillfully as the new helicopters. When they fly away, they disappear in the blink of an eye. I had never seen them before coming to the Mainland but, according to people from the Big Island, they can be found in Waimea. The camp was also visited by skunks, small animals that resemble squirrels. Their deep, glossy black-and-white fur is extremely beautiful. I almost wished to keep one as pet, but the smell the animal produces when its guard is up is offensive enough to make you feel sick. Since the middle of September, this "poisonous gas" wafted through the barracks every now and again while we were asleep. It woke us up and kept us wide awake. The skunks were probably driven into the barracks by dogs. Even now when I recall the smell, my nose begins to twitch.

Smoke without Fire

Those who were returning to Hawaii were ordered to get all their belongings (with the exception of two suitcases containing necessities) ready for inspection. These would be stored until departure time. The baggage check took three days, from September 17 through the nineteenth. Near the end, everyone was completely exhausted. There were performances at the theater on two nights, but no one was in the mood to see them. As the departure date approached, classes at the camp began to close. Rev. Dojun Ochi's "History of Japanese Culture" class, which had met eighty times since the previous January, held its last session on September 18. Mr. Ikeno's painting class closed on October 4. At the end of September, new Japanese books arrived at the camp library from Manzanar Center.

I ran into a not-so-bright young man from Tule Lake in the bathroom one night. He said that someone had received a letter informing him that the Japanese navy had entered Hawaii. I asked, "Who received this letter?" He said he could not divulge the details. I said, "That's nonsense. It's just a rumor." He argued that there must be some truth to it, because "where there's smoke there's fire" and this was the smoke. I guess he knew the common sayings, but he failed to realize that it was he who was stirring up smoke with nothing to start a fire with.

An exchange sale was held on September 22 and 23 in the east classroom. It was very successful and attracted many shoppers. The mysterious priest, Nisshu Kobayashi, "Saint of Honolulu," bought a large amount of fossils and semiprecious stones as souvenirs. One unfortunate internee who was going back to Japan was tricked into paying one hundred and fifty dollars for an inexpensive wristwatch. Some of the Japan Victory Party members had told him that one yen equaled fifteen dollars. He believed them and bought the watch.

Rev. Shigefuji contributed an article to the next issue of *Hikari* (a Buddhist publication) entitled "Four Years in Detention." In it he misrepresented the current situation entirely and slandered "those traitors behind barbed wire." The management staff of the Buddhist association warned that the article would cause a problem in camp and asked him to rewrite it.

A few returnees were told by the authorities that they had too many fossils and semiprecious stones, so they sent their souvenirs home by rail instead. The charge to send the stones from Santa Fe to Hawaii was fourteen dollars per ton, or seventy cents for one hundred pounds or less.

A memorial service for Mr. Riichiro Kanzaki, former owner of the Waimea Hotel on Kauai, was held at the Lower Town mess hall on September 28 with dozens of Mr. Kanzaki's friends in attendance. Rev. Kakichi Okamoto gave an impressive sermon. Mr. Kanzaki had been in a sanitarium with his wife for the past nine years and had passed away on September 14. He had been a deeply religious and charitable man.

On September 29 it snowed a little for the first time that year. Then it rained and hailed throughout the day. Winter had returned. We were all vaccinated for smallpox that afternoon.

On the night of the thirtieth, General Manager Koba invited about thirty people, including all department managers and Mr. Kuchiba, Mr. Minami, and me (advisers to the police and fire departments), to a special dinner at the "Udon Hall" in the sixty-fourth barracks. A *kaiseki* meal had been prepared by Chef Uemachi. The general manager gave a speech and Mr. Kuchiba and I expressed our thanks. The meeting ended at 8:30 P.M. That night it became clear that Mr. Kuchiba was among those who had misjudged the political situation, and I was quite disappointed. He had applied to return to Japan. He said to me, "I was once in the South Pacific and know the conditions there well. If you need work after the war, I hope to be of some help to you." It seems he did not know that Japan had lost her territories in the Pacific and Taiwan.

At midnight on September 30, 1945, daylight saving time ended, so we turned our clocks and watches back an hour.

Greed Accompanies the Return to Japan

Even those who should have known better were misinformed or deluded themselves. Around that time I met an uneducated but admirable young man. He had been in Honolulu in the old days and had worked for a while at the *Nippu Jiji* when the newspaper office was on Hotel Street. He told me that he had seen my arrest during the sugar plantation strike incident. Because we were in neighboring barracks, we became acquainted. He was a confirmed bachelor and had spent some time roaming the United States.

One morning in early October, the two of us were taking a walk. I asked if he wished to return to Japan. He answered that, because he was poor, he could not go back and wanted instead to remain in the United States, where many jobs would be available in restaurants. He continued: "Actually, one of my friends advised me to return to Japan with him. I said I would if I had the kind of money *he* had. He said looks were deceiving; in fact he was penniless and that was why he was returning to Japan. Since Japan had won the war, internees could expect reparations from the United States. Internees who went back now could receive as much as fifty thousand dollars. If they returned later, the money might no longer be available. My friend repeated that I should go back with him. I did not know what to say. There are so many such fellows who think Japan has won the war." And so many of them were greedily waiting to return to Japan.

On October 1 all residents of the sixty-sixth barracks boycotted the *Santa Fe Times* and suspended their subscriptions.

After Spain withdrew its offer to represent Japanese interests, Switzerland took over the responsibility. The Swiss representatives visited the camp with State Department officials on September 27. Mr. Fischer was among them. They met with General Manager Koba and other camp officers. A report of what had transpired, written in question-and-answer form, was mimeographed both in English and Japanese and circulated to all barracks on October 2. U.S.–Japan relations, the surrender of Japan, and the changed conditions in Japan were outlined in detail. I quietly noted the internees' responses to the report. Many said that talks between representatives of a small country like Switzerland and State Department officials could only be propaganda. They showed no further interest in the matter. The prevailing attitude toward the report was indifference.

On October 2, the camp population was 2,027, of which 106 were in the hospital and 3 were in the temporary holding cell. Those of us in the "traitors group" estimated that the number of internees who had any real understanding of the war and its aftermath was less than a hundred. Even Nisei who visited their parents in the camp around this time advised them not to worry, because Japan was winning the war. The purpose may have been to bolster the spirits of the internees, but it also seemed to provide fuel for the diehards who refused to accept Japan's defeat. In the end this sort of thing did more harm than good.

The cabinet of His Imperial Highness Higashikuni reportedly resigned on October 5. The night before, a young man at a barracks numbered in the fifties attempted suicide with a chisel. The temporary holding cell in Upper Town housed four or five internees who were mentally ill. On the night of October 9, five of these internees were suddenly taken to an insane asylum in Kentucky. One man kept shouting that he should not be taken because he was not a lunatic. All of them were from the Mainland, and each one probably has a sad story to tell.

Surrounded by Foes on All Sides

Several immigration officers who had been assigned temporarily to our camp began interviewing the remaining Hawaii and South America internees from October 11. Several internees were obliged to work as interpreters and typists. The officers' main task was to determine which internees wanted to be sent to Japan and which to Hawaii and, if the latter, why. They were in a great hurry and finished interviewing a hundred internees on the first day of the week-long investigation. Most of the interviews went smoothly. However, some of those who continued to talk about "Japan's victory" were given a severe talking-to. These men were full of bluster but were actually insecure.

Nisshu Kobayashi, the "Saint of Honolulu," responded to the immigration officer's questions on current affairs without incident, but when he was asked why he wanted to return to Hawaii, his answer seems to have invited trouble: "I, a humble priest, have a temple there, thanks to my ties to Buddha. I intend to work for the salvation and education of others when I return. To settle and live in Hawaii permanently, I plan to marry a Honolulu girl." The officer in charge went on to ask him many questions in a stern voice, referring to a thick report he had before him. He asked the minister how he expected to marry when he already had a wife in Japan. The Saint answered that his wife was dead, but this also got him into trouble. When the officer pressed him for letters or other evidence that would prove this allegation, the man sat in silence.

On October 12 someone received several recent issues of the *Kakushu Jiji* (Colorado News), which included transcribed editorials and detailed articles on current conditions that had appeared in the *Asahi* (a newspaper published in Japan). Not having seen or read a Japanese newspaper in more than four years, a thousand emotions filled my heart as I eagerly perused these issues. Later that day, in one of the Upper Town barracks, an argument over the question of Japan's victory or defeat resulted in some minor injuries. The number of false rumors circulating throughout the camp seemed to be increasing. I tried to clarify matters in careful detail, but some never fully understood the basic points I outlined. It was pathetic, but there was nothing more I could do. The "Number One Diehard" in our barracks, Rev. Nagamatsu, made a snide reference to us when he misinterpreted the news and said to his listeners: "Some people believe Japan has lost the war even though they read the English-language newspapers and magazines every day. I wonder how they are reading the articles . . . with eyes closed?" The question should have been directed to himself.

When the *Hawaii Times* arrived from Honolulu, everyone read it eagerly. However, one reader said: "Japan can never be defeated. This paper has nothing to offer but ads. I'd like to meet the publisher of such a newspaper." Surprisingly, this was a man who had been in the newspaper business. It was aggravating, but any further discussion would be a waste of time, so I said nothing. As a man of discretion, I felt it would be unworthy of me to challenge these people.

Around that time, *Life* magazine published a picture of General Mac-Arthur and the emperor. A Mainland man from my barracks said that the Japanese in the picture resembled a man he had seen in Hollywood. A man from Los Angeles, who lived in the barracks next door and claimed to be a director or something of the Hosai-kai (Worshippers Association) of the Meiji Shrine, argued, "It is impossible for Japan to lose the war in light of its 2,600-year history." Even if history does not "agree" with the present, you cannot deny reality. Only an extremely stubborn man would reason thus.

The Remaining Forty-one Internees

On the morning of October 17, 1945, the Japanese office announced that those returning to Hawaii would be leaving in the next five weeks. They also posted a list of thirty or more returnees, including Messrs. Ryoichi Tanaka, Mankichi Miura, and Makitaro Tamura, and Revs. Okamoto and Sugimoto, who had been waiting since July 17. The above list combined both the second and third returnee groups. With hopes of returning to Hawaii renewed, they were energized. I tried to send a cable by night letter (a telegram that costs less because it is sent during off-business hours), but the liaison office rejected it, saying it was against the rules to communicate the movements of internees.

At about this time, a list of forty-one internees who had been excluded from the above lists and denied permission to return to Hawaii was sent out by the government and military authorities in Washington. They included Messrs. Hatsuichi Toishigawa, Hideo Tanaka, Tsuruichi Sarae, and Katsuichi Kawamoto of my barracks; and Tsuneichi Yamamoto, Ichiro Nakamura, Haruo Koike, Kuwasaburo Sakaguchi, Daizo Sumida, Tetsuou Tanaka, Hiroshi Tamabayashi, and Jikai Yamasato. Some of these men had never experienced government red tape, so it was not surprising that they agonized unnecessarily over the possibility that they would be left behind, never to return to Hawaii. When I thought of their situation, I could not sleep a wink.

On the eighteenth, Mr. Ichiro Nakamura, who was one of the forty-one, was added to the list of returnees. Mr. Riichi Togawa, who was one the returnees, suddenly found himself among those denied permission. On the nineteenth, Mr. Togawa and the others received word that the original order had been cancelled and they were all free to return to Hawaii. A man in my barracks danced with joy. Nevertheless, the reasoning behind the flip-flop escaped me.

On the morning of October 18, the authorities began checking return-ees' luggage that had been in storage. First, they checked the baggage of fathers of U.S. soldiers. We were not allowed to take with us lists of intern-ees' names or issues of the *Santa Fe Times*. We were all relieved when we heard we could take whatever we had written while interned. Some Hawaii men had hidden in their luggage soy sauce, sporting goods, and books that had been donated by the Red Cross and others. The Japanese office sent out a circular cautioning internees about packing certain items. The Number One Diehard protested loudly, saying the donations had been given to each man as a gift. Actually, the office was afraid that the bottles of soy sauce might break during transport and cause damage to other belongings.

At that time I read in a newspaper that the memorable Lieutenant E from Sand Island Camp was still living, had been promoted, and was now stationed in Burma. The luggage inspection took a few days. It was mostly a formality, but we had to undo each piece, then redo it. This was heavy, hard work. I was very fortunate that young Mr. Thomas Okuyama from South America and Messrs. Toishigawa, Obata, Hinokawa, and Torii helped me with my bags.

The Saint and Dr. Kondo, an English teacher, had by far the most lug-gage. The Saint's bags weighed fifteen hundred pounds; the doctor had a complete set of the old *Encyclopaedia Britannica,* which you might expect of a scholar. I did not want to say more about the Saint, but there was an incident in which a man from Aiea named Yoshimura gave the Saint a hand with the latter's luggage. In the process the sixty-year-old gentleman injured his back and had to be hospitalized. Then he was told he could not move for six months. He became the focus of everyone's sympathy just before the return to Hawaii. The Saint later denied having asked for Mr. Yoshimura's help. However, we all agreed that, as a man of god, he should remain behind and take care of this unfortunate man and that, if he refused, the Buddhist federation should take appropriate measures against him. Fortunately, Mr. Yoshimura, wearing a plaster cast, was able to board the ship, and the matter was resolved.

Leaving Santa Fe At Last

On October 20, after everything had been packed for the journey, I went out for a walk with Doctor U. It was a beautiful night with a full moon. I became somewhat sentimental when I reflected that this was my last moonlit night in Santa Fe. The six Hawaii men who had been sent to work at Fort Stanton returned to the camp that day, possibly because their departure date was around the corner too.

On October 22 it was announced that, due to the shipping schedule, the groups would not be returning together. The second and third groups would depart between November 5 and 12. The fourth group of forty-two internees (one man had been added) would follow three weeks later. Mr. Schreiber, the assistant camp manager, reported that he was doing his best to arrange for the groups to travel together. The earlier elated group of forty-two became despondent again, and barracks spirits were low. That day I had my fingerprints taken—finally. My fingertips had been so smooth on two prior occasions that the imprint had been unclear. An immigration officer gave me a new ID number, 1275, and took my picture from the front and side. With that, procedures for my departure were finally complete.

October 23 began cloudy and chilly and remained that way. The Rocky Mountains were covered in glistening snow. The camp population then was 2,023. The second and third groups of 328 internees would leave for Honolulu soon, followed by the fourth group of 42. On the twenty-fourth there was a thick frost. When I went out for a walk, it was freezing cold and I had a difficult time breathing. According to a letter from home, Mr. Matsujiro Otani and Mr. Ichiro Konno had left Seattle on a military ship on October 10 and arrived safely in Honolulu on the morning of the sixteenth. An old friend, Mr. Alexander Hume Ford, who had been ill, died on the morning of October 14 at the age of seventy-seven.

We were later informed that the departure dates for the second and third groups had been moved up to Monday the twenty-ninth and Tuesday the thirtieth, and that we were sailing from Seattle. We were also told that the Japanese office would pay out thirty dollars from each account, with the remaining balance to be disbursed in Seattle. Everything was set. On October 26 I wrote to my family: "Do not send any mail." I was permitted to send this message by cable.

That night a meeting of the second and third groups of returnees was held at the Lower Town mess hall with Mr. Minoru Murakami as chairman. Mr. Kango Kawasaki was appointed spokesman during the journey; Messrs. Sawajiro Ozaki and Takeo Miyagi of Oahu, Mr. Kazuto Takeda of Kauai, Mr. Kosuke Hirose of Maui, and Mr. Masaichiro Shinoda of the Big Island, committee members representing each island; and Mr. Minoru Murakami, secretary. It was decided that we would each accept a nine-dollar dividend from canteen profits and make a one-dollar donation to the general fund for the various departments. Each of us would also contribute a dollar to cover expenses incurred during the return trip. We would collect additional money as needed.

Of the 328 returnees, 170 were from Oahu (124 from Honolulu and 46 from the other districts), 33 were from Kauai, 43 from Maui, and 81 from the Big Island. Mr. Chosuke Kayahara, who was hospitalized, decided to remain at Santa Fe for the time being; this brought the final number of returnees to 327. A few days before our departure, the number of bags we could take with us on the train was reduced from two to one, so we were quite busy repacking as well as making farewell calls on those who were still hospitalized. From the afternoon to the evening of October 27, the beer hall was jam-packed.

On the night of October 29, the day before I was to leave, the mustached Rev. Maeda came to say good-bye and asked me to step outside. He made a formal acknowledgment, saying: "I have you to thank for enlightening me on the current situation in Japan. I have decided not to go back there but to continue my missionary work among Nisei." He also wrote a poem in my notebook. This minister, who had enthusiastically spread false rumors, even from his hospital bed, had done a complete turnabout. I am glad I was able to see this side of his character. On October 30, after hastily bidding farewell to the remaining internees, we were temporarily isolated in the theater while our belongings were checked again. At two o'clock in the afternoon, we were directed to buses and made our way outside the barbed wire toward freedom.

7

RETURN TO HAWAII

Straight to Seattle

As we were driven out of the barbed-wire enclosure of Santa Fe Camp, the relief we felt showed in our faces. I inhaled deep breaths of freedom for the first time in four years. Of course we were not entirely free yet. Until our release from custody and the designation "internee" was struck from our records, we were still subject to many restrictions. In this way, life behind barbed wire continued for a while. Three hundred and twenty-seven internees exited the camp gates at 2:10 p.m. on Tuesday, October 30, 1945, and arrived at the station seven minutes later. Our train left the station at 2:32 p.m. It was a six-car train especially prepared for us, with freight cars attached. These held our luggage, all 150 tons of it. We were to travel north for fifteen hundred miles, directly to Seattle. The cars were considerably old and antiquated. We had sandwiches and fruit until dining cars were added in Denver. Several internees from each car were assigned KP duty. It turned out to be labor-intensive work, and I felt sorry for them. A ten-gallon can of milk was distributed to each car.

Traveling with us were Mr. Monroe, an immigration officer acting as transportation commander, and dozens of club-carrying guards. The sick were kept together in the Pullman car, attended by Dr. Masayoshi Tanaka, a white nurse, and a dozen rotating internee volunteer orderlies. The orderly's work was no easy task either. With the exception of the spokesman and committee members, no one was allowed to visit other cars.

At 4:35 a.m. on Wednesday, October 31, the train made a brief stop at Colorado Springs, where we saw many big glass buildings. Outside Denver at around 6:40 a.m., we entered a large industrial area lined with what looked like defense-related factories. We saw white female laborers for the first time. A streamlined Union Pacific train stopped beside ours; the white children in the train waved to us repeatedly. There were many overpasses in the area, and traffic seemed to be moving smoothly.

At 7:45 A.M. we left Denver. As soon as we pulled out of the station, we saw vast fields of beets. Dr. Tanaka, accompanied by the nurse and a few guards, moved about the train, checking on the internees. A blunt man, he was in a good mood that day and announced, "Everyone is homesick. Castor oil all around." Who was he kidding? I was *not* about to oblige him, and I refused. At lunch, seventy people passed through our car to go to the dining car. (Each group was given about thirty minutes to eat.) Our car was fairly dirty. On top of that, it was very difficult to rest, because we had to sleep in our traveling clothes with two of us sitting side by side and facing two others. Nevertheless, others envied us, saying their car was dirtier and must have been made in the Tokugawa era. Someone is always worse off, I suppose. Huge pastures appeared on either side of us. There were puddles as big as ponds and mobile fences here and there. We saw a huge herd of sheep.

When our turn came for lunch, we went to the dining car. We were served by black waiters and the tables were clean. The menu included beef stew, real coffee with cream, bread, and real butter. It was my first honest-to-goodness meal in four long years. The ice water and coffee were especially good. I did not know butter could be so delicious. In the camps, we had had coffee made from roasted beans and imitation butter. Now my dulled tastebuds had been reawakened. A few people in another car suffered food poisoning from sashimi they had brought from Santa Fe. They vomited and were plagued by diarrhea. This gave the authorities a bit of trouble.

The Vast Plain

At 2:12 P.M. we arrived in Laramie, a town of six thousand people and home to Wyoming University. Fish fossils could be found not far from here, so the fossil collectors among us looked out longingly. At 8:15 P.M. we passed through Rock Springs, a thriving town. Mr. Kyl So Han operated a coal mine farther beyond. It was said that he never hired Japanese workers and that one of the branch headquarters for the Independence for Korea Party was located on his property. At around 9:20 P.M. we passed a small town called Green River. There were many shops with neon signs, a café, and liquor stores on one side of a street. We were captivated by the female railroad laborers working diligently in twos and threes at the water tender behind the locomotive. Because we had been in a place without women for so long, we jokingly spoke of wanting to stop here awhile.

Our car, which had been the envy of others, showed signs of age too. The water and electricity stopped. The technicians could do nothing. At around midnight, Mr. Kawasaki, our spokesman, came around to inform us that the car would be replaced in Pocatello, at around four or five o'clock the next morning. Without water, the toilets stopped working and there was not even a drop of drinking water. I developed a headache from the bad smell and could not sleep however hard I tried.

It was Thursday, November 1, our third day in transit. After a light sleep I woke up at 2 A.M. It had snowed the previous night. The dinner menu had consisted of tomato juice, vegetable salad, pork, and tea. Thank goodness the meals at least were fit for humans. At 4:35 A.M. we arrived at a big station in Pocatello, in southeastern Idaho. At 6:55 A.M. we made a short stop in Minidoka. I wanted to see the Hunt relocation camp but was unable to. At 8:20 A.M. we arrived in Shoshone. The dining cars were changed and coupled in the middle of the train so we could get to them from both sides. For breakfast we had meatballs, mashed potatoes, rolls, coffee, and real butter.

"We will arrive at Seattle tomorrow morning. One more night and all of this will be over." Everybody brightened a little. The water and electricity in our car began working again somehow, so it was not necessary to replace our car. However, we could not change our clothes, shave, or shower, and we were not allowed to leave the train for a breath of fresh air while waiting at a station. We continued to endure the wretched lot of an internee. At 9:30 A.M. we arrived at the Glenns Ferry station. To the left we saw the grand, meandering Snake River, which we had not seen in a long time. (Also known as the Salmon River, it goes up to Salmon Falls.) Here, too, were several white women doing labor-intensive work. After a twenty-minute stop, the train started, not for Yakima as scheduled, but for Boise, the capital of Idaho, then Portland and Seattle. In whichever direction I looked, there was land and more land with unlimited resources. What is America going to do with all of it? They say land is power. This is true in America.

Spectacular Scenery

At 10:40 A.M. on November 1, we passed Mountain Home Station. At 12:30, while we were having lunch, we passed Nampa. Our route changed again; we bypassed Boise and took a shortcut. At 1:55 P.M., we passed Weiser Station and saw flocks of turkeys and pheasants. Beautiful mountains, valleys, and rivers dotted with railway bridges followed one after another. I only wish the sand hills could have been lush with trees, which would have greatly enhanced the scenery. As the train climbed up a mountain, the river narrowed into a swiftly running stream. We reached Huntington Station in Oregon at 2:25 P.M. In accordance with ID certificate regulations, we all filled out cards with our Hawaii addresses and handed them to our committee members. Since our departure from Santa Fe, the weather had been fine every day, but today was cloudy and a bit too warm. At 2:50 P.M., the train left Huntington.

Earlier all I had seen were vast plains. Now I was surrounded by nothing but mountains and valleys. The leaves on the trees were turning yellow and some were red. As far as I could see, mountains and fields were covered in golden yellow. It was a spectacular view. At 3:50 P.M. we passed a place called Durkee. I had counted seven connected valleys up to this point. From here the land leveled off into flat plains. After a while, the train began climbing again toward the Blue Mountains. While I was fascinated with the beautiful scenery, elderly Mr. Akimori was absorbed in a thick book of fiction. At around 4:20 P.M., I began noticing what looked like rain in the distant mountains. We put our watches back one hour and passed Baker Station. At 5:30 P.M. we waited almost two hours for another train to pass. That night, I was so tired I slept curled up like a lobster for at least three hours.

On November 2, Friday, the fourth day of our journey, we were scheduled to arrive in Seattle by noon. At 6:05 A.M., we crossed a massive bridge in Vancouver, Washington, located north of the Columbia River, and we proceeded along the riverbank. The fog was too thick to see anything, but the tall trees were green with foliage. We passed Longview Station at 7:10 A.M. We had a scenic view of fully grown fir trees, fertile land, mountains, water, fish, and other game. I thought to myself: This is where I would like to live.

The previous night someone had suffered a severe stomachache, so the authorities decided to forego Portland and make straight for Seattle as soon as possible. We passed through Chehalis Station at 7:55 P.M. and arrived at Centralia Station at 8:02 P.M., ninety-three miles from Seattle.

Detained Again

The scenery after we crossed the Columbia River was by far the most impressive on the entire trip. It was already November, but the trees were still fresh and green. Among them countless shrubs were dressed up in yellow leaves. The Reverend Okawa, who was sitting in my car, observed, "Just like the maples at Shiobara." I have never been to Shiobara, but scenes of autumn in Japan prior to the war ran through my mind. At 9:00 A.M., we saw something black moving along the Columbia River near Tacoma, which turned out to be several thousand ducks, and some common gulls flying among them. Sand, which would later be used in building materials, was being filtered in factories along the river.

The autumn scenery along the majestic Columbia River was beyond description. Abundant lumber from nearby mountains is gathered here using the waterways, so there were numerous lumber factories. At 9:10 A.M. we passed East Olympia. At around 9:25, we saw buildings with signs advertising the Tacoma Boat Mart and the Sperry Flour Co., Ltd. Five minutes later, we were in Tacoma. We had thirty-nine more miles to go, or about an hour. Tacoma's commercial area came up on the left side of our train, and there was a Union Pacific Station. Trees were withered but the grass was fresh and green. If it had been fair weather, the scenery would have been much better. At 11:10 A.M. we arrived at our final destination, Seattle Station. Our train stopped at the far corner of the yard. FBI officers and guards moved left and right, and it took a while before we could leave the train.

Now that we were in Seattle, I wondered where we would be heading. My group was transported by bus to the immigration office in the city. The building resembled a magnificent hotel, which was unusual. As soon as we were all gathered in a room on an upper floor, the door was closed and locked behind us, which came as a shock. Nothing is more psychologically unnerving than the clang of a door being bolted. Our natural reaction was one of crushing disappointment. We were still internees, but we had already been pardoned and were on our way home, yet here we were, locked up. Tired and almost dizzy with hunger, we were told that we had to wait until four or five o'clock for our next meal. Because it was a cloudy day, it was already getting dark. The switch was in the hall outside, so we could not turn on the light. Finally, sometime after five o'clock, a guard unlocked the door. We went to a dining room, which seated about a hundred people. Each of us received a dish of macaroni and a small dish of beans. Tea was served. The macaroni was not much, but we ate it up, thinking we might be given something else. We were a bit surprised when we were told there was nothing more.

Two Meals a Day

I had heard that a friend of mine in our group, Mr. F, was sick but, because he was in another room in the building, I could do nothing. We had not yet been given access to any of our belongings, so we spoke to the guards. They answered curtly, "We will do something about it tomorrow." Without a change of clothes or pajamas, we had no choice but to sleep as we were. After our meager meal, we were all still hungry, so naturally our talk focused on food. The dining room of the immigration office was contracted to an old Chinese couple with children. Between the dining room and the kitchen there was a small store where cigarettes, bananas, and so on, were sold. It seems they intended not to feed us but to sell us food. Late that night, our luggage, which had been piled up in the corridor, was handed to us. We shaved and showered, washing off three days of dirt. Wearing clean clothes at last, I lay down on the bed feeling as though I had been reborn. The bed had no mattress, but I was so tired I slept soundly from lights-out at 10:00 to around 4:00, thus reenergized.

On November 3, Saturday, I got up at 6:00 A.M., looked out the window, and saw the city through a thick fog. The temperature seemed comfortable. Breakfast at 8:00 consisted of coffee, bread, and two boiled eggs. Our representative, Mr. Kawasaki, sent a request for a meeting with the head of the immigration office. After a fruitful discussion he and a few others were allowed to visit returnees in other rooms. We had permission to go to the rooftop garden and walk around in the fog. From there, we talked to our friends in the infirmary through a window. I was relieved to see Mr. F doing well.

We learned that there were returnees from other camps staying here as well: Twenty-seven men from the Amache Relocation Center and the free zone, including Messrs. Yoichi Hata, Ryuten Kashiwa, Taichi Sato, Nishimoto, Morihara, and Yamada. These people were confined to the building only at night and took their meals in the city. They were free to come and go as they pleased during the day. About a hundred of the Santa Fe group were lodged at the Seamen's Institute some distance away. This big, magnificent building had hotel beds and even billiard tables. Although the men were not allowed to leave their rooms, they were not locked in and commuted to the immigration office for meals. I envied them a little. During their rounds, Representatives Kawasaki, Ozaki, and Takeda kept us informed of what was going on. According to them, the immigration office had had a two-meals-a-day policy prior to the war. Alarmed, we decided to buy provisions from the outside. With permission from the authorities, forty-nine of us in the first room contributed two dollars each and organized a cooperative group. We appointed Mr. Kusano chief, Mr. Ozaki accountant, Mr. Adachi bookkeeper, and Mr. Nishimoto purchase agent.

Although we were not yet allowed to send cables, we were now free to send as many letters as we wished by either air or surface mail. After being subjected to years of inspections and restrictions, it was like being in heaven. About a hundred airmail letters from our room alone were immediately dispatched. Most of them were addressed to loved ones in Hawaii. We had grown so accustomed to leaving our letters open for inspection that initially we felt uneasy about sealing them.

Apples and *Matsutake* Mushrooms

In the evening, Mr. Nishimoto returned with twenty-four-dollars'-worth of apples, oranges, cakes, cigarettes, and so on, which he had purchased in the city. We immediately opened a canteen in the room and began selling the items to "investors" in the order in which their names appeared on the list. Washington's famous large Delicious apples, as well as oranges, sold for ten cents each, and cake was fifteen. Everyone tried to be the first to buy. A Delicious apple really was delicious; I fully enjoyed the taste of the fruit. At the end of the sale, we showed a loss of one dollar. The event created such a commotion that grown men were acting like little boys. Thanks to the two-meals-a-day office policy, I was able to enjoy that wonderful apple. I am no longer certain what the prerequisites for happiness are. The second meal served that day was curry rice. There was no fruit that morning or evening.

Sunday, November 4. It rained for the first time. We had cereal and coffee for breakfast. Through the auspices of Mr. Nishimoto, a special arrangement was made with a newly opened Japanese restaurant, and he was able to obtain some highly coveted Japanese foodstuff just before noon. Mr. Taichi Sato, whom we had not seen since our days at Sand Island, paid us a visit. We feasted on rice balls, *kamaboko* (fishcake), prawns, lobsters, fresh oysters, and pickles. The canteen committee collected an additional dollar from each of us. Picture postcards and stamps were now available for purchase. The gamblers among us began to throw dice and play cards as soon as they filled their stomachs. They were full of energy and in a good mood so long as their stomachs were satisfied. After we arrived in Seattle, we were told that Dr. Tanaka, who had accompanied us on the train, had been sent back to Santa Fe. Dr. Kohatsu, from our group, was ordered to serve as the returnees' physician until our arrival in Honolulu, so he made his rounds, visiting each room.

Monday November 5. For the first time on this journey, we had fine weather in the morning, and it continued throughout the day. The view of the mountains from our room was beautiful. Breakfast was the usual coffee, bread, and two boiled eggs. Among the guards was a black sergeant, a smiling, likeable fellow. He cast dice with the returnees and lost one game after another, all the while holding his sides with laughter. An elderly white man and a young man of German descent stared at us coolly.

If I keep mentioning food, please forgive me. Lunch, which had been bought outside, was by far the best meal of the day: two big rice balls, fragrant *matsutake, kamaboko,* and cake. Seattle *matsutake* is famous. Harvested in the nearby mountains, its fragrance and taste are identical to the Japanese *matsutake.* Just like eels in New York, this mushroom is famous among Japanese. The season was already over, and the harvest was smaller than expected because of a shortage in transportation. However, next year, the harvesters said the market would be flooded with Seattle *matsutake.* I heard that Mr. Matsujiro Otani of Honolulu cabled an order for a thousand pounds, but it could not be met.

The apples and *matsutake* were so delicious that someone suggested we take them home as souvenirs. Many returnees bought a good supply of both items. Fresh *matsutake* sold for $1.75 per pound. The men had them boiled and packed in two-pound jars for $2.75. The bottled *matsutake* was just as tasty and was welcomed as a novelty in Hawaii.

Farewell to the Mainland

On the afternoon of November 5, Mr. Earl B. Bonham, head of the immigration office, disbursed our remaining camp savings. The largest amount received was $1,300, the least 40 cents. Most men received $200, $300, or $500. According to Mr. Saiki, a former assistant general manager who assisted Miss Carter with the accounting, the total amount paid was $75,000. Apparently surprised by the affluence of so many internees, Mr. Bonham asked Mr. Kawasaki if the savings were from work-related income. "No, most of this money was sent from Hawaii," Mr. Kawasaki answered. To this, Mr. Bonham asked jokingly, "Shall we play poker tonight?" The twenty-dollar and hundred-dollar bills we received were all brand-new. Not having seen money for so long, a few returnees laughingly said they hoped the bills were not counterfeit. Now that they were moneyed men, they were in an expansive mood.

Mr. Iwao Matsushita, an ex-Mitsui Bussan man and a former spokesman at the Missoula camp, had come from Montana to visit some of his Hawaii friends. A graduate of Tokyo Foreign Language College and a courteous gentleman, he now worked at the War Relocation Authority (WRA) in Seattle. After being introduced by a former coworker, Mr. Murakami, I had a good talk with him. According to Mr. Matsushita, the present population of Seattle was about seven hundred thousand, or twice that of the prewar period. The Japanese population was only three thousand. That evening, we were each handed a military embarkation permit. On it were listed the names of those permitted to board the ship to Hawaii; it included the name of Rev. Masahiro Himeno, who had been released earlier.

Tuesday, November 6 was cloudy but fairly warm. There were about twenty German internees and some young Chinese in our building, and they were given three meals a day. I could not understand the discrepancy, but now I did not care. We were sailing soon, so we ordered an extravagant lunch from Mr. Kanno: roast chicken, rice balls, and fresh oysters. When men have enough to eat but no work to do, they naturally seek an outlet for their energy. The gamblers in our room became absorbed in a 7-11 game from morning to night. Mr. B, Mr. C of Honolulu, and Mr. K of Kahului were in keen competition with each other. The game was interesting and they played like gentlemen; I was almost drawn into it.

Wednesday, November 7. After five days in Seattle, we were finally shipping out. It was a cloudy morning, and it began to snow at 7:30 A.M. It was the first snow of the year, a good omen. "After seeing the first snowfall in Seattle, I boarded the ship." I do not know if this is a poem or not, but it came to mind. At 11:30, we left the immigration office. The sick were taken first: Three or four people were carried out on stretchers. Then the forty-nine of us in the first room boarded a bus, followed by those in the fifth and sixth rooms. We traveled through the city in the rain. Seattle has many slopes, like San Francisco. We arrived at Pier 42, where 124 returnees who had arrived from various places were already waiting. We boarded the ship one by one after roll was called.

All Was Military Style On Board

Our ship, the SS *Yarmouth,* looked like a destroyer and was about the size of the interisland vessel the SS *Haleakala.* We sailed on November 7 at 4:30 P.M., on a voyage of twenty-five hundred miles to Honolulu. Passengers included five hundred Japanese returnees and military personnel returning to Hawaii, including some Japanese American soldiers. Rev. Himeno, whose name was on the passenger list, was not on board. I do not know what happened to him. When I heard that the view from port heading into the Pacific was splendid, I went out on deck, but had to leave quickly because of the cold.

The ship had been taken over for military use, so it was outfitted with three-tiered hammocks. There were not enough heaters, so it was fairly cold. At first we had no blankets, so we asked for some. Even then, it was cold at night. We had the same trouble with the toilets and water as we did on the train. What was especially bad was that we had only saltwater and it was cold, and the rusty plumbing reddened the water. Most distressing of all, however, was that we had no access to our trunks or bags, so we had no clean clothes. Our luggage had been inadvertently placed under other cargo, so it could not be delivered to us. We were going to meet our families for the first time in years in dirty, worn-out clothes. We made up our minds to endure the next seven or eight days like soldiers at the front.

As soon as we boarded the ship, we were ordered to fend for ourselves as we had in the camps. We had to take care of all the cooking, cleaning, and so on. An American mess sergeant took care of the menu and supplied the foodstuff, and we selected several helpers from among us. Under the supervision of Mr. Kango Kawasaki, our spokesman, various committees were organized. Mr. Minoru Murakami and his assistants oversaw everything proficiently and with military efficiency.

As far as foodstuff was concerned, the military was extravagant. They gave us a hundred-pound bag of sugar. Cream was plentiful, so we could use as much as we wished. The same was true of meat. There was a world of difference between the ship and the immigration office, where the authorities had been miserly. A no-smoking policy was in effect in the cabins and dining room, which I appreciated. However, when we were later caught in a storm and could not go out on deck, as expected this rule was overlooked in the dining room.

I met with Mr. Yamazaki of Waianae and Mr. Ozu of Honolulu and their families for the first time since we had parted at Sand Island, and I enjoyed talking with them. Some of the returnees from relocation centers or free zones had their families with them. Seeing children, looking like angels, made everyone think of his own family. Some members of the Japan Victory Party had been looking dismayed since coming aboard. They had expected Japanese ships, flying the Rising Sun, to pick them up in Seattle. Still clinging to hope, they claimed that we would soon learn the truth when we encountered the three hundred Japanese battleships currently surrounding Oahu. It was useless to talk to them.

The Return Voyage

On Thursday, November 8, I woke up at about 1:00 A.M. Apparently the ship had pitched and rolled considerably early on, but I had been so exhausted I had slept through it all. It was still cold, so I dozed off again until the light of day. In the morning, the weather was fine and the sea calmer, but the ship still pitched and rolled. Many people could not get up. I felt a little sick and did not eat much at breakfast and lunch. That day I heard news of some old friends from Mr. Takeo Inoue, who often contributed articles to the *Colorado Jiji News*. At night the sea grew more turbulent. The bow of the ship was heavier because of the cargo, and the stern propellers ran idle once in a while. Huge waves hit the side of the ship, sounding like powerful guns. It was my misfortune to be in the bow section, so I could not get a wink of sleep. I skipped dinner. On the ninth, the rough seas continued throughout the day. Most of the passengers were seasick, groaning in their hammocks. Since only a few could manage KP duty, those who went to the dining room had to serve themselves. I had heard that the Seattle–Hawaii crossing was bad. Now I knew it firsthand. I had been fairly confident that I was a good sailor, but I gave up completely that day. I did not eat at all and felt terrible. We were on a ship that was capable of doing twenty-one knots, but it could only manage to do nine knots during the storm. In the dining room, kitchen and eating utensils were tossed about.

Saturday, the 10th. The sea calmed and everyone slowly appeared on deck. Chaplain Captain Masao Yamada, who was on his way back from the European front, unexpectedly asked me, "Aren't you Dr. Soga?" Embarrassed at being addressed as "doctor" but pleased to see him after such a long time, I wanted to talk with him, but I was still feeling sick and excused myself. The storm had delayed our arrival in Honolulu; we were now scheduled to land on November 14.

The condition of the toilets worsened. Dirty water began backing up. Plumbers tried to repair the toilets, but they could not and never returned. Mr. Adachi, the washroom manager, had a talk with the captain, who said he could do nothing if internees threw cigarette butts and orange peels into the bowls. During the storm, Mr. Kawasaki bravely remained in the dining room and continued to issue directives in high spirits while his assistants fell to the wayside, seasick. His fortitude impressed me. Staff from each service department began returning to their duties the morning after the storm. Sick people were allocated cabins, and the orderlies who attended them worked extraordinarily hard. However, among the sick were a few brazen ones who never showed any gratitude. This was regrettable. That night I had dinner for the first time in two days; the stewed rice and tea were delicious. Later I saw a movie in the dining room.

Sunday, November 11. The sea began to pick up again, but the ship

was going at a faster clip. We were now seven hundred miles from Honolulu and were back on schedule to arrive on Tuesday, the thirteenth. We
were told that no more cables could be sent from the ship. Chaplain Captain Yamada gave a sermon in English in the ship's small chapel at 9:00
A.M. Thirty minutes later, the Reverends Ikezawa and Sugimoto held a
service in the dining room. At 1:30 P.M., Buddhists gathered in the chapel
and the Reverend Fujitani gave a short speech. That afternoon, all passengers were given thorough checkups. For dinner we had turkey and ice
cream, which I enjoyed after so many years. I engaged myself in a lengthy
conversation with Mr. Yoshinobu Sasaki, a schoolmaster, and Mr. Mantsu-
chi Hashimoto.

Dedicated Workers

Monday, November 12. I went to bed at around 8:00 P.M. and got up
just after 1:00 in the morning. Since the air in the lower cabin was stuffy,
I went up to the dining room. The waves were still high and the ship was
rolling considerably. Most passengers were still suffering from seasickness.
As was my habit, I dozed off in a chair in the dining room. People said
I was tough, but actually I still felt fairly sick. Just after 9:00 A.M., it was
announced that the ship was between 420 and 430 miles from Honolulu
and that we would arrive between 2:00 and 3:00 P.M. on the thirteenth.
We were not allowed to disembark with fruit we had brought from the
Mainland, but up to nine packs of cigarettes were permitted. Onboard
returnees and soldiers could purchase cigarettes at a discount. One carton
of Camels sold for sixty cents, other brands for ten cents less. Smokers
bought as much as they could.

The ship pitched and rolled so much that my seasickness returned.
The kitchen floor at the bottom of the ship was greasy and slippery in
the steamy air. The people who worked there began to succumb. We were
prepared to eat only bread and butter if necessary, but thanks to those
who worked in the kitchen, meals were somehow prepared and served.
Among the dedicated men who provided continuous service doing such
menial work were Mr. Yoshio Kobayashi of Kahului and Mr. Shozaemon
Masaki of Honolulu. There were of course other volunteers: Those on KP
duty served five to six hundred people in a small dining room and did an
excellent job.

Although I had no appetite, I went to the dining room. Ahead of me
was a sweet little girl with hair bobbed short, accompanied by her father,
who had been living in a free zone. In answer to my question, she said

she was five years old and her mother was so seasick she could not leave the cabin. The child herself was fine. Wives and children of internees, soldiers, and sick people were allotted cabins and had a separate dining room. Internees paroled from free zones and relocation centers had their travel expenses paid to Seattle, including an allowance of one dollar per meal per person regardless of age. On the way to Seattle, they stayed at hostels or immigration offices and the WRA paid them fifty cents per night. A family of nine was supposedly given six hundred dollars for traveling expenses.

The ventilation in our troop compartment stopped, and the room grew stuffy. I stayed on deck in the cold for about an hour and returned feeling refreshed. The movie *Show Business* was just beginning in the dining room. It was enjoyable. Before the start of the second show, I was back in my hammock. Eventually several strong sailors opened the door of the compartment beside ours and removed some of our luggage. They also restarted an electric fan, so the airflow improved greatly. I slept from 9:00 P.M. to 1:00 A.M. That night there were spectacular lightning flashes, and the seas remained high.

Beloved Honolulu

Naked girls were drawn on the walls of the ship's dining room along with some witty remarks. From a few of them I could guess when the average American sailor or soldier hoped the war would end or what they thought about postwar conditions. For example, "Golden Gate by 48" meant that those returning from the Pacific War expected to see the Golden Gate Bridge again by 1948. "Bread Line by 49" meant that a food shortage was anticipated sometime before 1949. There were also some silly remarks like "Today's Special: Pork and Beans. Tomorrow: Beans and Pork." Most Americans believed that Japan would not be defeated until 1948. In the end, Admiral Nimitz chose to attack the Japanese mainland directly rather than conquer the smaller islands one at a time. This unexpected strategy advanced the date of V-J Day. If the war had continued until 1948, Japan's defeat would not have been so devastating.

November 13, 1945. I woke up at 2:00 A.M. and went up on deck. Some of us discussed the best way to express our appreciation for the outstanding work of Mr. Kawasaki and the committee members. We decided to publish our thanks in two Japanese newspapers in Honolulu under the names of two representatives from each island: Mr. Sokabe and I (Honolulu and Oahu), Mr. Fukunaga and Mr. Sato (Maui), Mr. Seike and Mr. Horikawa (Kauai), and Mr. Saiki and Mr. Maehara (the Big Island).

It was a fine day. At 10:52 A.M. we spotted an island, which we thought was Maui but turned out to be Oahu. Everyone excitedly made preparations to go ashore. Just after 2:00 P.M. the ship slowly approached Pier 26. Mr. Olson, the Swedish consul, other consulate members, immigration officers, and Messrs. Katagiri, Miho, and Murai of the Emergency Service Committee of Japanese Americans came aboard to help us complete landing procedures. First we each received, in alphabetical order, a gangway pass giving us permission to disembark. Then we were handed our luggage and a release permit, officially ending our internee status, from the immigration officers and the consul. We were finally free of all barbed-wire fences, both visible and invisible.

The gentle sea breeze, unique to Hawaii, felt pleasant on deck. But the signing of documents and other procedures were completed in a stuffy cabin, so we were all uncomfortable and dripping with perspiration. Mr. Shu Nakayama, a schoolteacher, suffered from mild cerebral anemia and collapsed. Within a couple of hours of landing, we were told that the toilets did not pass inspection. Threatened with the possibility of not being allowed to land, the staff of the washroom department took off their ties and good clothes and began cleaning in their undershirts. At first we did not take the problem too seriously, but when the authorities began making arrangements for KP duty that evening, we grew uneasy. They announced that those from Oahu would be allowed to disembark later in the day, and that a specially outfitted ship would take everyone else to the other islands the following day. The second part of this announcement was later changed: Those from other islands could go ashore now with the others, but they had to return to the ship the next day before sailing time. Whoever was not back in time would have to pay his own passage home. The Hongwanji Betsuin Mission and the Jodo-shu Betsuin Mission provided lodging for those who had nowhere to stay overnight.

We disembarked in alphabetical order. It was after 6:00 P.M. before the "S" group touched land. Our families had been expecting us on the fifteenth; they were only informed that afternoon that we would be arriving two days ahead of schedule. They had been waiting since two in the afternoon to welcome us. After four long years of separation, we spent the next few days in a happy dream.

INTERNEES SENT TO THE MAINLAND ON THE FIRST SHIP BY OCCUPATION

The first ship, carrying 172 Japanese male passengers, left Sand Island camp in Honolulu port on February 17, 1942. Most of them were from Honolulu and other districts in Oahu. Twenty-nine German and Italian male internees were also on the same ship.

All individual names are omitted herein, because the translator cannot guarantee the accuracy of their transliteration or the absence of other mistakes.

Buddhist ministers and Japanese language teachers—57

Christian priests—2

Commerce and industry—56

Doctors—4

Hoteliers—2

Newspaper related people—6

Shinto ministers and related people—19

Others—26

INTERNEES SENT TO THE MAINLAND BY ISLAND
(INCLUDING JAPAN)

Males	Honolulu	Oahu	Hawaii	Maui	Kauai	Japan	TOTALS
1st Ship (departed February 17, 1942)	136	34	0	2	0	0	172
2nd Ship (departed March 19, 1942)	15	7	83	26	35	0	166
3rd Ship (departed May 23, 1942)	48	23	36	0	2	0	109
4th Ship (departed June 21, 1942)	14	3	12	1	9	0	39
5th Ship (departed August 7, 1942)	16	2	4	22	5	0	49
6th Ship (departed September 16, 1942)	8	3	12	1	4	1	29
7th Ship (departed July 11, 1942)	4	1	0	18	0	0	23
8th Ship (departed March 2, 1943)	18	1	11	6	6	1	43
9th Ship (departed July 1, 1943)	27	4	2	0	1	0	34
10th Ship (departed December 2, 1943)	19	6	0	3	2*	0	30
SUBTOTALS	305	84	160	79	64	2	694
Females	4	2	0	1	1	0	8
TOTALS	309	86	160	80	65	2	702

NOTE: Ships 1 through 8 departed from Sand Island Camp; ships 9 and 10 departed from Honouliuli Camp.

*One internee transferred to Santa Fe from Tule Lake.

STATUS OF JAPANESE AT SANTA FE CAMP AS OF AUGUST 10, 1944 (COMPILED BY THE JAPANESE OFFICE)

Deceased	6
Returned to Japan on first exchange ship	9
(SS *Gripsholm,* left New York on June 18, 1942)	
Returned to Japan on second exchange ship	71
(SS *Gripsholm,* left New York on Sept. 1, 1943)	
Relocated to Hawaii (U.S. citizens)	19
Paroled on the Mainland	103
Transferred to Kenedy Camp, Texas	1
Transferred to Kooskia Camp, Idaho	8
Transferred to Crystal City Camp, Texas	33
Male internees	444
Female internees	8
TOTAL	**702**

INTERNEES AT THE HONOULIULI CAMP

Honouliuli Camp opened on March 2, 1943, just as Sand Island Camp was closing. Only sixty-four internees from Honouliuli were sent to the Mainland aboard the ninth and the tenth ships; most were released. Both Issei and Nisei were interned, and their length of stay varied. I asked several former internees for recollections of their time at the camp. No exact records were kept. I was able to compile a list of 320 names, but there may be omissions and mistakes in the transliteration of names. On this point I beg everyone's pardon. (For the same reason, I do not give the names of the people interned at the temporary camps on other islands.)

LIST OF INTERNEES BY NAME

Family Name	Given Name	Group (1–10 are ship numbers)
Abe	Kiroku	Honouliuli
Abe	Sanji	Honouliuli
Adachi	Ichiji	6
Adachi	Tokuji	3
Aka	Ryosei	2
Akata	Kyu	Honouliuli
Akata	Tsutomu	Honouliuli
Akata	Yaichiro	8
Akegarasu	Takeo	2
Akimori	Daikichi	5
Akiyama	(Unknown)	Honouliuli
Akizaki	Takeo	Honouliuli, from 1
Akizaki	Yoshio	Honouliuli
Ama	Takao	2
Ando	Shigeru	3
Aoyagi	Seisaku	6
Aoyama	Takejo	Honouliuli
Aragaki	Kiyu	Honouliuli
Araki	Kazuma	1
Araki	Tadaichi	6
Arashiro	Munehisa	8
Arita	Gentaro	3
Arita	Nizo	9, from Honouliuli
Arita	Takazo	7
Arita	Tamaki	1
Asada	Shigeru	3
Asaeda	Horyu	1

Family Name	Given Name	Group (1–10 are ship numbers)
Asakura	Iwakichi	10, from Honouliuli
Asami	Shoichi	1
Asano	Kakusho	2
Asao	Shigeo	Honouliuli
Asaoka	Kakuho	2
Asato	Eishu	2
Asato	Shigeo	Honouliuli
Ashihara	Sokutaro	8
Atsuumi	Noriaki	1
Awaya	Shotaro	3
Baba	Tokuji	1
Bamba	Genko	3
Ban	Keiso	5
Chikuma	Masayuki	2
Chinen	Takahiko	5
Degawa	Rentaro	3
Deki	Ichiro	10, from Honouliuli
Deme	Jyosen	1
Egami	Jusabiro	Honouliuli
Endo	Sutematsu	3
Enogawa	Seiei	Honouliuli
Fuchino	Heigo	1
Fujihana	Kyodo	2
Fujii	Seiichi	1
Fujii	Sunao	8
Fujii	Teruji	Honouliuli
Fujiie	Shoho	1
Fujimoto	Kenkichi	1
Fujimoto	Kizo	Honouliuli
Fujimoto	Shigeki	Honouliuli
Fujimoto	Tadashi	Honouliuli
Fujimura	Masako	Honouliuli, woman
Fujino	Shigeo	2
Fujisawa	Hideo	1
Fujishiro	Utanosuke	1
Fujita	Kosaku	Honouliuli
Fujita	Masayuki	Honouliuli
Fujita	Sawaichi	3
Fujita	Yoshiharu	3
Fujita	Yoshinori	Honouliuli

Family Name	Given Name	Group (1–10 are ship numbers)
Fujitani	Kodo	3
Fujitani	Shiro	8
Fujiwara	Masao	Honouliuli
Fukuba	Kumaichi	6
Fukuda	Teiichiro	1
Fukuhara	Nao	2
Fukunaga	Zeichi	2
Fukutomi	Shinjiro	Honouliuli
Furukawa	Issaku	5
Furukawa	Shigeo	Honouliuli hospital
Furukawa	Masami	Honouliuli
Furuya	Kaetsu	2
Furuya	Kumaji	1
Genishi	Ichiro	10
Gibo	Anki	Honouliuli
Gibo	Eikichi	Honouliuli
Gima	Shinpuku	10, from Honouliuli
Goto	Mankichi	2
Goya	Kandoku	Honouliuli
Hagimoto	Toichi	3
Hamada	Itsuo	2
Hamada	Kango	3
Hamada	Otoshiro	9
Hamada	Takashi	10, from Honouliuli
Hamamoto	Kiyoto	Honouliuli
Hamamoto	Sadasuke	2
Hamamura	Chiyomatsu	2
Hamamura	Kyoichi	1
Hamano	Sobei	Honouliuli
Hamasaki	Yoshimatsu	3
Hamasaki	Yoshio	Honouliuli
Hanabusa	Minosuke	3
Hanada	Tessui	2
Hanamoto	Hitoshi	3
Hanzawa	Taichiro	5
Hanzawa	Tetsuji	7
Hara	Etsuji	Honouliuli
Harada	Shintaro	Honouliuli
Harada	Tsunetaro	1
Harada	Umeno	Honouliuli, woman

Family Name	Given Name	Group (1–10 are ship numbers)
Harimoto	Michinosuke	Honouliuli
Hasebe	Tatsuo	1
Hasegawa	Haruzo	7
Hasegawa	Kenryu	2
Hasegawa	Tsuruzo	2
Haseyama	Toso	Honouliuli
Hashibe	Shinichi	3
Hashimoto	Koji	Honouliuli
Hashimoto	Manzuch	1
Hashimoto	Yasuaki	Honouliuli
Hata	Yoichi	3
Hataishi	Kenichi	5
Hattori	Shigenari	1
Hayase	Ichiro	Honouliuli
Hayashi	Ichiro	10
Hayashi	Kenjiro	Honouliuli
Hayashi	Kyuhichi	2
Hayashi	Meijiro	8
Hayashi	Tomoichi	1
Hida	Sensei	5
HIga	Hideo	Honouliuli
HIga	Kamasuke	Honouliuli
Higa	Kamesuke	10
Higaki	Bunzo	Honouliuli
Higashi	Terumitsu	Honouliuli
Higuchi	Sakaye	4
Himeno	Masahiro	2
Hino	Shuzui	2
Hino	Yoshio	1
Hinokawa	Keiichi	4
Hirae	Gotaro	6
Hirae	Kei	5
Hirai	Katsutoshi	5
Hirai	Shinsho	Honouliuli
Hirama	Teruzo	1
Hirano	Keisaburo	3
Hirano	Naojiro	2
Hirano	Toshio	2
Hirashima	Kentaro	3
Hirashima	Masaichi	1

Family Name	Given Name	Group (1–10 are ship numbers)
Hirata	Jiro	Honouliuli
Hirayama	Shinsei	2
Hirayama	Unji	6
Hirokawa	Katsuichi	Honouliuli
Hiromitsu	Eiichiro	1
Hiroo	Jinsaburo	8
Hirose	Kosuke	2
Hisatake	Itsuei	2
Hishinuma	Jinjuro	Honouliuli
Honda	Eisaku	1
Honda	Eizo	Honouliuli
Honda	Gengo	10
Honda	Hiroshi	1
Honda	Hiroshi	9, from Honouliuli
Honda	Kaneki	1
Hori	Minetaro	1
Hori	Takunori	Honouliuli
Hori	Yasushi	8
Horibe	Kiku	Woman
Horikawa	Isuke	9, from Honouliuli
Horita	Kiyoji	5
Horita	Shigeru	Honouliuli
Horiuchi	Mitsutaka	2
Horiuchi	Takamori	8
Hoshide	Yoshio	3
Ichiba	Isao	1
Ichida	Heikichi	10
Ichikawa	Kiyoshi	2
Ida	Tadaichi	Honouliuli
Ida	Toka	1
Idemoto	Masao	Honouliuli
Iida	Koichi	1
Iinuma	Toshio	1
Ikeda	Chiei	3
Ikejiri	Daishin	4
Ikeno	Masao	2
Ikezawa	Shuntaro	1
Ikuma	Kinai	3
Imai	Toyoji	2
Imamura	Asataro	3

Family Name	Given Name	Group (1–10 are ship numbers)
Imamura	Teizen	5
Imamura	Tsutomu	1
Inasaki	Itsuo	2
Inokuchi	Kakuji	Honouliuli
Inokuchi	Uyemon	1
Inoue	Sadakichi	3
Inouye	Hideo	Honouliuli
Inouye	Jukichi	2
Inouye	Kumaki	2
Iohara	Masashi	1
Ipponsugi	Riuichi	4
Isa	Kashin	4
Isemoto	Hisato	4
Iseri	Torao	2
Ishibashi	Gakuji	6
Ishida	Heikichi	Honouliuli
Ishida	Kenji	Honouliuli
Ishida	Kyujuro	1
Ishigo	Inakichi	Honouliuli
Ishikawa	Kozo	1
Ishikawa	Masasuke	8
Ishikawa	Seifuku	Honouliuli
Ishiki	Gyuro	Honouliuli
Ishimoto	Masao	1
Ishioka	Yoshio	Honouliuli
Ishizaki	Raiji	2
Isobe	Hakuin	10, from Honouliuli
Isobe	Jusui	1
Isobe	Setsu	1
Isomura	Takasuke	5
Itagaki	Shigeichiro	Honouliuli
Itaoka	Seiichi	Honouliuli
Itaya	Torao	9
Ito	Choichi	2
Ito	Chuzo	6
Ito	Iwao	Honouliuli
Ito	Kanzan	Woman
Ito	Kiyoshi	Honouliuli
Ito	Tatsuo	5
Itsuno	Tokio	2

Family Name	Given Name	Group (1–10 are ship numbers)
Iwahara	Taketo	1
Iwahori	James	Honouliuli
Iwakami	Konosuke	7
Iwamoto	Masao	Honouliuli
Iwanaka	Satoru	Honouliuli
Iwasa	Shinzo	3
Iwasa	Sueji	2
Iwase	Shiro	10, from Honouliuli
Iwashita	Shigeo	2
Iwata	Masayuki	1
Izumi	Kakusho	2
Izumi	Kiyoto	2
Izutsu	Ryozo	6
Jimbo	Futoshi	Honouliuli
Kabashima	Suijo	1
Kagawa	Katsujiro	3
Kagawa	Takeo	1
Kagesa	Shikatsu	Honouliuli
Kageura	Chojiro	Honouliuli
Kageura	Nobuo	Honouliuli
Kageura	Tadao	Honouliuli
Kageura	Yutaka	Honouliuli
Kajiwara	Taryo	2
Kameoka	Sukeichi	9, from Honouliuli
Kamino	Tadami	7
Kamishiro	Noboru	Honouliuli
Kan	Buntaro	7
Kanazawa	Katsuo	8
Kanda	Michiro	4
Kaneda	Yohei	3
Kanemori	Shinroku	4
Kanemoto	Fukuji	Honouliuli
Kaneshiro	Masaaki	Honouliuli
Kaneshiro	Zensuke	Honouliuli
Kanja	Yonezo	2
Kanno	Sakugoro	Honouliuli
Kanno	Tomizo	3
Kasai	Ichiro	9
Kasamoto	Mitsuji	8
Kashima	Ryuichi	1

Family Name	Given Name	Group (1–10 are ship numbers)
Kashiwa	Ryuten	3
Kashiwabara	Ryuju	2
Katamoto	Usaburo	3
Kato	Isoo	3
Kato	Shu	9, from Honouliuli
Kato	Yoshinobu	8
Katoda	Tetsuei	2
Katsuno	Asaichi	9
Kawahara	Toraji	4
Kawakami	Shozo	1
Kawamata	Sadaji	5
Kawamoto	Katsuichi	1
Kawamoto	Shigeo	Honouliuli
Kawamoto	Takuzo	Honouliuli
Kawamura	Daizo	Honouliuli
Kawamura	Shodo	7
Kawano	Kazuyuki	4
Kawano	Shoichi	8
Kawasaki	Kango	3
Kawasaki	Kashu	1
Kawasaki	Miyuki	Woman
Kawasaki	Ryosaku	3
Kawashima	Masagoro	Honouliuli
Kawauchi	Kichitaro	2
Kawazoe	Zenichi	Honouliuli
Kayahara	Chosuke	1
Kida	Katsukichi	3
Kikuchi	Chigyoku	2
Kimura	Akio	1
Kimura	Hideji	3
Kimura	Katsuzo	5
Kimura	Kenji	1
Kimura	Muneo	Honouliuli, from 1
Kimura	Tomiji	1
Kimura	Toraki	1
Kimura	Toyoki	5
Kinjo	Chin-ei	3
Kinoshita	Hideo	9, from Honouliuli
Kinoshita	Ichiji	3
Kinoshita	Masaru	Honouliuli

Family Name	Given Name	Group (1–10 are ship numbers)
Kinoshita	Takichi	8
Kinoshita	Uichi	10, from Honouliuli
Kirita	Kamekichi	2
Kisada	Zenzo	6
Kishida	Eiichi	1
Kitajima	Masao	2
Kitano	Masaichi	Honouliuli
Kitayama	Yoshio	2
Kiyohara	Tetsuei	1
Kiyotsuka	Tetsuzo	3
Kobata	Mitsugi	Honouliuli
Kobayakawa	Tomikichi	8
Kobayashi	Enjo	2
Kobayashi	Keinosuke	9, from Honouliuli
Kobayashi	Masaichi	6
Kobayashi	Motoichi	2
Kobayashi	Nisshu	1
Kobayashi	Shokichi	3
Kobayashi	Yoshiemon	Honouliuli
Kobayashi	Yoshio	2
Kodama	Masayuki	1
Kodama	Yoshiharu	Honouliuli
Koga	Masao	Honouliuli
Kohatsu	Yukihide	1
Koide	Hideo	Honouliuli
Koide	Kiyoichi	3
Koide	Shoichi	2
Koide	Yuichi	Honouliuli
Koike	Haruo	5
Koike	Yoshio	3
Koizumi	Gensaku	3
Kojima	Hikoji	2
Kojima	Sadakichi	1
Kokuzo	Zenkai	2
Komagata	Zenkyo	Honouliuli
Komatsu	Taichi	1
Komine	Heisuke	Honouliuli
Komo	Kakuro	8
Komu	Mannosuke	3
Kondo	Kikujiro	9, from Honouliuli

Family Name	Given Name	Group (1–10 are ship numbers)
Konno	Ichiro	1
Konno	Manjiro	7
Koyama	Tomiichi	8
Koyanagi	Fukuo	Honouliuli
Koyanagi	Kiyomi	Honouliuli
Kubo	Hisaichi	Honouliuli
Kubo	Kazuo	Honouliuli
Kubo	Shinsaku	Honouliuli
Kubokawa	Kyokujo	1
Kubota	Ryudo	2
Kubota	Saichiro	2
Kuchiba	Gikyo	1
Kudo	Isamu	2
Kumasaki	Tamotsu	Honouliuli
Kunimura	Kichijiro	Honouliuli
Kuniyoshi	Choin	10
Kuniyuki	Aisuke	3
Kuniyuki	Ikuzo	2
Kuniyuki	Takeo	Honouliuli
Kuraishi	Tomomichi	Honouliuli
Kurakake	Toraichi	3
Kuramoto	Tameto	Honouliuli
Kurisu	Koichi	3
Kurita	Yasuro	3
Kuroda	Keisei	1
Kurohira	Hosho	3
Kurokawa	Tetsuji	1
Kurozawa	Zensuke	3
Kusano	Ishima	6
Kusao	Takegoro	3
Kusuda	Kakushin	1
Kuwahara	Gunichi	2
Kuwahara	Shigeru	2
Kuwahara	Tsuyoshi	Honouliuli
Kuwaye	Ryozen	Honouliuli
Kyosaki	Masato	2
Maeda	Hikoemon	5
Maeda	Kametaro	2
Maeda	Yoshihisa	5
Maehara	Kenichi	3

Family Name	Given Name	Group (1–10 are ship numbers)
Maehara	Teiichiro	5
Maehokama	Shobun	5
Maekawa	Shigezo	1
Maemoto	Isamu	Honouliuli
Maeno	Waichi	Honouliuli
Makihira	Tamehachi	8
Mamiya	Toshio	2
Manju	Eiji	5
Marumoto	Masaichi	10
Marutani	Matsuo	6
Masaki	Jikyo	1
Masaki	Shozaemon	1
Mashimo	Junzo	2
Masuda	Gosaku	2
Matano	Konin	1
Matayoshi	Shinjiro	4
Matsubayashi	Shoten	7
Matsubayashi	Shushin	1
Matsuda	Genichi	1
Matsuda	Ihichi	1
Matsuda	Rikichi	3
Matsuda	Ryugen	2
Matsuda	Toshiji	Honouliuli
Matsuda	Toyoki	Honouliuli
Matsui	Kakusuke	2
Matsui	Totaro	1
Matsui	Yuutetsu	2
Matsumoto	Kazumi	2
Matsumoto	Kuramatsu	8
Matsumoto	Masato	Honouliuli
Matsumoto	Shigeichi	Honouliuli
Matsumoto	Toramatsu	8
Matsumoto	Yozaemon	3
Matsumura	Tamotsu	1
Matsumura	Tomoji	2
Matsunaga	Nobusuke	9, from Honouliuli
Matsuo	Keijiro	Honouliuli
Matsuo	Umesuke	2
Matsuoka	Buichi	Honouliuli
Matsuura	Gyokuei	2

Family Name	Given Name	Group (1–10 are ship numbers)
Matsuura	Kakichi	Honouliuli
Matsuura	Shuun	2
Matsuura	Toshiyuki	Honouliuli
Matsuzaka	Shigeru	Honouliuli
Mende	Tazo	3
Miake	Eimu	5
Mihara	Sensuke	Honouliuli
Miho	Katsuichi	2
Mikami	Kakai	7
Mikami	Shuji	1
Miki	Yasuzaemon	1
Mikuni	Matagoro	1
Mitose	Masayoshi	Honouliuli
Mitsunaga	Manabu	Honouliuli
Miura	Genpei	2
Miura	Mankichi	4
Miura	Sadahichi	6
Miura	Shinichi	2
Miura	Takeo	5
Miura	Toshio	Honouliuli
Miwa	Shogo	3
Miyagawa	Shintaro	1
Miyagi	Genei	1
Miyagi	Takeo	1
Miyahara	Manabu	Honouliuli
Miyama	Masao	Honouliuli
Miyamasa	Kaichi	3
Miyamoto	Buntetsu	2
Miyamoto	Isamu	Honouliuli
Miyamoto	Jinpei	1
Miyamoto	Kazuo	1
Miyao	Shigemaru	1
Miyao	Yoshie	Woman
Miyao	Yuki	Woman
Miyashiro	Kaoru	Honouliuli
Miyata	Kyoichi	2
Miyazaki	Hiseki	2
Miyazaki	Kazuo	4
Mizumoto	Shigeki	1
Mizuta	Tadashi	Honouliuli

Family Name	Given Name	Group (1–10 are ship numbers)
Mizutari	Yasuyuki	3
Mochizuki	Tanryu	2
Mori	Ishi	Woman
Mori	Motokazu	6
Mori	Shigeo	Honouliuli
Mori	Tenran	4
Moribe	Ryuichi	3
Morifuji	Sadato	3
Morihara	Usaku	3
Morikawa	Eitsuchi	Honouliuli
Morikubo	Shigetsuchi	Honouliuli
Morimoto	Tatsuji	7
Morimoto	Uichi	Honouliuli
Morishige	Kenji	9, from Honouliuli
Morita	Hideo	Honouliuli
Morita	Koetsu	1
Morita	Makoto	Honouliuli
Morita	Zenkichi	8
Moritsugu	Tokuemon	Honouliuli
Moritsugu	Yasuichi	9, from Honouliuli
Moriyama	Sadao	Honouliuli
Motoda	Chester	Honouliuli
Motoshige	Hiroshi	1
Motoshige	Tatsuo	1
Mukai	Yoshizo	6
Mukuda	Shinichi	Honouliuli
Murahama	Hatsujiro	Honouliuli
Murai	Masao	2
Murakami	Jinji	6
Murakami	Kanato	Honouliuli
Murakami	Minoru	2
Murakami	Shigeru	7
Murakami	Taiji	Honouliuli
Murakawa	Masaru	Honouliuli
Murakawa	Takeo	Honouliuli
Murashima	Tateo	5
Murata	Ryuichi	5
Murata	Yasumasa	Honouliuli
Muroda	Toshio	Honouliuli
Mutobe	Ryujun	1

Family Name	Given Name	Group (1–10 are ship numbers)
Nada	Yujiro	1
Nagakura	Eizo	2
Nagami	Genichi	5
Nagasawa	Shukichi	4
Nago	Ninryo	1
Naito	Rikio	Honouliuli
Naitoh	Kyojyo	2
Nakagawa	Akira	Honouliuli
Nakagawa	H. Shizuko	Honouliuli, woman
Nakagawa	Koichiro	3
Nakagawa	Sawaichi	8
Nakagawa	Shiro	Honouliuli
Nakagawa	Takejiro	3
Nakahara	Buntaro	3
Nakaichi	Yuichi	8
Nakama	Ginpachi	1
Nakami	Hyotaro	8
Nakamoto	Hidekichi	1
Nakamoto	Tokuji	Honouliuli
Nakamura	Chusaburo	10, from Honouliuli
Nakamura	Ichiro	9, from Honouliuli
Nakamura	Koichiryu	1
Nakamura	Kokichi	2
Nakamura	Mitsugu	Honouliuli
Nakamura	Tamio	5
Nakamura	Tomoaki	1
Nakamura	Yuichi	3
Nakano	Chikao	5
Nakano	Kyoichi	1
Nakano	Minoru	3
Nakano	Tamejiro	1
Nakano	Yunoshin	4
Nakao	Toshio	Honouliuli
Nakaoka	Tayori	Honouliuli
Nakashima	Hisajiro	8
Nakashima	Mari	Honouliuli
Nakata	Tadashi	Honouliuli
Nakata	Toshiro	8
Nakatsu	Tsunazo	3
Nakatsuka	Ichiro	2

Family Name	Given Name	Group (1–10 are ship numbers)
Nakayama	Chikashi	5
Nakayama	Dengo	1
Nakayama	Hozui	2
Nekomoto	Shunichi	3
Niimi	Tokuichi	1
Niino	Katsuichi	Honouliuli
Niisato	Shigeru	Honouliuli
Niitani	Kazuo	Honouliuli
Nishi	Hatsutaro	Honouliuli
Nishi	Masashi	Honouliuli
Nishida	Biho	2
Nishii	Kokyo	2
Nishikawa	Toru	Honouliuli
Nishiki	Kakujiro	1
Nishimoto	Goichi	Honouliuli
Nishimoto	Hajime	3
Nishimura	Masao	Honouliuli
Nishimura	Takao	Honouliuli
Nishimura	Yonesaku	Honouliuli
Nishino	Yoshinori	8
Nishioka	Hikoyoshi	Honouliuli
NIshioka	Kuniaki	Honouliuli
Nishiyama	Kanesuke	Honouliuli
Nishiyama	Kansuke	9, from Honouliuli
Nishizaki	Nizo	6
Nishizawa	Kozan	2
Noda	Inazo	Honouliuli
Nomura	Giichi	9, from Honouliuli
Nonomura	Yuuko	2
Norinobu	Takeshi	Honouliuli
Nose	Masaru	Honouliuli
Obata	Soichi	1
Ochiai	Ekichi	2
Oda	Hakuai	1
Oda	Junji	3
Odachi	Kinzaemon	3
Odate	Chikai	4
Odo	Shunichi	1
Ogata	Kazuhiko	1
Ogawa	Yoshiro	1

Family Name	Given Name	Group (1–10 are ship numbers)
Ogi	Koichi	2
Ohama	Futoshi	3
Ohara	Kenjyo	4
Ohashi	Mohei	Honouliuli
Ohata	Seiichi	2
Ohta	Toshiichi	Honouliuli
Ohye	Honi	2
Oi	Jyoei	1
Oi	Tetsuo	Honouliuli
Oikawa	Tokuji	2
Oishi	Kichiji	Honouliuli
Oka	Wahei	9
Okabayashi	Toshiichi	Honouliuli
Okachi	Toyomi	2
Okada	Isao	Honouliuli
Okada	Jiro	3
Okamoto	Kakichi	4
Okamoto	Nanshin	4
Okamoto	Tokuichi	7
Okamura	Juichi	2
Okamura	Keiichi	3
Okano	Ryoshin	1
Okawa	Gendo	1
Okazaki	Seishiro	Honouliuli
Oki	Iwao	Honouliuli
Okimoto	Sakatsuchi	10, from Honouliuli
Okimura	Kazuo	Honouliuli
Okumoto	Yoshimi	2
Okura	Seido	2
Omiya	Manjiro	9, from Honouliuli
Omizo	Kyoichi	Honouliuli
Omura	Sodo	Honouliuli
Onaga	Rincho	2
Onoda	Torataro	1
Onodera	Tokuji	5
Onoue	Hikohachi	8
Onoyama	Ken	Honouliuli
Ooka	Hiroshi	2
Ooka	Suekichi	1
Orimoto	Kozo	Honouliuli

Family Name	Given Name	Group (1–10 are ship numbers)
Orita	Isaku	1
Osaki	Yojiro	5
Oshima	Kanesaburo	2
Oshima	Shigeo	1
Oshio	Munetaro	8
Oshiro	Hirosuke	10
Oshiro	Shinko	Honouliuli
Osumi	Sutekichi	4
Ota	Gentaro	2
Ota	Kunio	2
Otake	Tatsujiro	7
Otani	Genji	1
Otani	Matsujiro	4
Otomo	Kenju	10, from Honouliuli
Otsuka	Hikoju	8
Otsuka	Wahei	Honouliuli
Oumae	Masato	Honouliuli
Oyama	Shuhei	10
Oyama	Shuhei	Honouliuli
Ozaki	Ichitaro	Honouliuli
Ozaki	Otokichi	2
Ozaki	Sawajiro	2
Ozawa	Gijo	2
Sadanaga	Minoru	Honouliuli
Sado	Takeshige	5
Saegusa	Zenko	4
Saiki	En-ichi	4
Saiki	Takaichi	2
Saito	Haruto	2
Saito	Seigan	1
Saito	Toshio	Honouliuli
Saito	Yukihei	7
Saito	Yukio	Honouliuli
Sakaguchi	Kuwasaburo	9, from Honouliuli
Sakaguchi	Toshio	6
Sakai	Futoshi	Honouliuli
Sakai	Kunisuke	2
Sakakihara	Tameichi	Honouliuli
Sakamoto	Kyuichi	2
Sakamoto	Masao	Honouliuli, from 1

Family Name	Given Name	Group (1–10 are ship numbers)
Sakamoto	Munetaka	2
Sakamoto	Sanji	1
Sakamoto	Seiichi	2
Sakata	Shizuo	Honouliuli
Sakimizuru	Atsuo	2
Sakuma	Takeo	Honouliuli
Sano	Waichi	Honouliuli
Sarae	Tsuruichi	4
Sarashina	Shinri	1
Sasai	Akihide	2
Sasaki	Giichi	1
Sasaki	Tadao	1
Sasaki	Tokuro	3
Sasaki	Yoshinobu	1
Sato	Eita	3
Sato	Giichi	10, from Honouliuli
Sato	Heikichi	4
Sato	Ichiro	Honouliuli
Sato	Katsuzo	4
Sato	Taichi	1
Sato	Yazo	1
Sayegusa	Kinzo	1
Seike	Takeo	4
Seki	Kosaburo	4
Sekiya	Kichitaro	1
Sekiya	Yoshio	6
Serizawa	Hideyuki	1
Seto	Naoichi	10, from Honouliuli
Seto	Taichiro	10
Sezoko	Shoichi	Honouliuli
Shiba	Kakuo	2
Shigekane	Juzo	2
Shigekuni	Aisuke	1
Shigemoto	Osuke	1
Shigenaga	Kakuro	1
Shigenaga	Shigeo	3
Shiigi	Kenji	6
Shiigi	Ryoichi	Honouliuli
Shimamoto	Seiichi	Honouliuli
Shimizu	Kiyoshi	9, from Honouliuli

Family Name	Given Name	Group (1–10 are ship numbers)
Shimizu	Masatoshi	Honouliuli
Shimizu	Matsutaro	4
Shimoda	Keifu	Honouliuli
Shimoda	Shigezo	1
Shimokawa	Hanzo	2
Shimomura	Kisei	Honouliuli
Shimonishi	Iwataro	2
Shinagawa	Tetsuo	Honouliuli
Shindo	Takuji	3
Shinno	Minoru	Honouliuli
Shinoda	Masaichiro	2
Shinohara	Masami	9, from Honouliuli
Shintani	Ichiro	6
Shintani	Ishimatsu	2
Shiotani	Motoi	2
Shiraishi	Tadatoshi	Honouliuli
Shirakata	Tamiichi	Honouliuli
Shirasu	Jukaku	2
Shiratori	Shunsei	3
Shishido	Genkichi	Honouliuli
Shoda	Seiichi	2
Sodetani	Koho	2
Soga	Yasutaro	5
Sogawa	Masao	1
Sokabe	Ko	2
Sone	Tetsunosuke	5
Sonoda	Nejio	6
Sonoda	Santaro	1
Sueoka	Tameju	3
Suetomi	Koten	1
Sueyasu	Yonezo	1
Suga	Mamoru	9, from Honouliuli
Sugimoto	Seiichi	Honouliuli, from 1
Sugimoto	Tokikichi	2
Sugimura	Iwata	2
Sugiura	Yonematsu	9
Sugiura	Yoshinori	Honouliuli
Sumida	Daizo	1
Sumida	Shinzaburo	Honouliuli, from 1
Suyemura	Takeo	Honouliuli

Family Name	Given Name	Group (1–10 are ship numbers)
Suzuki	Eijiro	1
Suzuki	Genzo	3
Suzuki	Kazuo	Honouliuli
Suzuki	Masaru	7
Suzuki	Sadaichi	2
Suzuki	Seihei	Honouliuli
Suzuki	Tajiro	9, from Honouliuli
Suzuki	Teruchiyo	Honouliuli, woman
Suzuki	Tsuneo	Honouliuli
Tagashira	Yoshio	5
Tagawa	Shizuma	2
Taguma	Rintaro	Honouliuli
Taguma	Toichi	Honouliuli
Tahara	Hiroshi	2
Tahara	Jyoichi	Honouliuli
Tahara	Kameo	2
Taira	Kotaro	Honouliuli
Taira	Yojyo	2
Takabata	Yoshio	4
Takahashi	Haruko	Honouliuli, woman
Takahashi	Hideki	3
Takahashi	Izumi	3
Takahashi	Naoichi	Honouliuli, hospital
Takahashi	Rien	1
Takahashi	Shoichi	Honouliuli
Takahashi	Shozo	Honouliuli
Takahashi	Tokue	1
Takahashi	Tokushi	Honouliuli
Takahashi	Umon	9, from Honouliuli
Takahashi	Yasue	Honouliuli, woman
Takahashi	Yoshio	Honouliuli
Takahashi	Zenji	4
Takaki	Suekuma	2
Takakuwa	Shujiro	1
Takamoto	Wataru	3
Takanishi	Kazuichi	2
Takara	Kometaro	Honouliuli
Takasato	Morikame	10
Takashima	Shigeto	5
Takata	Keizo	3

Family Name	Given Name	Group (1–10 are ship numbers)
Takata	Toichi	3
Takayama	Shoji	Honouliuli
Takei	Nekketsu	5
Takei	Tokiji	7
Takei	Torao	2
Takei	Tsuyoshi	1
Takemori	Tamezo	3
Takemoto	Hikoju	2
Takemoto	Seiichi	Honouliuli
Takeshita	Kenichi	7
Takeshita	Wataru	8
Taketa	Kazuto	5
Taketa	Torao	2
Takeuchi	Kunitaro	3
Takeuchi	Naoji	8
Takezono	Seikaku	7
Takitani	Kanichi	Honouliuli
Tamabayashi	Hiroshi	3
Tamanaha	Tentoku	Honouliuli
Tamashiro	Shigeru	Honouliuli
Tamayose	Houn	Honouliuli
Tamekuni	Shonen	2
Tamura	Giichi	9, from Honouliuli
Tamura	Iwakichi	Honouliuli
Tamura	Makitaro	2
Tamura	Masao	Honouliuli
Tamura	Shigeki	Honouliuli
Tamura	Yoshihisa	9, from Honouliuli
Tamura	Shigeo	Honouliuli
Tanabe	Sannojo	3
Tanada	Gihei	8
Tanaka	Haru	Woman
Tanaka	Henry	Honouliuli
Tanaka	Hideo	5
Tanaka	Jitsuryu	7
Tanaka	Kanji	8
Tanaka	Katsuichi	1
Tanaka	Kazuaki	3
Tanaka	Kazuhiro	Honouliuli
Tanaka	Kyuhachi	2

Family Name	Given Name	Group (1–10 are ship numbers)
Tanaka	Ryoichi	3
Tanaka	Sueki	Honouliuli
Tanaka	Tamaichi	1
Tanaka	Tetsuo	3
Tanaka	Yaroku	2
Tani	Shigeki	5
Tanigawa	Tomizo	10
Taniguchi	Shinshi	Honouliuli
Tanisako	Saburo	6
Tanizaki	Hisatoshi	4
Tanji	Shizuma	2
Tanji	Yukio	Honouliuli
Tarasawa	Heitaro	1
Tarimizu	Tadayuki	8
Tasaka	Yoshitami	Honouliuli
Tashiro	Manabu	1
Tatsuguchi	Goki	1
Tatsuguchi	Zenkai	4
Tatsuhara	Koshi	3
Tatsutani	Genshin	1
Tawada	Shinryo	Honouliuli
Terada	Kyuzo	Honouliuli
Terada	Shigeji	7
Teraoku	Masutaro	10
Toda	Shoshin	2
Toda	Sosuke	5
Toda	Taiyu	1
Tofukuji	Koshiro	2
Togawa	Riichi	3
Togioka	Setsugo	2
Toishigawa	Hatsuichi	4
Tokairin	Jinhichi	1
Tokumoto	Eikichi	Honouliuli
Tokumoto	Mitsuo	Honouliuli
Tokushiro	Nobuji	3
Tominaga	Asahei	2
Tomioka	Sakae	Honouliuli
Tomita	Kazuo	1
Tomoyasu	Matsutaro	Honouliuli
Torii	Chuji	8

Family Name	Given Name	Group (1–10 are ship numbers)
Torii	Ginpei	5
Toyama	Takinosuke	1
Toyama	Tetsuo	1
Toyofuku	Hatsutaro	1
Toyofuku	Masaji	5
Toyota	Junichi	9
Toyota	Setsuzo	1
Tsubaki	Edward	Honouliuli
Tsuchiya	Seiichi	Honouliuli
Tsuda	Tatsuto	Honouliuli, woman
Tsuge	Giko	2
Tsuha	Kenjitsu	1
Tsuji	Kokichi	6
Tsuji	Tokuichi	Honouliuli
Tsukamoto	Kenneth	Honouliuli
Tsukamoto	Toku	Honouliuli
Tsunoda	Kensaku	1
Tsunoda	Takayuki	2
Tsushima	Genpachi	9, from Honouliuli
Uchida	Kinji	Honouliuli
Uechi	Kenji	8
Ueda	Ichiro	2
Ueda	Kyoichi	2
Ueda	Toraichi	1
Uehara	Masao	Honouliuli
Uehara	Masayoshi	6
Uehara	Yokichi	6
Uemori	Shigeyuki	Honouliuli
Ueno	Kenji	Honouliuli
Ueno	Sakujiro	1
Ueno	Takeshi	Honouliuli
Uenoyama	Shutetsu	2
Ueoka	Isamu	5
Ueoka	Sokan	1
Uesugi	Hitoshi	10, from Honouliuli
Uezu	Yasumatsu	Honouliuli
Umehara	Shodo	2
Uranaka	Wasaburo	3
Urata	Masaru	Honouliuli
Urata	Minoru	Honouliuli

Family Name	Given Name	Group (1–10 are ship numbers)
Uyehara	Saburo	1
Wada	Ichiro	2
Wada	Takashi	1
Wada	Umeo	1
Wakamoto	Giichi	Honouliuli
Wakayama	Jitsuji	2
Wakimoto	Katsuichi	3
Wakukawa	Seiei	4
Watanabe	Akimasa	10
Watanabe	Ittetsu	2
Watanabe	Iwaki	2
Watanabe	Tamasaku	3
Watanabe	Yakichi	5
Watanabe	Zennichi	9, from Honouliuli
Yama	Manabu	1
Yamada	Kaoru	Honouliuli
Yamada	Saburo	Honouliuli
Yamada	Shigeki	3
Yamada	Tomokichi	2
Yamagata	Heiji	3
Yamakawa	Yoshinobu	3
Yamamoto	Genzo	Honouliuli
Yamamoto	Gunichi	Honouliuli, hospital
Yamamoto	Hatsukichi	4
Yamamoto	Hiroemon	4
Yamamoto	Kazuo	Honouliuli
Yamamoto	Kazuyuki	3
Yamamoto	Kiyoshi	Honouliuli
Yamamoto	Kizo	2
Yamamoto	Ryotaro	Honouliuli
Yamamoto	Takeo	Honouliuli
Yamamoto	Toyosuke	9, from Honouliuli
Yamamoto	Tsuneichi	8
Yamamoto	Yaichi	8
Yamamoto	Yozaemon	8
Yamanaka	Heiichi	1
Yamane	Goichi	1
Yamane	Mitsuomi	3
Yamane	Seigi	1
Yamane	Tsuta	Woman

Family Name	Given Name	Group (1–10 are ship numbers)
Yamasaki	Hiroshi	Honouliuli
Yamasaki	Jisei	Honouliuli
Yamasaki	Katsutaro	4
Yamasaki	Sam	Honouliuli
Yamasaki	Takejiro	Honouliuli
Yamasato	Jikai	1
Yamashiro	Shusei	Honouliuli
Yamazaki	Zenichiro	3
Yanagi	Tokujiro	6
Yanagihara	Kaneichi	2
Yano	Shigeru	8
Yasuda	Satoshi	Honouliuli
Yasunaga	Tokuichi	5
Yoda	Kichisuke	2
Yogi	Seisaburo	3
Yokota	Kazuto	6
Yokoyama	Shinajiro	7
Yonahara	Ryosen	1
Yonemura	Isamu	Honouliuli
Yonemura	Kiyoshi	8
Yonesaki	Ushitaro	3
Yoshida	Goro	Honouliuli
Yoshida	Hannosuke	9
Yoshida	Shinobu	3
Yoshikane	Teruo	Honouliuli
Yoshikawa	Yuichi	Honouliuli
Yoshimasu	Masayuki	2
Yoshimasu	Shinjiro	5
Yoshimoto	Asami	10, from Honouliuli
Yoshimura	Kohee	10
Yoshinaga	Shigeru	10, from Honouliuli
Yoshinaga	Sogi	Honouliuli
Yoshioka	Masuo	Honouliuli
Yoshioka	Yoshio	9, from Honouliuli
Yoshiura	Kenji	5
Yoshizawa	Jiro	7
Yoshizumi	Kogan	3

POSTSCRIPT

Three years have passed since those of us who were sent to camps on the Mainland returned to Hawaii. This book stems from a series of articles I wrote for the *Hawaii Times* from January to July 1946. I received encouragement for these pieces as well as criticism. (Some readers felt I had been too candid.) However, many friends advised me to publish the articles in book form—the first public record of the wartime experiences of Japanese in the United States. I followed their advice, although I may have taken longer than they had anticipated.

I would like to express my gratitude to Mr. Akira Furukawa, who took care of the book binding, and to those who helped me compile information for the appendices.

November 1948

Production Notes for Soga / Life behind Barbed Wire

Designed by Liz Demeter with text in Garamond
and display in CgGothic

Composition by Josie Herr

Printing and binding by Versa Press, Inc.

Printed on 55# Glat Writers Book, 360 ppi